S0-AEU-081

DATE DUE

NOV 1 7 1976			
JAN 0 5 1977 BR			
JAN 3 1977			
FEB 1 8 1986			
MAR 1 2 1986			

The Spoiled Child of the Western World

THE MISCARRIAGE OF THE AMERICAN IDEA IN OUR TIME

By the same author

THE KENNEDY PROMISE
THE LIFE OF POLITICS

The Spoiled Child
of the Western World

**THE MISCARRIAGE
OF THE AMERICAN IDEA
IN OUR TIME**

HENRY FAIRLIE

DOUBLEDAY & COMPANY, INC.

GARDEN CITY, NEW YORK

1976

Grateful acknowledgment is given to the following for permission to reprint:

Excerpt from *The Human Condition* by Hannah Arendt. Reprinted by permission of the University of Chicago Press.

Two lines of verse from *Epistle to a Godson and Other Poems* by W. H. Auden. Copyright © 1972 by W. H. Auden. Reprinted by permission of Random House, Inc. and Faber & Faber Ltd.

Excerpt from *Democracy and Education* by John Dewey. Copyright 1916 by Macmillan Publishing Co., Inc. Copyright renewed 1944 by John Dewey. Reprinted by permission of Macmillan Publishing Company.

Excerpts from *Individualism Old and New* by John Dewey. Copyright 1929, 1930 by John Dewey. Reprinted by permission of G. P. Putnam's Sons.

Random quotations from *The Revolt of the Masses* by José Ortega y Gasset. Copyright 1932 by W. W. Norton & Company, Inc. Copyright renewed © 1960 by Teresa Carey. Reprinted by permission of W. W. Norton & Company, Inc. and George Allen & Unwin Ltd.

Excerpts from *On the Democratic Idea in America* by Irving Kristol. Reprinted by permission of Harper & Row, Publishers, Inc.

Lines of poetry from "The Kallyope Yell" in the book *Collected Poems* by Vachel Lindsay. Copyright 1914 by Macmillan Publishing Co., Inc. Reprinted by permission of the copyright owner.

Excerpts from *America in the Fifties and Sixties* by Julián Marías. Copyright © 1972 by The Pennsylvania State University. Reprinted by permission of The Pennsylvania State University Press.

Excerpt from *Tradition and Revolt* by Robert A. Nesbit. Reprinted by permission of Random House, Inc.

Extracts for *Do It!* by Jerry Rubin. Copyright © 1970 by the Social Educational Foundation. Reprinted by permission of Simon and Schuster and Jonathan Cape, Ltd.

Library of Congress Cataloging in Publication Data
Fairlie, Henry, 1924–
    The spoiled child of the Western World.

    Includes bibliographical references and index.
    1.   United States—Social conditions.   2.   National characteristics, American.   3.   United States—Foreign relations.   I.   Title
HN57.F34   309.1'73
ISBN 0-385-04936-6
Library of Congress Catalog Card Number 73–15337

THIS BOOK IS FOR
TUCKA
IN MEMORIAM, 1930–1975

384223

Contents

can Revolution in the New Man — The Country That Must Constantly Be Remade — The Past That Is Present — The I Released in the En-Masse — The Imagination of Jefferson — The Creative Tension in American Life

PART I

The Spoiled Child of the Western World

"We are what we get high on."[1]

—JERRY RUBIN, in *Do It!*

CHAPTER 1

The Incitements to Permissiveness

On June 6, 1944, Dwight Eisenhower led what he later described as a "whole host" of men into Europe; a host of Americans, in particular, to march over the bones of their fathers which still lay in the soil of the continent that they or their fathers or their forefathers had once left. Twenty days later, the first objective had been accomplished; Cherbourg had fallen; the way to the heart of Europe was not yet open, but the footing on the continent had been secured. In the intervening years, the course of the United States at home and abroad has been astonishing. To look back now is to find a landscape that is barely recognizable, yet one in which the signs were already posted to the landscape of today. It is there that we may start. Of whatever else we are the children, we are certainly the offspring of our immediate past; yet it is the immediate past that we often have the most difficulty in understanding.

America was turned outward to the world. The shelves of bookstores were filled with books of maps that seemed to announce a new world, of which the New World had become the centre. Richard Harrison in *Look at the World,* Erwin Raisz in *Atlas of Global Geography,* O. M. Miller in *World Maps and Globes,* Nicholas Spykman in *Geography of Peace:* these and a score of others all presented a new projection of the world's surface in which Europe and even Australia were shrunk to the size of frankfurters, as someone said at the time, whereas the American continent was so enlarged that Winnipeg "suddenly showed up as the centre of the world." The revolution was Copernican in its nature: America had become the sun round which its satellites revolved.

It was not just an advent of power that was being celebrated, but a sense of mission in the world, and of confidence in its success. Bonwit Teller advertised a new perfume that was called "Bretton Woods"; across Central Park a new saloon opened on the corner of Broadway and Seventy-third with the name of "Dumbarton Oaks." At a more serious level, Thomas E. Dewey declared, three weeks after the invasion of Europe: "I say to you: our country is fighting its way to new horizons. The future of America has no limit."[2] Playing in *A Guy Named Joe,* Spencer Tracy gave the mood a characteristic utterance: "Everything's going to be prettier, you're not going to have any more bad dreams, you're going to have all the things people have, your life is going to be living, laughing, fighting, and loving." Thirty years later, there seemed to be nothing but bad dreams in the land, and everything did not seem to be prettier; or so at least we have been persuaded.

It was a time when even the most traditional institutions in the country were trusted to cope with the new international responsibilities. The citizens of New Hampshire met, in March of 1945, in their town meetings, more than two hundred of them. Pembroke determined that it would auction its police station; Weare decided to sell its tramp house; Manchester recessed at midday for a hot dinner and homemade fudge. But at the foot of every ballot was an identical question: "To see if the town will vote to support United States membership in a general system of international cooperation"; and the answer from the towns was that they would. A year before, the American Communist Party, by a unanimous vote of its national committee, had dissolved itself into the Communist Political Association, as Earl Browder told of the virtues of the two-party system, "traditional in our country," and of a system of free enterprise which could "beyond question" be made to operate "to the benefit of labor, farmers, and capital"; asking only that "some extraordinary means . . . be found to double the buying power of the individual consumer." It was one of the earliest prescriptions for the politics of the "affluent society."

WHEN THE MIDDLE CLASS WAS CONFIDENT

The confidence of the United States was the confidence of its middle class. "The middle class was the great architect of political democracy," said a writer in the *Antioch Review* in the spring of 1945; "it can become an architect of supplementary economic democracy."[3] It was with this sense of social responsibility, international and domestic, that the middle class was looking forward. It was not satisfied when Franklin Roosevelt told Dilworth Lupton that he wished that reporters would stop talking about the New Deal, because "there is no need of a New Deal now." In particular, the professional leadership of the middle class was seized by a progressive spirit that was unusually generous in its estimate of the American people, their needs and their capacities; it had not yet cultivated a disdain for the ordinary people of the country and their cares.

It was the last time that the professional middle class felt itself to be, firmly and creatively, in alliance with the organized working class. The Political Action Committee of the CIO had held its first conference in New York early in 1944; by May of that year, with the defeat of John M. Costello in the Democratic primary elections in California, the third member of the Dies Committee in the House of Representatives was eliminated in four weeks; and no one doubted that this was the work of the PAC under the leadership of Sidney Hillman, who could say with reason, two months later, that "the most important politician at the Democratic Convention in Chicago this week is, very probably, a labor leader."

The method was, not manipulation, but education. The trade unions were interested in, and believed in the efficacy of, the education of their members to their opportunities and responsibilities as citizen voters. A characteristic publication of the CIO was an eight-page "comic book" pamphlet, distributed at one cent a copy and meant for the lunch box of every worker, which explained the need for postwar planning in terms that would make sense at the factory gate. This belief in not only the efficiency but the worth of political education was one of the strongest bonds which joined the working class to the professional leadership of the middle class. The alliance was not only concerned with "who gets what, when and how," and with helping each other to get it; there was a deep sense of a shared citizenship, of the general capacity of the ordinary citizen for political sense and even wisdom. Middle-class organizations such as Americans for Democratic Action were not yet contemptuous or supercilious in their attitudes to the working class; it was assumed that each needed the other.

The confidence of the middle class—in themselves and their country, its institutions and its people—rested to a large extent on the fact that it could still draw on the resources of its conventional morality. Even its professional and intellectual leaders, who might not observe its traditional standards in their private lives, and sneered with Mencken at the "booboisie," were in fact sustained by the awareness that the morality and the standards were nevertheless secure—somewhere. In 1944 alone, the Watch and Ward Society in Boston was able to enforce the banning of Lillian Smith's *Strange Fruit,* of Kathleen Winsor's *Forever Amber,* and of Joseph Pennell's *The History of Rome Hanks;* and it tried to ban Erskine Caldwell's *Tragic Ground.* The police in Boston required Katherine Dunham to omit two of her numbers from *Tropical Revue,* and refused permission for the performance of Stravinsky's arrangement of "The Star-Spangled Banner"; a play about lesbianism, Dorothy and Howard Baker's *Trio,* was not allowed a performance in New York; and the library of the U. S. Naval Academy ruled that *Forever Amber* should not be issued to anyone of the rank of midshipman or lower. These were not representative actions; but they were symbolic of a persistence in the middle class of traditional values.

"There was not the slightest evidence in the 1930s, or even in the decade following," wrote one of the most distinguished of American sociologists in 1971, "that the time would shortly come when to be middle class would mean being indulgent, permissive, tolerant, in a wide range of political, social, and moral matters to a degree that can only be called radical (and to a degree that would certainly have appalled either Marx or Freud)."[4] But perhaps the evidence was there, if only the signs had been read; perhaps the change, as the argument of this book will suggest, did not come out of the blue. The signs of experimentation, of a straining to be free from the standards and morality of the past, were already to be discerned.

In short, the spoiled child of the Western world was about to arrive, exactly as had been predicted by Ortega y Gasset, and we must first try to locate the child where it may most clearly be observed: in the vast commonalty of the middle class of the United States.

THE COMMONALTY OF THE MIDDLE CLASS IN AMERICA

As early as 1940, observers were already commenting on the extraordinary growth of the middle class in America. During the preceding seventy years, whereas the working class had multiplied only six times, the middle class had multiplied eight times, and the new middle class of salaried employees no less than sixteen times. In the 1950s it was this vast commonalty of the middle class that took the stage. The wide range of occupations and incomes and status that is now included in the middle class may seem to make the term meaningless; it is not. To the outsider, at least, it is clear that the middle class in the United States is a commonalty. Writing of Amherst College at the beginning of the 1890s, Calvin Coolidge said in his autobiography:

> About ten fraternity houses furnished lodgings for most of the upper class men, but the lower class men roomed at private houses. All the students took their meals in private houses, so that there was a general commingling of all classes and all fraternities around the table, which broke up exclusive circles and increased college democracy.[5]

By the 1950s, with the exception of a few relics, these patterns had dissolved in the general expansion of the middle class; and the "common man" made his appearance in the great commonalty.

The phrase "the common man" was offensive even at the time, and it has now almost disappeared from the political vocabulary. But we must understand why it was necessary in the 1940s and the first half of the 1950s. Today the rhetoric of Henry Wallace seems strange to us:

> Some have spoken of the "American Century." I say that the century on which we are entering—the century that will come out of the war—can and must be the century of the common man. The people's revolution is on the march, and the devil and all his angels cannot prevail against it. They cannot prevail, for on the side of the people is the Lord.[6]

That was in 1942, and the phrase travelled into the literary as well as the political mind of the country. In 1949, Dwight Macdonald said of F. O. Matthiessen that he "talked about Emerson, Thoreau, Whitman and Melville as the Henry Wallaces of their day," and that his high point was his reference to Captain Ahab as a "common man."[7] As late as 1958, Arthur M. Schlesinger, Jr., was still saying: "The century of the common man has come into its own"[8]; and one wonders if he thinks that it is still here.

The phrase was necessary because it was no longer possible to talk about the commonalty of the American people in terms of class. As early as 1907, William Graham Sumner—that gifted and perverse observer of societies and cultures—had said: "The man in the mode is the 'common man,' the 'average man,' or 'the man in the street' "; and he was not referring to any class. When he remarked that "suddenly we are told that the common man is wise beyond all philosophers,"[9] it was not of a class that he was speaking; in fact, he was adumbrating the concept of "the masses" as it was elaborated by Ortega a quarter of a century later, who insisted that he was not talking of a social class. But it was Julián Marías, the friend and disciple of Ortega, who made the finest distinction between the proletariat and the common man, during a visit to the United States yet another quarter of a century later. The significant feature of the common man, he said, is that he "possesses a way of life within which to install himself and to which he adheres; he believes his condition an honorable and estimable one, and he aspires to what he desires within that framework."[10] By and large, this is still true of the commonalty of the middle class in America.

We may look to England for a contrast. George Melly, one of the most acute observers of, even as he has been a participant in, the "pop scene" in that country, wrote in 1962:

Teenagers are not everyone in their teens. There are very few teenagers in the full meaning of the term at Grammar or Public [i.e., private] Schools. The teenagers proper belong by origin to the lower middle or upper working class—not that there is for them any clearly defined class boundaries. One can place them only if one meets their parents. As soon as they can, they leave school and earn.[11]

The observation was exact; and it is inconceivable, of course, that the teenager in America could ever have been described in terms of class. Like his parents, he belonged to and was a product of the commonalty.

PREPARING THE GROUND FOR THE TEENAGER

It was this that was important as the 1950s gave way to the 1960s in the United States. If the "pop scene" of the teenager was transformed, it meant that the transformation must touch, as it had its origin in, the entire commonalty of the middle class. This was notably not true in England, in the second half of the 1950s, where the pop music had to force its way into the established middle class, either from below or from outside. Even the success of the Beatles, although they were celebrated and even honoured by their sovereign, was regarded, certainly at first, as something of a class phenomenon: the lower middle or upper working class of the country advancing from the provinces on the metropolis to claim their overdue patrimony.

Many of the most original writers of pop lyrics in England—John Lennon and Peter Townshend and Ray Davis—had been students at the art schools which had multiplied after the war, attracted those who would not otherwise have had a higher education of any kind, stood in opposition to the academic education that was offered by the traditional universities, and became "a kind of forcing ground for nonconformity and dissent." It would be impossible to describe the development of pop music in America in terms of such minute specifications of class and upbringing: the early pioneers of rock, such as Bill Haley or Elvis Presley, or the Everly Brothers or the Kingston Trio, were conventional members of the commonalty of the middle class.

Let us listen to Jerry Rubin:

The New Left sprang, a predestined pissed-off child, from Elvis's gyrating pelvis. . . . Elvis Presley ripped off Ike Eisenhower by turning our uptight young bodies around. Hard animal rock energy beat/surged hot through us, the driving rhythm arousing repressed passions. . . . Buddy Holly, the Coasters, Bo Diddley, Chuck Berry, the Everly Brothers, Jerry Lee

Lewis, Fats Domino, Little Richard, Ray Charles, Bill Haley and the Comets, Fabian, Bobby Darin, Frankie Avalon: they all gave us the life/beat and set us free.[12]

All that Rubin is describing, in himself and in his heroes, is nothing more than the popular culture of the middle class from which he had sprung; after all, the intermediary between him and them was as conventional a figure as the disc jockey.

There is much to be said about the close association within this culture between the attitudes of the parents and those of their children. But for the moment the point to be grasped is that by the 1950s the middle class in America was a social phenomenon of considerable novelty and interest. It was in many respects the entire society, and those who did not yet belong to it were soon to be called "the minorities" or "the disadvantaged." It was composed of "the common man" as we have described him, who was installed in a way of life to which he adhered; and it was within this way of life, rather than against it, that he was, in the figure of his children, to appear to rebel. There was no profound social protest to make, no protest of a class on its own behalf, or on behalf of another. In these circumstances, it could be a rebellion only of the self and, as we will see, the ground for such a rebellion in the popular culture had in the high culture been prepared for a long time and in many ways.

THE END OF THE STRUGGLE FOR EXISTENCE

If the middle class in the United States at the end of the Second World War was about to become "indulgent, permissive, tolerant, in a wide range of political, social, and moral matters," it was because two influences were already at work: a science that was creating the *opportunities* of permissiveness, and a culture that was encouraging the *experimentation* of permissiveness. Although science and art have been believed to be opposed to each other, they have in fact worked to the same ends. Science (with its handmaiden, technology) has said: "We have freed you from the physical constrictions of the past." Art has said: "Freed from the constrictions of the past, you may now experiment with your freedom."

Permissiveness is too slight a word to describe the kind of freedom which, by 1945, could be imagined as a result of the advances in science and technology. Life itself was being reshaped in no obvious mould. At the end of 1943, for the first time in its history, the American Medical Association published a list of approved contraceptives in its journal. This was a concession by medical science to the new morals that science itself had made possible. As if to demonstrate the breadth of the possibilities that were opening, John Rock and Miriam F. Menkin in 1944 reported in *Science* the first recorded fertilization of a human ovum outside the mother's body. To talk of permissiveness in such a situation is to miss the depth of the challenge.

Fresh news of the discoveries and inventions of medicine was brought almost every day. In May of 1944 alone, it was announced that penicillin would at last be available to civilians; that the first eye bank in the country had been established at New York Hospital; and that three new methods—one of surgery, one of drugs, one of technology—were already being used in the fight against tuberculosis. As the announcements were made, week by week, the impression was left in the mind of the ordinary person that he might be freed even from the threat of crippling disease. Instead of talking of permissiveness as if it has been no more than a rather frivolous abandonment of conventional moral standards, we need to understand that it has been in part a response to the removal, and the promise of the removal, of many of the physical restrictions of the past.

In 1944, the censorship was lifted at last from the news of the discovery of DDT, and the U. S. Surgeon General's Office said that it "will be to preventive medicine what Lister's discovery of antiseptics was to surgery." Even at the time there were warnings that its nonselective killing power was dangerous, but it was also a symbol of the ability of man to free even his agriculture from the constrictions of nature. If the food could be produced in abundance, it could be stored with ease. The first quick-freezing process had been patented by Clarence Birdseye in 1925; by the end of the Second World War, the American people were already consuming nearly a billion pounds of commercially frozen foods each year. The conditions of the individual's everyday life were being altered, touching him directly in a way that had not often been true in the past, altering his conception of himself and his expectations.

There is no need to list all the inventions and discoveries that were to transform the everyday life of the ordinary American. Some were as significant as the development of air transport for passengers and freight; in 1944 Howard Robard Hughes piloted a four-engine, sixty-passenger Lockheed Constellation from Burbank, California, to Washington, D.C., in six hours and fifty-eight minutes, reducing the previous time for a transport plane by three and a half hours. Others were less significant but, in a way, no less symbolic. In 1944 a Hungarian named L. J. Biro announced that he had invented what he called a Stratopen, which used a ball bearing in place of a nib point, fed by a fine coiled tube in its barrel with a gelatinous instant-drying ink. (In Britain, ball-point pens are still known as "Biros.") Whatever the other consequences of his invention, it provided the kind of inexpensive convenience which is itself a release from past constrictions.

In ways both large and small, the opportunities of permissiveness have been the creation of our science and technology, and the consequences have often been as far-reaching as they have been indirect and unintended. In 1944, 16,000,000 women in the United States had jobs; almost 4,000,000 of them were employed in war industries. Observing these figures, Fannie Hurst commented on the opportunities for the further emancipation of women after the war, but immediately added: "I am beginning to doubt whether we want it. Home fires are going to roar"; and roar they did, although the metaphor seems a little inappropriate to most American homes. But what were the women to do in their homes? Even those home fires did not need their attention. Increasingly the freedom from the physical constrictions of the past had given their lives not so much a new shape as no recognizable shape at all.

One of the answers was given by Alexander Wiley in 1948, when he was the U.S. senator from Wisconsin, in words that can be cherished: "When I see my grandchildren, these lovely clods of human clay given to us by God, I reflect that each of us is a sculptor of that soft, receptive clay. We can fashion it whichever way we will. We can make of it a masterpiece of human art." But this attention to the child, having become the primary if not the sole occupation of the woman in her home, in fact yielded a generation of parents who were more permissive than could have been imagined only a generation earlier. The clay was not shaped, it certainly was not fired; and the most important of the reasons was that life had ceased, as a result of science and technology, to be as hard and earnest as before; and it was understood that it would be even less hard and earnest for the new generation when it reached maturity.

"The life of man in society, just like the life of other species, is a struggle for existence," Thorstein Veblen had written in 1899[13]; but fifty years later the struggle for existence had ceased to be a preoccupation in the lives of the majority of the American people. Even the vogue of existentialism at that time, which could be interpreted as recommending a kind of permissiveness, had its origin in this fact: since the struggle for existence had ceased to be a problem, one's existence in itself became the problem. Existentialism is not a philosophy for someone who lacks a crust of bread.

The voice of an earlier generation, pointing the contrast, may be heard in an answer that Patricia Nixon gave to Gloria Steinem during the 1968 election campaign: "I never had the time to think about things like that—who I wanted to be, or who I admired, or to have ideas. . . . I've never had it easy. I'm not like all you people . . . all those people who have had it so easy."[14] She was not talking of the increase of affluence in merely economic terms: as will be argued later, that has been greatly exaggerated. The real affluence, if we must use the word, in contemporary society is that which has been the endowment, almost willy-nilly, of our science and our technology.

Venereal disease may still be a problem to the ignorant or the careless, but it is no longer the agent of an avenging god; contraceptive techniques may not be foolproof, but on the whole they have released the individual to explore, without inviting the risks, and possibly the agony, of accidental conception. In these circumstances, it is not really a question of permissiveness, but of recognizing the need for a morality that is more appropriate to them. By and large, until the end of the Second World War, it was imprudent for the majority of young women, but not for the majority of young men, to engage in premarital intercourse. Many contraceptives were unreliable; female contraceptives were hard for the unmarried woman to obtain; abortion was illegal and dangerous; to give birth to a bastard was a stigma; and, on the whole, custom was generous in excusing the male from his responsibility. "Manifestly, in these circumstances," Ronald Atkinson has said, "although prudence would not require a man to refrain from intercourse outside marriage, considerations of beneficence and fairness would."[15] It may be that we need to discover a new morality to determine when "considerations of beneficence and fairness" ought still to rule in a sexual relationship—people still get hurt, after all—but the change in the old morality is not one that we can refuse, or glibly describe as permissiveness, when our science and our technology have so altered our lives.

THE TRANSFORMATION OF POP CULTURE

Art was to become the accomplice of science. Since the struggle for existence was over, the effort could begin to remake that existence. As we have noticed, by the end of the Second World War it was already clear that the urban middle-class popular culture was straining at its ties, that it was in the mood to experiment, to try new things. In 1944, Alfred A. Knopf made the surprising announcement that his second best seller of the year, after *A Bell for Adano,* was *The Prophet* of Kahlil Gibran; and at the same time there appeared the first English translation of the *Bhagavad-Gita* that was both authoritative and readable, with a foreword by William Ernest Hocking, the professor emeritus of philosophy at Harvard University, who prayed, "May this majestic poem find its way into the literary friendship of many readers." Immediately it did, having been reviewed in the news magazines, whose editors did not seem to regard it as a provocation to their readers. Eastern religions have always been given a hearing in the United States, but this was the first time, at least since the days of the Theosophical Society, that there was evidence of their attraction for the popular mind, of its willingness to experiment with them, as it was also beginning to experiment with drugs. One of the first popular news stories about the use of marijuana appeared in *Newsweek* as early as 1945, which called it "a notoriously troublesome civilian problem," no longer confined to jazz singers and black ghettos.

The audiences of white people for jazz itself had been small and rather private, until Eddie Condon in 1942 started his Saturday-afternoon concerts at City Hall in New York. Week by week, the lines at the doors grew longer and longer, until in 1944 a network radio station took the decision to broadcast them and they won an even wider audience. "In order to preserve the unrestrained and ad-lib qualities of the music," he warned at the beginning of each concert, "the artist may depart from the following program at any time." He disdained the big bands—"the melody fellows," as he called them, Harry James and Benny Goodman—and he found an audience for a kind of music that until then had been thought to have only an esoteric appeal. The widespread interest that was shown in the success of his concerts was given in part to the still unexpected readiness of the popular culture for experiment and complication, to try new things and discard old forms.

It was, after all, less than thirty years since the first jazz record had been made by the Original Dixieland Jazz Band, a group of white players from New Orleans, to be released on March 7, 1917, by the Victor Talking Machine Company. They were at the time playing to the rich and the elite in the 400 Room at Reisenweber's in New York. Ten years later, when Eddie Condon and the Chicagoans recorded "Nobody's Sweetheart," the audiences for the Chicago jazz of the 1920s were still comparatively small and esoteric. That was the significance of his concerts in the 1940s: jazz and all that it meant, in itself and in its influence, had travelled into the popular mind of the urban middle class of America. What it meant, among other things, was described by a British critic, Peter Worsley, in 1963. It was "specifically the idiom of modernity: smart modernity, deviant modernity, the modernity of new generations, the modernity of new and attractive civilizations. In particular, it has been the music of American modernity. . . . The spread of jazz has reflected the dynamism of America in the twentieth century."[16]

The readiness to experiment . . . the idiom of modernity: but something else was happening, of which the examples that have been given are in a way illustrations. The messages of the high culture were being more rapidly transmitted than before to the popular mind. Indeed, it began to seem that there was none of its messages that could not be transmitted and absorbed. After the liberation of Paris in 1944, lines of American soldiers filled the Rue Saint-Augustin to pay tribute, not to Charles de Gaulle, not to a nightclub singer, but to Picasso, who in the end had to plead that they would honour him more if they left his studio to him. The master could not make a remark so silly that the news magazines would not print it. Art had become a celebrity, and leading the way was the advertising industry. "The unassailable fact," said *Printer's Ink* in

1944, "is that one of the most conspicuous trends in advertising today is the adoption of surrealist techniques in advertising illustrations"; and it added that it was odd that such a "radical, eccentric art form should have been embraced by the most conservative element in the American community, i.e., business." We do not find it odd; we are well aware of the role of "Madison Avenue" in the culture. But the phenomenon was then new.

We are now used to the rapidity with which the messages of the high culture are transformed into the codes of the popular culture; and, since the high culture has for long been experimental, the popular mind has in turn been attuned to experiment. What was happening by the end of the Second World War was that the radical dissociation that had taken place in the high culture, between the created worlds of art and the actual world in which we live, was beginning to take place in the popular mind. In the actual world, men would conform, because there was nothing much else that they could do; in the created worlds, they would rebel, and imagine themselves to be free spirits. A small event that passed unnoticed in 1950 was the innovation of Decca in putting its records into hard jackets; a quarter of a century later, a display of these jackets is enough to demonstrate how deeply this dissociation, between the actual world and the created worlds, had driven into the popular culture. By the time in 1949 that Andy Warhol moved to New York, "frail and pallid, raggedy and poor," the stage had been set for him.

The urban middle-class popular culture of the United States had already gone before, preparing the way for him to take the actual world and, by painting his signature on it, to turn it into a work of art. Freed from the struggle for existence, each man might be an artist, and the artist in particular of his own life. It is in this sense that one speaks of him as a spoiled child: freed from the physical constrictions of the past, he gives himself now to the gratification of himself in his-self, the immediate satisfaction of what he conceives to be his vital desires.

THE OBVIOUS SYMBOLS OF CONTRIVED ALIENATION

By the end of the Second World War, existentialism was already beginning its spectacular career from the high culture of Europe into the semiliterate culture of the United States. "There is much talk in

Paris, in Greenwich Village, even in the center of Manhattan, about existence and existentialism," Jean Wahl wrote in 1945[17]; and again the news magazines bent their energies with a grotesque earnestness to expound the "philosophy." A reader of *Time* would by 1947 have grown facilely familiar with the vocabulary of "anxiety" and "absurdity" and "being in the world," and the associated vocabulary of "alienation." By 1948, Kafka had become a hero, not only of the literary critic, but of the popular culture, celebrated as the archetype of the contemporary man, the dedicated artist, and The Victim. Any pressure of society on the individual was described as "Kafkalike," and the incitement of the individual to defiance was implicit.

It is difficult for the outsider to understand why the American mind should have fallen so abjectly for the European import of existentialism—which might have been thrown into Boston Harbor without much loss—unless it is that *Moby Dick,* which sometimes seems to have been translated into a holy myth of the American experience, was already being represented as a mythical representation of that experience, or of man in general, even of life, each of them to be hunted as "a mighty and mysterious whale," so that "man is once more a mystery to us, and a greater mystery than ever before,"[18] which is one of the earlier and more restrained abasements before "the mighty and mysterious soul" of Herman Melville that have now been a common currency for two generations.

There were many influences, some of which are the subject of this book, but at any rate Moses Herzog had every reason to complain in Saul Bellow's novel a few years later, about the "safe, comfortable people playing at crisis, alienation, apocalypse and desperation." "The Movement," when it came on the scene in the 1960s, seemed determined to try to follow Norman Mailer's prescription for acting out one's life, so to speak, on one's existential nerves. What was to be found in both was a "hopeless displacement of the boundary between literature and life," as Graham Hough once called it in another context; and Mailer no less than "The Movement" in the end left his work no more than a wasted battleground, on which he had ordered the imaginary armies of himself into battle with the imagined armies of his genius, throwing in more and more battalions, to dispute a no-man's-land. "I am imprisoned within a perception," he wrote, "which will settle for nothing less than making a revolution in the consciousness of our time," and both he and "The Movement" would try it by meeting each circumstance with nothing more substantial than the existential gesture.

It was the facility of this gesture that travelled into the mind of the spoiled child, telling him of his solitude in his situation, and of his ability to meet it with a self-mustered honesty that issues in a gesture, for it is rarely more, of the solitary and self-mustered will. The use which Ingmar Bergman has made of the island—men and women working out their salvation, never in any genuine public, but always in a place in which the isolation is contrived—is characteristic, and it enabled *Time* to exclaim of *The Shame* that "what matters is the body of his work—comprising 29 films—which now amount to a great literature of heroic despair."[19] But what we in fact are given—in another film, *The Silence,* for example—are obvious symbols of contrived alienation: whether in the arrival of the travellers in a city in which they understand nothing, or in the dwarfs who cannot inhabit the ordinary world, or in the sister making love to the waiter even though they cannot converse, or in the country itself that has no contact with the outside world, and so on. What matters is this is not any heroic despair, but that there is little in it that is describable as real life.

Yet we have plenty of evidence that to many the tedium of this idiom was made to seem more real than the idiom of their own lives. There is always the contrived isolation, as in *Jealousy,* the short novel of Alain Robbe-Grillet, in which the man lives isolated on a banana plantation. There is always the gesture of rebellion, as in Anouilh, for example, whose Antigone does not rebel to a purpose, but only absurdly. In a milder form, there is the comic lore of the anti-hero, who is not asked to make the effort to confront his own environment and negotiate with it, but manages to survive like Lucky Jim by slipping under the wire of reality in the nick of time. In perhaps the most popular form of all, there is the meaning we give to the roles of a Humphrey Bogart, the misfit as gangster who, according to one critic, "is the 'no' to that great American 'yes.' " The spoiled child is upheld in the "absurd" rebellion to which he is provoked.

There can be no doubt that, as it travelled from the high culture of Europe after the Second World War into the popular culture of America, existentialism had a profound effect on its middle class, detaching the individual, even as other ties were being loosed, from the commonalty, and from his feeling of commonness with others in its social relationships. The spoiled child was taught to despise both the reality and the ordinariness of the human situation, and to meet it with an invigorating even if superficial conviction in the possibility of his personal salvation. By a "wild leap of the will," as Iris Murdoch puts it, he could even fly in the face of facts.[20]

THE FALLACY OF THE "GENERATION GAP"

If we are not, in all this, talking of a specific social class but of a commonalty, we are also not talking of a generation. The idea of the "generation" is elusive. Let us take, for example, this from John Stuart Mill:

> In each successive age, the principal phenomena of society are different from what they were in the age preceding, and still more different from any previous age; the periods which most distinctly mark these successive changes being intervals of one generation, during which a new set of human beings have been educated, have grown up from childhood, and taken possession of society.[21]

But, since human beings are being born in every hour, and are from year to year at different stages of their development as they are raised, how do we mark the moment when a new generation has "arrived"?

There is obviously a new generation in a family; it is clearly marked. But how can we talk of a new generation in a whole society, and say that it has "taken possession"? Perhaps the clearest answer was given by Walter Bagehot, when he said that the passage of the Second Reform Bill in England in 1867 marked the arrival in office of a new generation that had risen to power since the passage of the First Reform Bill in 1832: a period, it is worth noticing, of thirty-five years. They had been shaped by a great event. Jefferson appeared to be using the term in a similar way when he wrote to St. George Tucker in 1797 of the "generation of 1776." But on another occasion he said that "We may consider each generation a distinct nation," reckoning that the length of a generation was nineteen years, which would seem to suggest that a "generation" is not necessarily separated from the preceding one by the influence of a determining event, that a new one simply arrives every nineteen years as a "distinct nation."

The trouble that we can get into is clear if we examine the remark of Ralph Headstrong, in Richard Chase's symposium *The Democratic Vista,* when he says that "[Maggie's] attitudes were formed in the 1920s, as mine and Dorothy's were in the thirties, and the Middlebys' were in the forties."[22] It is a comparatively new idea to parcel our own time into decades like this; it is hard to think of any "decades" in this sense before the Naughty Nineties. It is a misleading habit, weakening our sense of the continuity of our societies, which Tocqueville characteristically regarded as a peculiarly American weakness: "the tie that unites one generation to another is relaxed or broken; every man there loses all trace of the ideas of their forefathers or takes no heed of them."[23]

Whether it is American or not, we need to resist it. The continuity is at least as important as the break, as Antoine Cournot noted in 1872: "Each generation transmits to the one immediately following a certain wealth of ideas through education; and while this educative process or transmission is taking place, the educating generation is still present and is still influenced by all the survivors of a previous generation which continues to play an important part in the government of the society and in the flow of ideas and business."[24] There is even a sense in which the rebellion of a new generation is in fact made by what it has been taught by the previous generation, and is not only a reaction against it.

From this point of view, we may see why the idea of the "generation gap" was a misconception. The story of the United States from, approximately, the beginning of the 1950s until, approximately, the end of the 1960s was the story of the increasing separation of a popular culture that was assertively experimental from a political society that was unquestioningly traditional. In the second half of the 1960s, they collided; and the impact of the collision was shattering for one simple reason, whose significance is still not clearly understood, and which one has been trying to explore here. It took place inside the vast commonalty of the urban white middle class of the United States, even inside individual members of that commonalty. That was the arena of the struggle, and from it were drawn the gladiators. That is why it looked as if there were a "generation gap"; but it was not primarily a matter of age.

The morals and manners of "the young" were those in which, more by example than by precept, they had been instructed by their parents. They merely took those morals and manners, carried them into the open, and used them as a gesture, rather than as a rebellion, against the conservatism of the political society, as contrasted with the experimentation of the popular culture. When the young of this period turned to their parents and said, "But look at *your* drugs, at *your* marriages, at *your* affairs; we are merely copying you," they had a point. They were talking about the values—or lack of values—in which they had been reared: about the experimentation and freedom from constrictions that were already the marks of the lives of their parents.

The meaning of it may again be grasped by contrasting what happened in America during this period with what happened in Britain. During the 1950s, it was in Britain that a new radical movement seemed to be emerging with most confidence. It was there that the "Angry Young Men" made their appearance, and that the New Left was born; *Look Back in Anger* was produced at the Royal Court Theatre in 1956, and was soon followed by *Declaration,* the first manifesto, as it seemed at the time, of a new radical generation. But it all came to nothing; the littleness of it—one might even say, its Little Englishness—soon began to tell. It amounted in the end to little more than a few pinpricks of protest against the stubborn peculiarities of the class structure in England. The kind of victory that it won was celebrated in 1962, when Marylebone Cricket Club announced that at Lord's Cricket Ground no distinction would henceforth be made between the Gentlemen (the amateurs) and the Players (the professionals), who would even be permitted to enter and leave the field by the same gate.

The radical movement in England was indeed a cultural movement, in many of its manifestations; but the only place to which it could look for the popular culture that it needed, to inspire and sustain it, was to a reimagined culture of a working class that even in Britain was ceasing to have any cohesion or genuine vitality. But in America the popular culture was that of the urban middle class, which meant that it was the popular culture of a society, rather than of a particular class. It was this that gave "The Movement" an appearance of much greater depth than it in fact possessed. The fascination of the writings of Jerry Rubin, for example, is not that they displayed any genuinely revolutionary impulse or political concern, but that they were a sustained hymn to the popular culture of the middle class in which he was reared; he adhered to that culture, in which he was installed, rather than being separated from it by his generation.

PERSONAL MALAISE AS A SOCIAL PROTEST

With this insight, it is easier to understand the most striking characteristic of many of today's movements. Cushioned by his upbringing, Rubin beat out his tunes on the pillow with his fists:

> TV is raising generations of kids who want to grow up and become demonstrators. . . .
> You can't be a revolutionary today without a television set—it's as important as a gun. . . .
> The Marx Brothers are our leaders as they run through restaurants cutting off people's ties. . . .
> I got my ideas from the Lone Ranger. You know the Lone Ranger always fought on the side of good against the forces of evil and injustice.

His gratitude to his culture was unbounded.
He was even more explicit:

> Affluent culture, by producing a car and car radio for every middle-class home, gave Elvis a base for recruiting.
> While a car radio in the front seat rocked with "Turn Me Loose," young kids in the back seat were breaking loose. Many a night was spent on dark and lonely roads, balling to hard rock beat.

Those who had grown up before the 1950s, he said, lived in "a mental world of Nazism, concentration camps, economic depression and Communist dreams Stalinized." But those who had grown up in the 1950s or later lived in "a world of supermarkets, color TV commercials, guerrilla war, international media, psychedelics, rock'n'roll and moon walks. For us *nothing is impossible.*"[25] The struggle for existence was being replaced by a concern for new ways of personal living, however juvenile and inept.

Irwin Siller, the former editor of *Sing Out,* once remarked of folk rock that it was "basically a middle-class trip"; and Irving Louis Horowitz said much the same of hard rock: "Unlike jazz, hard rock is basically a white music. A strong connection does exist between soul music and hard rock, but hard rock is a sound apart: white, youthful, disengaged, sexually blunt, and for the most part ideologically closer to pantheism than to socialism."[26] Even when it has been socially concerned, Andrew Weiner has put it, rock "reflects social change to a far greater degree than it shapes it," and the example that he offers is revealing: "Rock did not, for example, begin the American craze for surfing in the early sixties. But performers like the Beach Boys promoted surfing into a proportionately greater role in the imagination and the reality of the nation."[27]

With the mention of surfing, we are firmly in the popular culture of the more affluent element of the white middle class of America, just as we were with Charles Reich, when he put at the head of his list of the "human experiences" that are "either missing altogether from our lives or present only in feeble imitation of their real quality" the need for adventure and travel, including in particular: "The Yukon, the Hebrides, a blizzard, fog on the Grand Banks, the lost cities of Crete, climbing a mountain on rock and ice in its elemental cold and wind."[28] This is the sentimentality of the individual members of a leisured class, freed from the struggle for existence, and from the physical constrictions of the past, who have ceased to have any genuine concern for the condition of the human estate in which they live, and who in fact have ceased to be able to imagine their personal attitudes in social terms at all. When they wished to regard themselves as a class that was oppressed, they had to reach outside their own experience, and talk of themselves, with a fatuity that was as great as the impertinence, as "white niggers," claiming that their long hair was their black skin and that they "felt like" Indians and blacks and the Vietnamese.

Given the nature of the commonalty of the middle class of America, it has not been surprising that most of the movements that have demanded our attention during the past few years, including "The Movement," have been expressions of the personal malaise of some of its individual members. It is this extreme personalism that has rendered them ineffective as social influences; and this personalism has its origin in the total failure, during the past half century, to discover what is the meaning of this new phenomenon, the commonalty of America. The only attempt that has been made is to describe it as the "mass society," and the ordinary man in it as "the masses." That is the only picture we have, and against "the masses" in this picture is pitted the individual, isolated and with no sense of his community of interest with his fellows: the self, as we have been taught to conceive it, in rebellion against a society we have similarly been taught to conceive as impersonal and unfriendly.

CHAPTER 2

The Godfathers of the Child

Although he may not know it, the spoiled child of the Western world has been largely made by four men: Darwin and Marx, Freud and Einstein. The influence of none of these is much more than a hundred years old; and, when we consider the havoc that they wreaked in almost every field of traditional attitudes and ideas, we ought to be surprised, not that we live in a tempestuous time, but that our societies have held so well together. It is the effect of these four men and their collaborators on all the generations that have followed, and not particular influences on individual generations, that we need now to consider. These are our godfathers—if the term can still be used as once it was—responsible for our instruction.

DARWIN AND THE REMOVAL OF PURPOSE

First to the cradle of the spoiled child came Darwin, with his announcement, as one evolutionary theorist has put it: "Man is the result of a purposeless and materialistic process that did not have him in mind. He is a state of matter, a form of life, a sort of animal, and a species of the Order Primates."[1] An even more contemporary interpretation has been given by the geneticist S. E. Luria:

By integrating man into his comprehensive record of evolution, Darwin dispelled the hope of some immanent purpose in history. However unique man's endowment with consciousness might make him, his past and future represented only the passing of one species on the surface of the earth. They had no reason, no goal, no meaning except what man in his existential freedom might choose to set for himself.[2]

This is not so much an inaccurate statement as an extreme one and provocatively worded. The suggestion of "existential freedom" as the only alternative to purposelessness is gratuitous, and ought not to be in a scientist's interpretation of a scientific theory. Yet the passage is interesting because it illustrates exactly how a message from the high culture can travel into the popular mind.

The fact that the process of natural selection is thoughtless and random in the most obvious of its operations is not where we ought to stop. Equally important is that man's evolution at some point ceased to be as thoughtless and as random as that of any other species. It is part of the unique status of man that in him, as George Gaylord Simpson put it, "a new form of evolution begins, overlying and largely dominating the old, organic evolution which nevertheless continues in him. . . . Plan, purpose, goal, all absent in evolution to this point, enter with the coming of man and are inherent in the new evolution, which is confined to him."[3] In this more confident view, the freedom available to man—his power to choose and to plan—is not merely existential.

Yet there can be no doubt that in the spoiled child of today it is the extreme interpretation of Luria that holds sway. This is what justifies Bruce Mazlish when he speaks of "our Heraclitean period," pointing out that the greatest effect of Darwinism was to introduce the idea of "constant and unremitting change" as "the dominant mode of viewing the world. The result was that, throughout the world, all things, man included, had now to be conceived of as being in a perpetual state of variation."[4] Here indeed is the excuse or the incitement, whichever way one looks at it, for the spoiled child to reduce his life to a series of existential gestures in the flux of the universe. What is neglected is that man has managed to establish himself, alone among animals, against nature in his societies, in what are later described as the human estate. There he has purpose, there his intentions have a meaning, there he can plan. His social evolution is as much a part of his evolution as his organic evolution, "and it depends on learning, the inheritance of knowledge, as the old does on physical inheritance."[5]

It is clear that a crude Darwinism—we are *nothing but* animals—has surged again in the popular mind of today. It places man in nature, but not in history. (It is one of the curiosities of the theory of evolution that, in spite of its insistence on movement and change, it is unhistorical and in at least the extreme forms of the theory it makes man as unhistorical a creature as the animals.) Under its impact, the spoiled child is excited to follow exactly the prescriptions of Luria, as he expounds the meaning of evolution: "the substitution of reasons for survival in place of reasons for having been born; of cause in place of purpose; of an all-determining past in place of an all-important future."[6] To talk of an all-determining past is unhistorical; there could be no history—man could have had no history—if everything had been determined in the past. It is also an incitement to men to cease to try to be moral: in a world in which everything is caused, all is determined, the behaviour of men is reduced to little more than a series of expedients for his "survival in place of purpose," which is a form of existentialism.

MARX AND THE INCITEMENT TO CHANGE

Then to the cradle came the many-tongued Marx. Outside the societies that claim to be following his prescriptions, if not fulfilling his prophecies, it is as a moral influence that Marx has had, and still has, the greatest impact. No man in the modern age has done more to undermine the justifications of injustice in human society. Even the conservative, wishing to argue that some injustice is defensible or unavoidable, has to cast his arguments in terms that he would not have been forced to choose if Marx had not lived and written and inveighed. Marx has to be met.

Again, we are concerned with the influence that his ideas have had on the popular mind; and, if one selects only one, it is deliberately to simplify, deliberately to show how, apart from any of his particular diagnoses and prescriptions, the spoiled child of the Western world is bound to respond to him. The deep and continuing moral force of Marx is to be found in one of his many tongues: his insistence that men can and may, indeed that they must, *act* in their societies and in history. The fact that this will to action was contradicted, and in the end betrayed, by his historicism and determinism does not alter the fact that the insistence that goes on and on reaching the popular mind is the cry in his *Theses on Feuerbach:* "The philosophers have only interpreted the world in various ways; the point however is to *change* it." He wished to change it, to improve it, to enable men to enjoy more freedom, more equality, more justice, more security; he wished them no longer to be oppressed, and he urged that men could act to accomplish these changes.

In this tongue, what Marx proclaimed was that man could become the "master of his own social environment." Thirty years ago, in his searching criticism of Marx, Karl Popper said that contemporary Christianity, in its concern with the injustices in society, owes much to "the moral reformation brought about by Marx"[7]; and he was referring to this idea that men can be makers of their social environment. Striking confirmation of this was given in the extraordinary pronouncement, *Lumen Gentium,* that accompanied Vatican II, and which will be noticed more fully later in this book. Its statement that men and women today think of themselves, more and more, as "the artisans and authors of their culture and their community" is a remarkable tribute to the depth of Marx's influence. "In this sense," said Popper, "Marxism with its ethical rigour, its emphasis on deeds instead of mere words, is undoubtedly the most important corrective idea of our time"; and he added, "This moral radicalism is still alive."

This is the strenuous voice that persists in spite of the falsehoods —even the heresies—of scientific Marxism. Men are capable by their own willed acts to change history and their societies. We have lived through the vulgar version of it in the spoiled child. The message that one would expect him to take from Marx would be exactly the *Do It!* of Jerry Rubin, who was leaning ritually on a vulgarized Marxism when he said: "You gotta be born a Kennedy. Anybody can become a Che."[8] He can become Che by acting: do it! If it turned out that everyone could not become a Che, then everyone might, as Rubin in fact urged, drawing on his culture, become a Bonnie and Clyde. In this way, the act for which Marx called is turned into no more than gesture, and another existential influence is added.

FREUD AND THE LIBERATION FROM REPRESSION

To the cradle then came Freud: and one must once more emphasize that it is the manner in which his ideas have reached the popular mind that is our concern. In 1895, for example, he introduced the notion of repression as a contributor to neurosis; and it was this notion that later emerged in the popular culture as the *necessary* cause of unhappiness and ill health. Yet, between 1900 and 1905, Freud has passed beyond his initially simple observation, and begun to demonstrate that the mechanism of repression that he had identified in hysteria was in itself a normal part of the functioning of the human psyche. Indeed, the position at which he at last arrived was that repression in itself is not necessarily pathological, and that it is not repression as such that creates neurosis, but unsuccessful repression.

It is clear that in the scientific theory there is nothing to justify the abandonment of all moral restraints. Yet it is to the notion of repression as it has entered the popular mind that we owe a great deal of the permissiveness in the popular culture. Many of the contemporary ideas of sexual morality and of child rearing—the actual rearing of the spoiled child—spring from the misrepresentation that repression must always prevent the full and spontaneous, healthy and happy, development of the individual, child or adult. Indeed, the spoiled child of today seems less and less inclined to join with Freud in saying that emotional spontaneity and instinctual gratification are worth sacrificing to some extent for the rewards of "civilization," for the stability and security of civilized life.

Perhaps the most general influence of Freud as his ideas have entered the popular mind is to be found in the concentrated attention that is given to what is individual and biological, to the consequent neglect of what is social and historical. The repressive forces in the individual are studied so exclusively that no genuine effort is made to examine the oppressive forces of society. Attention is not given to the working of society, and the improvement of it, because it is considered to be either unimportant or important only in the sense that the individual must free himself from it. Part of the importance of Women's Liberation, it may be said in passing, is that, when it is true to itself, it tries to define some of the problems of individual women in social and not in personal terms; it might almost be said that its true purpose is to get women out of the psychiatrist's office into the political and social arena.

This concentration on the individual instead of the social is particularly noticeable in the influence of those—Wilhelm Reich is an obvious example—whose psychological interpretations of man's social condition mean that the remedies that they propose amount to little more than a series of personal acts of the individual by which he is supposed to achieve his own liberation. One of the faults in these prescriptions is that, the more closely one looks at them, the clearer is the implication that perhaps only a few individuals are capable of this kind of liberation. In this way, freedom is made the property of an elite, and this assumption lurks in Reich's own interpretation of *The Mass Psychology of Fascism,* where "the masses" are characteristically said to long for authority and be incapable of freedom. In the works of Norman O. Brown, this self-liberation is really little more than a fetish for a privileged minority.

A. S. Neill, who became one of the cultural heroes of the spoiled child, had by 1945 become a disciple of Reich and openly espoused the theory that sex repression is a device to dispirit the working class, and thus preserve the capitalist system. If one were a capitalist, one would pay Reich or Neill to expound such a theory. What could make capitalism more secure than to let those whom it oppresses find their "liberation" in the obsessed and tolerated gratification of their sexual appetites? It may even be that the commercial emphasis on sexuality in the popular culture is just such a device. Those who are in authority would much prefer that "the masses" run around naked than armed, that they read *The Joy of Sex* rather than *The Rights of Man.* They did not call out the National Guard to stop the "streakers" at the state universities.

The attempt that has been made here has been, not to show full range of the influence of these three men, but to demonstrate that their impact on the popular mind of all the generations that have followed them has been far more important than any "generation gap." Day by day, the spoiled child of whatever age reacts to their messages as they reach him: messages whose full significance is still undisclosed after approximately a century. To talk of the changes in attitude and morality that have followed as nothing more than permissiveness is not to understand the size of the shock.

The influence that is common to them all, and that has been singled out here, is the separation of the individual from his society. Insofar as the spoiled child is a Darwinian, he returns himself, "the human animal" of Weston La Barre, the "naked ape" of Desmond Morris, from his society to nature. Insofar as he is a Marxist, he stands ready to pit himself, by act or by gesture, against his society. Insofar as he is a Freudian, he is tempted to question the restraints of society on his personality, and to regard his problems as personal rather than social, so letting his society take care of itself while he absorbs himself in his-self.

EINSTEIN AND THE ALWAYS CHANGING UNIVERSE

But the fourth who came to the cradle, although he is not usually taken into account in such a context, was the most important of all. Our picture of our world and of ourselves has been altered more, in this century, by Einstein than by any other of the godfathers; and we must make the effort to understand what his influence, more ambiguous than any other, on the spoiled child has been.

In 1924, a front-page article in the *Times Literary Supplement* proclaimed: "We are living in one of the great ages of science." It spoke of "the enthusiastic optimism of our men of science," and of "the full vigour and joyfulness of another renaissance."[9] But its faith was already out of date, and one may observe the decline of that faith in the work of Ortega. "Science alone is not bankrupt. It is, then, without a competitor," he wrote in 1932; but in 1941 he was saying, "Science is in danger," and that man should be on his knees before its "majestic power," but, "on the contrary, he is beginning to turn his back."[10] Ozenfant was near the truth when he wrote in 1931: "It is said, idiotically enough, that science has gone bankrupt, whereas what went bankrupt was the faith we had in it."[11] It is in fact dangerous that we should have so powerful a force in our culture as science, and have no faith in it, for it means that we will not trouble to understand how it shapes our lives.

What has happened? In the first place, science is itself less certain that it can be certain. From the time, on November 10, 1619—when Descartes closed his eyes, stopped his ears, shut off all his senses, and even effaced "all images of corporeal things" from his thought, and dreamed his dream of the "Admirable Science," his vision of one science by which everything that we can know might be comprehended, as Jacques Maritain put it, by the same light, with the same certitude, and on the same level of intelligibility—to the beginning of this century, science was confident in its ability to find the fixed and regular laws of the universe, of nature, and even of all life. Its own faith was the faith of our civilization; and the scientific method could for three hundred years be seen as "that keen, levelling sovereign, refuge and comforter, of the modern world,"[12] or equally, if one chose to look at it differently, as its tyrant. It was not merely that science was certain, but that we were made certain by it of our knowledge of the universe.

The certainty of the universe of Descartes and Newton was a comfort; and Calvin Coolidge described how his generation was introduced to it at Amherst:

> . . . we learned of the universal application of the laws of mathematics. We saw the discoveries of Kepler, Descartes, Newton and their associates bringing the entire universe under one law, so that the most distant point of light revealed by the largest reflector marches in harmony with our own planet. We discovered, too, that the same force that rounds a tear-drop holds all the myriad worlds of the universe in a balanced position. We found that we dwelt in the midst of a Unity which was all subject to the same rules of action.[13]

It is fascinating that this vivid description is given to us by Coolidge, because the picture of a fixed and ordered universe could of course be translated into a political conservatism upholding a fixed and ordered society.

A few years later, the Unity—the order—was destroyed by science itself. Men such as Henri Poincaré and Albert Einstein, in effect, turned our science back on itself by envisaging a space that our senses cannot know, an infinite world in spite of its finiteness. The business of science was no longer thought to be the discovery of fixed and universal laws in nature, but the never ending, always changing attempt to understand nature by concepts that were created in men's minds. Einstein himself wrote, as if challenging the Newtonian image of "God the Clockmaker":

> Physical concepts are free creations of the human mind, and are not, however it may seem, uniquely determined by the external world. In our endeavor to understand reality we are somewhat like a man trying to understand the mechanism of a closed watch. He sees the face and the moving hands, even

hears its ticking, but he has no way of opening the case. If he is ingenious he may form some picture of a mechanism which could be responsible for all the things he observes, but he may never quite be sure his picture is the only one which could explain his observations. He will never be able to compare his picture with the real mechanism and he cannot even imagine the possibility or the meaning of such a comparison.[14]

The *Times Literary Supplement* might say in 1924 that "it is now pretty generally understood that the theory of relativity has come to stay," but Einstein himself declared that "There are no eternal theories in science. . . . Every theory has its period of gradual development and triumph, after which it may experience a decline"; and late in his life he confessed that his own theory was inadequate, but that he was by then too old to make the effort to rethink it.

This rejection by science of its own claims to certitude is the most shattering event in the contemporary world; and we have not yet come to terms with it. We ought to have found it an inspiration, but we have not done so. The scientific method itself is no longer the inexorable dictator of fixed laws that it had been since Descartes and Newton. "Science apart from its application is *pure game*," said Simone Weil,[15] and she could not have said so in any of the three preceding centuries. In fact, the scientific method which once seemed so forbiddingly different from other intellectual pursuits now appears to be less unlike them, despite the fact that so many of its "truths" can no longer be given expression in normal speech. C. Day Lewis once wrote of the simple truths that "the poet seems to have hit upon . . . while looking at, or for, something else; but he could not have hit upon them, just at the right moment, unless the looking had been wonderfully attentive and devoted."[16] Einstein could have accepted that as a description of at least part of his activity.

Much of the fury of the "counterculture" of the 1960s—as in Theodore Roszak's critical vindication of it—and much of its sentimentality—as in Charles Reich's testament to a third consciousness—was misdirected against the presumptuousness of a scientific method that no longer ruled. As an artist, Ozenfant could speak of the "untrammelled and lyrical imaginings" of Poincaré and Einstein; and Einstein himself talked of the "creative imagination" that is required in the great scientist if he is to raise new questions, see new problems, look at old problems from a new angle. To distrust this method—disdain it as it was disdained by the "counterculture"—is to refuse one of the most vigorous displays of the human imagination; and this refusal, transmitted from the high culture to the popular culture, has done much to weaken the imagination of our times.

Since the beginning of this century, as Maurice Merleau-Ponty said, "many great books have expressed the revolt of life's immediacy against reason. Each in its own way has said that the rational arrangements of a system of morals or politics, or even of art, is valueless in the face of the fervor of the moment, the explosive brilliance of an individual life, the 'premeditation of the unknown.'"[17] But much of our difficulty in this, and much of the wrongheadedness of the remedies that are proposed, would be avoided if we understood that reason itself has been in revolt against an excessive rationalism. "To have led so many reasoning animals around to a hatred of reason," said Maritain, "is another of rationalism's misdeeds." The rationalism of Descartes was intended to give man mastery over nature, and over his own nature, by the use of his reason alone, and the effect of this, of course, was to set man against nature, including his own nature. The reason was removed from the senses. The pretension of Descartes, of "rising to the plane of the intellect without passing through the gate of the senses, the way fixed for us by nature," was the "cockcrow of rationalism," its "early-morning presumptuousness"[18]; and it laid a curse on us and on our reason, which we have not yet escaped.

Nevertheless, we will not understand the spoiled child of our times if we do not realize that he does not altogether like the release that science has given him. He is at a loss when confronted by science's inability, or refusal, any longer to provide him with absolute explanations of the world. He hankers after the unity and order in which someone as recent as Coolidge was instructed. Having been released from the "reality" that was once imposed by science, he is unhappy that science now openly admits that it is only with reality's illusion that it deals. "Science is concerned not with things but with the systems of signs it can substitute for things,"[19] said Ortega; and the spoiled child in fact feels betrayed that it has so humbled itself; and he goes in search, as we will see, of other gods to substitute, not only for the One God who now is dead, but also for God the Clockmaker, who could once open the case and let us see how it worked.

THE RELEASE FROM THE MECHANICAL VIEW OF MAN

But there is more. What the science of our own century has done is destroy forever its own previous effort to give a mechanical explanation of the universe. As he moved deeper and deeper to his realization that the classical concepts of physics were not adequate to explain the observed phenomena of nature, Einstein came to the point where he recognized that "all the fruitless attempts . . . seem to indicate that the fault lies in the fundamental assumption that it is possible to explain all events in nature from a mechanical point of view. Science did not succeed in carrying out the mechanical program convincingly, and today no physicists believe in the possibility of its fulfilment."[20]

The mechanical world of Newton was perhaps comprehensible but it was also repellent, and it increasingly became so to the modern sensibility. The romantics inveighed against it; it was "an empty generalization, an abstract, inane Utopia," said Ortega; and the "counterculture" continued to inveigh against it even when science had itself disposed of it. One would have expected our imaginations to feel a sense of release at being freed from the Newtonian universe, and this was the reaction of the *Times Literary Supplement* in 1923, as it contemplated, in its article on Melville, the new universe of Einstein, "whose matter, space, and time, it appears, are largely creations of our own. Such ideas do not nestle isolated in the mind. They subtly modify the whole of a man's outlook. . . . It is a characteristic of our time that there is a sense of unlimited possibilities; the firm lines of our actual world are growing indistinct. . . . we get glimpses of greater and perhaps more lonely seas than man has ever adventured on before." But in the fifty years since then we have reacted in the opposite way, as if made anxious by living in a world of which our explanations are only relative.

Science "may take Nature apart," cried Frank Lloyd Wright in 1949, "but cannot put Nature together again for the growth of the human soul"[21]; and it had of course been the genius of the Newtonian synthesis that it did put the world together again. Yet at the deepest level at which we imagine ourselves the sense of release should be invigorating. For what we have been witnessing is the collapse, not only of the mechanical view of the world, but of the mechanistic study of man, the picture of man as given by Descartes:

> The body of a living man differs from that of a dead man just as does a watch or other automation (i.e., a machine that moves itself, when it is wound up and contains in itself the corporeal principle of those movements for which it is designed along with all that is requisite for its action) from the same watch or other machine when it is broken and when the principle of its movements ceases to act.

The neatest riposte was given by Queen Christina of Sweden when she remarked that it was all very well, but that she had never seen her watch give birth to infant watches.

In a brilliant lecture that he gave at the University of Chicago twenty-five years ago, Alexandre Koyré said that "The overwhelming success of Newtonian physics made it practically inevitable that its particular features became thought of as essential for . . . all the new sciences that emerged in the eighteenth century—sciences of men and society." The order and harmony that had been found in nature must be discoverable also in human nature, and discoverable by the same methods. According to this prescription, "we have to find out, by observation, experience, and even experiment, the fundamental and permanent faculties, *the properties of man's being that can neither be increased or diminished;* we have to find out the patterns of actions or laws of behavior which relate to each other and link human actions together. From these laws we deduce everything else." (Italics added.) "A magnificent program!" exclaimed Koyré. "Alas its implications did not yield the expected results." In fact, it produced "rather bad results."[22]

But it is precisely this idea that has exhausted itself. We no longer have any measure to decide what in any individual can be "increased or diminished." Our understanding of man's nature has become as unlimited as the universe into which the science of this century has pitched him. Again one would have expected us to respond to this new apprehension of ourselves with exhilaration, but we have not done so, and at least a part of the reason may be found in the fact that we disdain the science which, correcting itself by its own method, has given us this release. We cannot hope to understand our world or ourselves unless we acknowledge how deeply our views of them are shaped by our science, and so reach to it for assistance in comprehending why we imagine ourselves as we do.

The profound shift in the attitudes of ordinary men and women that was traced at the beginning of this chapter was caused, at least in part, by the unexpected disclosure of an unlimited world of unprecedented possibilities by contemporary science. By the middle of this century it was the influence of this disclosure that was, as much as anything else, reaching into the popular mind, telling of the unprecedented possibilities of man. "I am not stressing the fact that the physics of Einstein is more exact than the physics of Newton," wrote Ortega, "but that the man Einstein is capable of greater exactitude and liberty of spirit than the man Newton"[23]; and we are also this "man Einstein," it is to this enhanced "liberty of spirit" that we are heir in this century. The tragedy has been that, ceasing to have a just respect for the science that is a creation of our own minds, we have looked elsewhere for explanations of our new apprehensions of our world and ourselves, and thus have forfeited the intellectual corrections that our modern sensibility has so desperately required. There is a literal sense in which it may be said that our culture, high and popular, is out of its mind.

EVERYMAN THE ARTIST OF HIS OWN LIFE

That sensibility has been in large part the creation of our art. "More and more mankind will discover that we have to turn to poetry to interpret life for us," said Matthew Arnold in 1880, "to console us, to sustain us. Without poetry our science will appear incomplete; and most of what now passes with us for religion and philosophy will be replaced by poetry." This is no longer thought to be true: for one thing, which belief or speculation of which poet or artist is supposed to be the interpretation of life that we require? Although it is untrue, however, it has come to seem to be true. At least since the proclamation of Nietzsche, "I am convinced that art represents the highest task and the truly metaphysical activity of this life," the capitulation to art, which has meant also the imposition on it of a burden that it cannot bear, has been so consistent a theme that it is even today a popular habit. Busloads of housewives from the suburbs will arrive at an exhibition of modern art, persuaded that they can—and indeed must—discover a meaning in a painting that will bestow a meaning on their lives.

"I saw in pictures—not necessarily those which deal with religious subject-matter—a revelation of the meaning of life," says the theologian Paul Tillich.[24] "The artist is the most sensitive individual in society," echoes the chemist Eugene Rabinowitz. "His feeling for change, his apprehension of new things to come, is likely to be more acute than that of the slower-moving, rational, scientific thinker."[25] According to the critic Susan Sontag, "The subject of literature has pre-empted much of the energy that formerly went into philosophy. . . . Art is seen as a mirror of human capacities in a given historical period, as the pre-eminent form by which a culture defines itself, names itself, dramatizes itself."[26] Infected by this spirit, it is no wonder that Harold Rosenberg could present the moderate talent of Barnett Newman to the readers of *Vogue* as "a man of spiritual grandeur" and his work as "forms of the sublime."

Anyone may listen to music, or read a poem, or gaze on a painting, and imagine that he has found its meaning, or at least a meaning for him. In this way, countless people today lead the kind of double lives of actual conformity and fantasized rebellion that we have already noticed, and which have been described by Merleau-Ponty: "in their roles as citizens, husbands, lovers, or fathers, they follow the rule of a fairly conservative reason, locating their revolt in literature or poetry, which thereby become a religion."[27] This has been exactly the fallacy in the "counterculture" of recent years. It has been imagined that a revolution in aesthetic sensibility can be translated into an actual revolution. It has not happened, and there is no way in which it could have happened. Art does not have the capacity to make us *in our living* as wild and free as ponies.

But there is a further curiosity in all this: while we demand from art a revelation of the meaning of life, art seems determined to retreat from the burden. In spite of its prominence—itself a celebrity—art has withdrawn to the margins. From the sidelines, the artist waves his pompoms, no longer a part of the game, but a part of the intervals. Because of its unseriousness, there is nothing that art can do to astonish us that we will not accommodate. There is no artist that we will not tolerate, no confection of his that we will not put on a wall, on the floor, or on the ceiling. Art offers us the bizarre and the unexpected, the peculiar and the whimsical, the impermanent and the valueless. "What I am chiefly conscious of is a loss of resonance," says Richard M. Weaver, "and I think that this loss is owing mainly to the fact that the modern style shuns things suggestive of values."[28] Art will *play*, because only in play can it be autonomous, open to no judgment but its own, with no obligation but to itself. The world asks for a meaning; from the margins, art laughs and spits in the world's face.

Is this not the profound dissatisfaction that one must in the end feel at the work of Mark Rothko, for example? The form is reduced to an exquisite contemplation of its own achievement, as is the colour to an intense preoccupation with its own beauty. But there it stops; the space moves in and out, as the art critic tells us as if he were describing a breathing exercise, moving to no depth of observation of anything. It appears to be a habit, in Washington and Houston at least, to hang his pictures as if in a chapel; but to what are we meant to pray? (One notices that people in these galleries talk to each other in whispers.) "If he doesn't pull out soon," said Frank Getlein in 1961, "the wallpaper people will get him, same as the linoleum man got Mondrian"[29]; and Rothko of course did pull out. After all, where was there left for his art to go? It was annihilating itself.

This double position of art, autonomous but on the margins of life, has affected the actual living of the spoiled child. In place of the familiar image of Everyman as the passive consumer, Rosenberg once said, it is as realistic to imagine Everyman as his own artist; and all that this can mean, of course, is that each may be the artist of his own life. The autonomy that has already been claimed for art is thus claimed for the individual; an image of art itself has been transposed into an image of our real lives; its potentiality is our potentiality.

THE TEMPTATIONS TO HALLUCINATION

To use hallucination as a way of seeing things may be profitable, for example; but it is not profitable as a way of living one's own life. "I habituated myself to simple hallucination," said Rimbaud; "I would see quite honestly a mosque instead of a factory, a school of drummers composed of angels, barouches on the roads of the sky, a drawing room at the bottom of a lake," and there he arrested his art. "Then I explained my magical sophistries by the hallucination of words!" The words are not allowed to intervene with their own art, and from that point the conclusion is inevitable: "I ended by finding sacred the disorder of my mind." We must ask of the life as well as the art of Rimbaud, for he made both short, whether he could not have done better by them.

We have seen the results of the confusion of hallucination with art, and of art with life, in recent years. Through psychedelics, one of their celebrants has said that the world may be experienced— presumably by anyone—as some great writers are supposed to have experienced it, and one is familiar with the claims that follow: the apparent transfiguration of the ordinary world, the sense of timelessness, the realization of Self by the loss of Self, identification with the universe, and peace and joy. All this—in fact, heaven—for the price of a joint or a fix. What is altogether absent from this description is any sense of reality, of a correspondence between the created world of art and the real world in which we live. We are not even given reality's illusion; only hallucination.

Again we find it in *Do It!*—that sustained incantation of the spoiled child:

> Marijuana makes each person God. . . .
> Get high and you turn on the world. . . .
> Pot transforms environments. . . .
> Grass travels around the room like a continually moving kiss. . . .
> When you're high on pot you enjoy only one thing—the moment. . . .
> Marijuana is the street theater of the mind. . . .
> Pot scrambles up our brains and presents everything as one perfect mess. . . .
> Grass destroyed the left as a minority movement and created in its place a youth culture. . . .[30]

What is pathetic in these ejaculations is that there is absolutely no sense of anyone or anything but the self, which itself is hallucinated; the kiss that continually moves can be the kiss of no other person;

the other is not present. There has again taken place, under another inspiration, "a hopeless displacement of the boundary between literature and life."

"The literary mind has a unique power today," Martin Green has said. "I mean, people believe James Joyce's account of Dublin in 1904 rather than that of a Lord Lieutenant of Ireland or an Archbishop or a philosopher."[31] Insofar as this is true, it is a calamity. It means that we are deprived of a great part of our humanity: our sense of the actual, our ability to see commonplace things in a commonplace way in order to perform commonplace deeds to achieve a commonplace good. In fact, what is common to us in our everyday lives is too often represented to us as inauthentic in contrast with our authentic selves. This is one of the heresies of our time, and it has been carried from our art and our literature into life, so that the spoiled child is given one more excuse or incitement to dissociate himself from his society, from his obligation to it and the fellowship it has to offer.

THE SMASHED FORMS OF TRADITION

We must notice at the beginning one more influence. The unseriousness of the art that was to come was described long ago by Hegel: "an inexhaustible self-abandon of the imagination, an innocent frolic, and with it an inward warmth and joy of sensibility . . . raising the soul, through serenity of form, above any painful involvement in reality." This lack of seriousness and disengagement from reality—the fact that art, as he said, would never be dangerous again—he thought would be its splendour, in fact its final splendour. This is seductive, but it must be remembered that he was writing in a certain place at a certain time, in Europe when it was, he believed, in a period of transition, the birth time of a new order: ". . . the spirit of the time growing slowly and quietly ripe for the new form it is to assume, disintegrates one fragment after another of the structure of its previous world. Frivolity and again ennui, which are spreading in the established order of things, the undefined foreboding of something unknown—all these betoken that there is something else approaching."[32]

Was not the old order that had to be destroyed the old order of Europe? "The lamps are going out all over Europe," said Edward

Grey at the outbreak of war in 1914; "they will not be lit again in our lifetime." We need to understand that he was lamenting more than the beginning of a holocaust. By the time that war had broken out, Europe had already smashed almost all of its forms. Almost all the important experimenting had been done before 1914. "Cubism, futurism, dadaism, and surrealism, and various forms of abstraction," Herbert Read once wrote, "had already proliferated their main features" by the 1920s, "and it may be doubted if forty years later the confused manifestations of contemporary art contain anything essentially new."[33]

By 1914 the same had happened in all the arts in Europe. After Rimbaud and Mallarmé, there had come Eliot in 1913 with "The Love Song of J. Alfred Prufrock," with its broken lines and succession of dissociated images, the indecision of the man an echo of the dissolution of the will of a civilization. After Debussy and Wagner, there had come Schönberg in 1912 with *Pierrot Lunaire,* with no key, and its "weird wandering and haunting sense of homelessness," and Stravinsky in 1913 with *Rites of Spring,* its dissonance and bitonality. In 1907 had come Picasso with "Demoiselles d'Avignon," showing the influence of a primitive art from outside Europe, and prefiguring the cubism which was to exhaust its creativeness in a few years. Even in architecture, "about 1900 to 1914," Nikolaus Pevsner has said, "a race of giants arose and created a new style for a new century, a style which was completely independent of the past. . . . By 1914 that style was complete."[34] Before its political order was destroyed in the First World War, the cultural order of Christendom was already being fragmented.

It was at this time that the Armory Exhibition of the modern art of Europe was shown in New York, and it has since been the seat of a legend. By a single exhibition of the work of European artists the American artist is improbably supposed to have been released. An early statement of the legend was given by Ralph Adam Cram in *The Atlantic Monthly* of February 1917, on the eve of America's entry into the war:

Then, in the latter days on the very eve of Armageddon, came over to us the anarchy of Europe, one preposterous absurdity after another, fruit of a righteous, if riotous, rebellion against Salon and Royal Academy, and Fifth Avenue seethed

with heresy and schism. . . . the new anarchy of Europe—
not to achieve a following, for we have at least the saving sense
of humor, but to break down the smug self-complacency that
had become a mode, and open up still unexplored reaches of
individualism.

But at least this early rendering of the legend recognized that what
was being brought from Europe was the expression of its own
anarchy at the moment of its dissolution and self-destruction.

What was unfortunate in the event and the legend was that at the
very moment at which American art might have been expected to
achieve its own form and even its own subject, and in fact was
beginning to demonstrate its own vigour, it tied itself again to the
tail of European art; and the story of American painting during the
years of its dominance since 1940 has been the story of a succession
of valiant but rarely successful attempts to untie itself from that tail.
One of the major works on abstract expressionism is called *The
Triumph of American Painting*. The celebration is premature. There
has yet been no triumph, because the painting has not yet become
American, it has only made the painful effort.

Again and again, which was perhaps not surprising in a painter
who had Thomas Hart Benton as his teacher, Jackson Pollock
refused to go to Europe, in body or in spirit: one has the impression
that, on the eve of each visit, he failed to get his passport, or managed to lose it. Even he, as he laboured for a form, none with more
energy, felt the oppression of Europe, and still at the end was not
free. Old forms can be replaced only by the creation of new forms.
But the besetting fault of American art, in its quandary, has been
to rely, for the breaking of old forms, too much on improvisation.
The temptation to improvisation has indeed been one of the experiences of the American. But there is a form in American life which
not only is not improvised but is not European; and it is to this
that we are about to turn.

EUROPE IN ITS DEATH THROES, ITS FINGERS AT AMERICA'S THROAT

But let us make our approach from another angle. "The true business of literature is to remind the powers that be, simple and corrupt

as they are, of the turbulence they have to control," said R. P. Blackmur. Well, yes! But an obsession with turbulence is a recipe for inaction. Our reality is in fact not so turbulent as we have been taught to imagine, precisely because a great part of that reality is in our human estate, fenced against nature on the one hand and against our-selves on the other. "One cannot unceasingly," as Camus warned in the voice that is too often unheeded in his work, "suffer from cold." The pleasure of our lives, for which the pain of our births and our deaths is acceptable, is in the ways of other men and our association with them: not always in their whole souls, their whole hearts, their whole minds, but in their own everyday corrections of the turbulence of their human existences. Can these not also be the subject of our art and our literature?

One of the answers is that which is being given here. The art and the literature of turbulence are primarily the art and the literature of Europe in decline. Perhaps the most athletic worshipper of art in our time, Herbert Read said that modern art "shares those elements of revolt and dissolution, of violence and fragmentation, of destruction and reconstruction, that give the political development of Europe in our time its intrinsic meaning. But that does not make the art less 'human'; on the contrary, it gives art its relevance, its significance, its intrinsic honesty."[35] This may well be true of Europe, as sadly true as the art and the literature of decay have proclaimed. But what in that case, one must ask again, are the art and the literature of America doing in following suit, in being indeed the suitors to the decline, surrendering their youth to an aged and painted courtesan? Life is short, Europe cries at the end of its millennial supremacy, so let art be shorter, that it may correspond: broken and fragmented, let it mirror our shiftiness.

"It is one of the great points of Conrad's story," Lionel Trilling has said of *The Heart of Darkness,* "that Marlow speaks of the primitive life of the jungle not as being noble or charming or even free, but as being base and sordid—and for *that* reason compelling. . . . Is this not the essence of the modern belief about the nature of the artist, the man who goes down into that hell which is the historical beginning of the human soul?"[36] Insofar as this is a theme that has been celebrated in the literature of our time, it represents a sickness of the imagination, and the sickness had a cause. In its failing years, with a failing strength, Europe went forth in the nineteenth century to subdue the continents to which it had roamed, and it encountered their vastness and their intractability: the menace of the jungle and the desert, the sierra and the pampas. What a speck of dust, blown down the khud, as Kipling said, was the civilized European man before these inert continental masses of the wilderness and the primitive; and into their ears, as they stood dumbfounded at the jungle's terrors, Darwin breathed to them of the shortness of the span of their civilization, and Freud of the Eros that they had repressed so that they might be civilized.

But that was not the experience of the American: he gazed on his continent and its wilderness, and determined that it should be won and farmed. No matter what the cost in human life, that was his achievement. At least the Europeans in the eighteenth century understood the nature of the experiment. As is revealed in their writings, they wondered at the size of the new world and imagined that it was inhabited by animals and men of monstrous proportions. Men such as Jefferson and Franklin had patiently to send to Europe specimens of animals and men that were of ordinary size and unexotic garb in order to convince even the *philosophes* that in America also man could find his measure. Was the discovery of America a mistake? This was one of the questions that disturbed the European mind until shortly before the Revolution, when the proclamation of the new man with his hope for all men was taken as an answer that it was not.

Whenever he strayed from the garden he had made in his peninsula, the European was in danger of being overcome by terror and superstition: but not the European who became an American. The poet and the artist in America will not be true to themselves until they travel back to their own revolution and their own enlightenment, to make again the break from Europe that still has its fingers to their throats even in its death throes. It was not by superstition or myth that America was made, but by the rejection of them; not out of a nightmare of "that hell which is the historical beginning of the human soul," but out of an awakening of the human reason which was the historical beginning of our democratic societies. The history of the United States has yet to be long; its art and its literature should be preparing to be long as well, to march with it in step, and not always to be shifting their feet from experiment to experiment, movement to movement, fragment to fragment, accomplishing only the ruins, only an imitation of the ruins, among which the ghosts of European culture are now doomed to exercise. If the United States is at the prow of today's world, as Marías said, it is certainly at the prow of our culture, and we can look only to it for redress. It is to the presence of the American that we must now turn.

PART II

The Presence of the American

One's-self I sing, a single separate person,
Yet utter the word Democratic, the word En-Masse.

—WALT WHITMAN; the opening lines of *Leaves of Grass*

CHAPTER 3

The Beginning of American Time

From the moment the country was invented, the dominance of the United States in the world was foretold by Americans and Europeans alike. Thomas Pownall, an English colonial statesman of unusually refreshing insight, wrote in 1783, in a memorial "Addressed to the Sovereign of America," that the Americans "will become a Nation to whom all Nations will come; a Power whom all the Powers of Europe will court to Civil and Commercial Alliances; a People to whom the Remnants of all ruined Peoples will fly,"[1] and he was not alone in his prediction.

THE AMBIVALENT RESPONSE TO AMERICAN DOMINANCE

The inevitability of the dominance of the United States was one of the great themes of the political literature of Europe in the nineteenth century: in Tocqueville, of course, who confessed that "in America I saw more than America; I sought there the image of democracy itself . . . , in order to learn what we have to fear or hope from its progress"; in Marx, who more than once spoke of the cause of America as the cause of mankind, and who remarked that Benjamin Franklin's description of man as a tool-making animal was characteristic of "Yankeedom" and therefore of modern man, as it had been characteristic of antiquity to speak of man as a political animal; in Hegel, who wrote that America is the land of the future where, "in the ages that lie before us, the burden of world history shall reveal itself." The theme was sometimes only adumbrated, as if the writers found it too grand and even too terrible to contemplate, but for almost a century after 1783 it was consistent: the American was the precursor of modern man, the modern age would be the American age; for better or for worse.

Towards the end of his life, John Adams exclaimed of the American Revolution: "Its effects and consequences have already been awful over a great part of the Globe; and when and where are they to cease?" Until the Civil War, no European seriously doubted the claim of Daniel Webster that "We are placed at the head of popular governments"; and, as late as February 1, 1862, Marx wrote in the New York *Daily Tribune* of "the natural sympathy the popular classes all over the world ought to feel for the only popular government in the world." Throughout this period, for eighty years after the end of the War of Independence, a strenuous debate was conducted in the political reviews in Britain about the meaning of the American experiment. Should it be welcomed or disdained? Was it relevant to other countries or did it owe its success to the "propitious circumstances" which existed in the United States? One thing was agreed. For good or ill, America was the omen of something new that was happening in the world.

Then the theme began to fade. As popular governments were established in Europe, the popular government of the United States no longer seemed to be so singular an experiment; as the power of the aristocracies in Europe was broken, the absence of an aristocracy in the United States no longer appeared to hold so novel a promise. In fact, when the popular movements in Europe at last turned from disputing with monarchs and aristocrats to disputing with industrialists and capitalists, the appeal of the United States was reversed, or at least it seemed to be. Engaged in the industrialization of a continent—throwing roads of iron, to echo a phrase of Emerson, east and west between two oceans, north and south between the tropics and the snows; and transporting across these roads the plenty of nature and an abundance of manufacture—America seemed to be a land of unlimited wealth and uninhibited energy, but the land also of E. H. Harriman and John D. Rockefeller, whom the popular government which had once humbled a monarch and repudiated an aristocracy now seemed unable to control. From being the head of popular governments, it has become the head of capitalist societies, to be welcomed or disdained as such, as once it had been welcomed or disdained as the hope of "the popular classes."

During the first century of American time, the promise of the United States was represented as idealistic; during the second century, as materialistic. By the end of the nineteenth century, the political reviews in Britain spoke in wonder of the resources and wealth of the United States, and of the ingenuity of its people, but also with a sniff of self-conscious (rather than effortless) superiority. It was, after all, rather difficult to be effortlessly superior when the most imaginative way in which the heirs of the landed class in England could save themselves and their estates from extinction was to marry the heiresses of the capitalist class in America.

It was conceded that Britain and Europe were being Americanized, but by American commerce rather than an American idea. This was an Englishman's description of the process at the end of the nineteenth century:

> In the domestic life we have got to this: The average man rises in the morning from his New England sheets, he shaves with "Williams" soap and a Yankee safety razor, pulls on his Boston boots over his socks from North Carolina, fastens his Connecticut braces, slips his Waltham or Waterbury watch in his pocket, and sits down to breakfast. There he congratulates his wife on the way her Illinois straight-front corset sets off her Massachusetts blouse, and he tackles his breakfast, where he eats bread made from prairie flour . . . , tinned oysters from Baltimore, and a little Kansas City bacon, while his wife plays with a slice of Chicago ox-tongue. The children are given "Quaker" oats. At the same time he reads his morning paper, printed by American machines, on American paper, with American ink, and probably edited by a smart journalist from New York City.

W. T. Stead quoted this passage from the writing at Fred Mackenzie in 1901, in his book *The Americanization of the World;* and in the same year Goldsworthy Lowes Dickinson wrote from the United States to E. M. Forster: "The two things rubbed into me in this country are (1) that the future of the world lies with America, and (2) that radically and essentially America is a barbarous country.

. . . The life of the spirit . . . is, not accidentally or temporarily, but inevitably and eternally, killed in this country."

Here is the root of the ambivalence towards the United States which has been characteristic, on the part of many Americans as well as most Europeans, of the second century of American time. The future of the world lies with America, yet in America the life of the spirit is killed, "not accidentally or temporarily, but inevitably and eternally." If one believes this to be true, the prospect is bleak, and much of the despairing literature of Europe during the past century, the literature of the "decline of the West," may be explained in terms of this overwhelming recognition, on the one hand, that it is in the United States that henceforth "the burden of world history shall reveal itself," and the no less overwhelming (and undermining) belief that in America the life of the spirit, nourished for so long by Europe, will at last be extinguished. To understand that the leadership of the West had passed to the United States, but not to believe in the spirit of America, or even that the spirit could live in America: Was this not the empty valley of the hollow men; the broken column, the lost kingdoms, the dead land, the broken jaw, the whimper at the world's end? The decline of the West, as it was described by Oswald Spengler at the end of the First World War, was the decline of Europe; he barely mentioned the United States.

THE END OF EUROPEAN TIME

Moreover, this attitude had been complicated at the beginning of the century by the recognition that, immediately and practically, Europe needed the power of America. The meaning of the outbreak of war in 1914 was that the European system had collapsed; and of the inconclusive slaughter between 1914 and 1917, that the system could no longer correct itself. No political review in Britain, perhaps not in Europe, understood this more clearly than *The Spectator* under the editorship of John St. Loe Strachey. With the outbreak of war, it urged on the United States a policy of neutrality, but only in the letter. A month after the outbreak of war, it looked beyond the fiction of neutrality to a reserve of American power on which the European allies could draw:

England is not going to perish, and we believe that we can guard the English ideals of freedom and independence by ourselves and without help. Nevertheless, since all human calculations are fallible, we want to know that at any rate there shall be some other place in the world where those can be maintained, and some other Power strong enough to maintain them. But America cannot do that unless she secures her independence and liberty by providing the men and rifles and the equipment which are required to protect her against a *coup de main.*

There could have been no clearer admission, as early as September 10, 1914, before the slaughter had begun, that Europe had started a war which Europe would not be able to conclude. The clock had struck the end of European time.

Three years later, on October 23, 1917, in the trenches southeast of Nancy, a gun of Battery C of the Sixth Field Artillery of the 1st American Division fired the first shot from an American fighting force into the German lines on European soil; and with it the United States entered history. It was exactly in this manner that *The Spectator* welcomed the American Expeditionary Force, pointing out that many of the men who were embarking for Europe had never seen the sea before, but that they would now become "citizens of the world, and heirs of the great tradition of history." "It is our war, America's war," Theodore Roosevelt had declared from the beginning; and so it became.

The men poured across the Atlantic, from states which had only recently been territories, even from territories which had not yet been admitted as states, and the bald record of their transportation is a sufficient commentary on the magnitude of what was occurring:

In 1917:   1,718 men in May
            12,261 men in June
            12,988 men in July
            18,323 men in August
            32,523 men in September
            38,259 men in October
            23,016 men in November
            48,840 men in December
In 1918:   46,776 men in January
            48,027 men in February
            83,611 men in March

117,212 men in May
244,345 men in June
297,000 men in July
283,000 men in August
258,000 men in September
159,000 men in October

Men of the regular army at first, then men of the National Guard, then men of the conscript army; the National Guard of one or two states able in the beginning to field an entire division—the 27th from New York, the 32nd from Wisconsin and Michigan—until its reserves were so depleted that the famous 42nd (Rainbow) Division was composed of men from the National Guards of twenty-six states.

What could be more astonishing? The path of the immigration was retraced; two million men returned to the continent from which their forefathers and their grandfathers, their fathers and even they, had set out, in many cases so recently; from the New World they returned to succour the Old World which had not succoured them. There could be no doubting the meaning of such a saga. The beginning of American time, dimly realized for a century and a half, could no longer be denied. Yet even *The Spectator,* which had looked so openly and so confidently to the "physical strength and moral resolution" of the United States to save the world, could write in 1921, "We are too proud to be helped by the daughter country," and publish an article, a year later, under the title "Mother's Eldest Daughter." The wealth—the energy—the power—of the United States, these were not questioned; what was questioned was its maturity. Its resources were physical like a youth's, and like a youth it did not know what to do with them.

THE SEARCH FOR THE LIFE OF THE SPIRIT IN AMERICA

This attitude has been persistent, and it is worth dwelling on it at the beginning, when we first encounter it. Materialism without the grace of the spirit: this was the image that was created. "The man who dictated the policy of more miles of railway than exist in the United Kingdom," *The Spectator* wrote on the death of E. H. Harriman, "was a singular example of the omission to enjoy all those graces and compensations in life which were potentially his." Twelve years later, it explained the success of the Prohibition movement in the same terms: "In Britain there is what might be called an art of drinking. . . . In America . . . meditative, reflective and critical drinking [is] not the habit." It smiled at the effort of Richard Croker, the former boss of Tammany Hall, to transport the Temple of Philae from Egypt to Central Park, and at the offers of contractors "to transport the ruins and tastefully supervise their re-erection" in New York.

What was being denied was the existence of any culture in the United States, whether in literature or in drinking habits. Culture was something—a thing—which Americans came to Europe to gaze at and, if possible, to purchase and to carry home as a trophy, like the Temple of Philae. The familiar story in English literary circles at the time was of the American woman who was presented with her small son to Matthew Arnold, and whispered to the brat: "Here he is, Lenny, the leading poet and critic, somewhat fleshier than we had been led to expect." Individual writers and works were praised, but their "Americanness" was questioned and in the end disputed. If they were good, they were "European." (Poe was generally looked at askance as a rather unwholesome poet over whom the French had characteristically lost their heads.) Indeed, the American writers themselves seemed to take their lead from Europe in their own debate about their "Americanness." To Europe, the recognized canon of American literature was small, a few handfuls of works, with no central concern to which the world need attentively listen.

Yet it was at just this time that a few English writers, and one English literary review, the *Times Literary Supplement,* understanding the significance of America's entrance into history, went in search of American culture and, not only found it, but experienced it with a thrill. At the beginning of 1925, the *TLS* was not content to observe only the political and commercial dominance of America:

With America lies, after all, the future of the world; with her, at present, are the most fruitful opportunities for expansion and experiment *in spiritual things.* [Italics added.] If human life is to be changed for the better, new reserves of power must somehow be brought into action, and our trouble in the Old World is that our human material, like all the rest of our material, is exploited. We have made every possible mistake and encumbered ourselves with all the resulting inhibitions. The Americans constantly attempt new things, which we are prevented from attempting; they attempt and succeed.

Immediately before and during and immediately after the First World War, *Times Literary Supplement* sustained this attitude, alert and responsive to the new American literature, and welcoming it as new and American.

In 1913, in the manuscript of *Patria Mia* which was not discovered and published until 1950, Ezra Pound had proclaimed: "I have declared my belief in the imminence of an American Risorgimento. . . . A Risorgimento means an intellectual awakening. . . . Hence, when I say that there is more artistic impulse in America than in any country in Europe, I am in no peril of being believed."[2] But there were some in England who believed the same. His own early poems were noticed, as were those of Vachel Lindsay, with whom for a time he was linked, and was willing for a brief time to link himself. Lindsay may not have been a great or even a good poet, but he was an important poet of America at a crucial moment, and his Kallyope Yell was heard across the Atlantic:

> I am the Gutter Dream,
> Tune-maker, born of steam,
> Tooting joy, tooting hope.
> . . . .
> I am the Kallyope, Kallyope, Kallyope,
> Tooting hope, tooting hope, tooting hope, tooting hope.

He visited England in 1920, "where he converted a sceptical Oxford University," says one of his biographers, "to the Higher Vaudeville, and he was lionized."[3] The hope of a New World was welcomed.

But it is to the *TLS* that one can go, in a review of Lindsay's *The Golden Book of Springfield* on February 25, 1921, for a perceptive reading of his work, and for an image of America which, in its similarities and its differences, must evoke in the reader today his own vivid image of the United States, now halfway to 2018:

> So in the Springfield of 2018 there is a kind of religion of apples, half pagan, half Christian, and oddly mixed up with

movies, aeroplanes, a religion of the League of Nations, and a counter-religion of a Green Glass Buddha from Singapore, which in that age is the mysterious power of darkness, of the past, of magic and drugs, and consecrated vice of all kinds. . . .

One curious and American characteristic of the book is its large and loose impartiality. Mr. Lindsay seems to sympathise with all the contending powers in his dream because they all express some real force or tendency, whether good or bad. . . . There we see the American in whose country there is ample room and verge for all men and things, and who is unacquainted with failure and fear at the heart of the world.

Vachel Lindsay was one of the few genuine ballad makers in American poetry—some of his best work, and even some of his worst, should be part of the baggage of every American child—but what is of interest to us is the seriousness with which a number of English critics at the time were inquiring into the nature, not only of the material expressions of American power, but of the American spirit.

ITS DISCOVERY

It was for this that the *TLS* searched at the beginning of the 1920s, and the record of its findings, immediately after the First World War, reads like the log of an explorer, eventually sighting land:

—January 20, 1920: "There is every reason to believe that America can bring something new to literature; it is high time, we may add, that it did."

—May 7, 1920: "We have looked in vain to America for the *instauratio magna* of a new poetic era. . . . the verse in both these volumes . . . is traditional in form, conventional in language, obvious and ordinary in thought and feeling."

—November 26, 1920: "During the last few years, America has developed an interest in experimental literature which is quite remarkable. The writers of the 'extreme left' are printed and discussed with a serious energy very much unlike the apathy and ridicule with which such writers are generally treated in this country. . . . what it does mean is that American intellectuals are extremely anxious that there shall be an American literature, and that they have set about creating this literature with characteristic impatience. . . . [*The Dial* and *Poetry*] have succeeded in their primary design— to create a poetry which should be American in thought, feeling, subject, and form." (This was the real turning point; thereafter, it never really doubted again.)

—January 21, 1921: ". . . modern American poetry ranges from an almost narrow localism to a cosmopolitan freedom, from the most faithful adherence to the Anglo-Saxon tradition to the most violent revolt against it."

—November 17, 1921: "American poetry has vividness, sincerity and vitality. . . . at its best it has a subtlety of perception, a delicacy of expression, a mastery of technique, greater than that of any younger English poet."

These amounted to more than literary criticism: a new spirit in the world was being looked for, slowly recognized, and at last apprehended. "The world continues there," wrote the *TLS* in 1920, as it gazed on America, "keeps an inexplicable coherence of its own." Five years later, Ortega proclaimed, in one of the passages in which he seemed to be whistling in the dark to keep up his spirits: "No doubt, Europe is entering upon an era of youthfulness"; but the *TLS* in 1923 had already said, more tentatively and with more precision: "Europe, under American tuition, may become young again."4 The rejuvenation of a whole civilization, the dying civilization of Europe, was what was wanted from the entrance of the United States into history.

It is important to have made this plain: to understand that, at the beginning of this century, the materialistic image of the United States was not the only one, and that in fact it was severely challenged. Forwards and backwards, in the intervening years, the struggle between these two perceptions of America, materialistic and idealistic, physical and spiritual, has swung, and it is time that a resolution was attempted: that it was recognized, once and for all, that the United States is the bearer of its own idea to the world, not in spite of its materialism, but with its materialism; that with the voyaging of its power and its riches there flows also a traffic of the spirit. Until the American idea is thought and felt, once more, in the mind and heart of the world, as it was thought and felt at the beginning of American time—to be welcomed or resisted, celebrated or scorned, it does not matter, as long as it is thought and felt—our civilization will be craven. Perceived as old, with no new idea to impel it forward, old it will be. We will gather what we deserve, a literature and an art and a philosophy of decline and dissolution, and see ourselves reflected in it; we will have condemned ourselves to live in a world which will never be young again.

CHAPTER 4

The Country Which Is an Idea, the Idea Which Is a Country

To the outsider, as he travels into America, there comes a moment when he severely doubts that the country exists. How can its immense spaces be a nation? His ambition is to reduce it, to scale it down to a size which he can comprehend. Even *The Economist,* writing from London after the election of 1972, said that it had been "raining in America" on polling day. Bitten by the frost at one extremity while it is burned by the sun at another, great rivers in flood while its earth is somewhere parched, how can it be understood as a land?

At the Democratic National Convention of 1960, when he entered the name of Adlai Stevenson in the lists, Eugene McCarthy drew a picture of Barry Goldwater as a man who came from a land—he spoke of it as if it were foreign—where the sun stood always at high noon, casting no shadow. Was it any wonder, he asked, that in such a light the pale horse of death was mistaken for the white horse of victory? As if in reply, at the Republican National Convention in 1968, Barry Goldwater told how he had gone to bed the night before, the dust of the desert in his throat; but during the night a storm had swept across the land, and by dawn the desert had been cleansed and the air was sweet. Was it not time, he asked, that the whole of America was so cleansed—by a desert storm? The voices of Minnesota and of Arizona: How could they be more different, and yet be speaking from the same country, of the same nation? This is the doubt that the stranger will at some point encounter.

Regions which are like provinces, as apart as those of Rome; states which might be regions and, within the states, divisions so marked that they might be countries. If one rests in Colorado for a while, it is hard to believe that Nebraska *and* Wyoming *and* Utah *and* Arizona *and* New Mexico *and* Oklahoma *and* Kansas are all its neighbours, their own territories stretching from the Missouri, where it turns east to join the Mississippi, almost to the tip of the Gulf of California. The manner of the land is not the same in Virginia as in North Carolina, in South Carolina as in North Carolina, in Georgia as in South Carolina; and at Atlanta one may turn south to Florida or west to Alabama but, whichever way one chooses, it will be to a different country. There is not one Illinois, there are three; not just one Arkansas, but an Arkansas that is southern and an Arkansas that is western, so that at times during an election in his own state, William Fulbright seemed to be campaigning in two countries, speaking two tongues.

IN THE BEGINNING OF AMERICA WAS THE WORD

One can stand in Colorado on one of the great passes of the Rocky Mountains—places so bleak, as one pioneer wrote, that even the crow does not come—and contemplate, in the reach of a single state, the stretch of an entire continent. Straight and flat across the plains runs the highway from Kansas, straight and flat into Colorado, until it meets the mountains; and there the arm which has driven from the east must spread itself into fingers, each to clamber to the west, over the Continental Divide, a mile above sea level, then two, at last almost three. On the Divide, two raindrops fall, settle at one's feet, and sink into the earth, one to flow east to the Atlantic, the other west to the Pacific, to wash on the western coast of Europe, perhaps, or on the eastern shore of Asia. In two raindrops, the reach of a state, the stretch of a continent, the expanse of the oceans, the limit of the globe. This is a nation? The stranger must entertain his doubt but, believing that it could be, the pioneers made it so. Nothing was less manifest than the destiny which they imagined for the land, believed and accomplished.

To the north of this Colorado, one state among fifty, was carried the culture of the Anglo-Saxon outcrop of Europe and its Celtic fringes; to the south, the culture of the *conquistadores* and the missionaries. In the north, towns that are called Greeley and Lupton, Buckingham and Windsor, Craig and Moffat; in the south, Trinidad and Durango, Cortez and Monte Vista, Alamosa and San Luis. Jackson, a county, in the north; Montezuma, a county, in the south. In the north, on the ranges, still the cowboys; in the south, on the reservations, still the Indians. From west to east one may cross the state, and pass in a direct line from Montrose, where the Scot has been, to Salida where the Spaniard has been, to Pueblo, where the Indian has been, each leaving his signature. In the south, a city called Del Norte, for to the Spaniard coming from the south it was "the north"; in the north, seven thousand feet above sea level, a town called Nederland, for to the Hollander coming from the peaks, it was the "low land." All of this history to be heard day by day in the place names of a single state, which was not even a state a hundred years ago. The stranger must entertain his doubt but, believing that it could be, the pioneers made it so; by a vote, they made of their territory a state, in a land which by a vote had been made a nation.

At the constitutional convention of Colorado in 1874–75, these grubbing pioneers, resolving to order paper and ink and pens to record their solemn deliberations, took the words of the Declaration of Independence—the right to life, liberty, and the pursuit of happiness—and transformed them into the unique promise of the constitution of their state—the right to life, liberty, *and happiness*. Was it a slip, or did they mean it?—one cannot tell. But what they were doing, these digging and earnest men, was claiming a territory, not for a sovereign or for a church, not in the name of a god or of a king, but for an idea. The stranger must entertain his doubt but, believing that it could be, the pioneers debated and resolved in their convention, and made it so.

An idea! In one state or in the whole nation, that is all there really is which seems to have made them so. Wherever one gazes in America, there are always people, constitutionally assembled, resolving first to purchase a said quantity of paper, a said quantity of pens, a said quantity of ink, to scribble down, in one form or another, the same idea. No wonder, whether they invented it or not, it was they who *needed* the typewriter; and there is an irresistible symbol in the fact that the first contract for the commercial manufacture of the typewriter was placed, in 1875, by C. L. Sholes and G. Golden with Messrs. E. Remington & Sons, gunmakers, of Ilion, New York. With the gun, and with commerce, must travel the idea. In the beginning of America was the word, and the word must be replicated. To as many as are citizens, the idea must be given; by as many, it must be reproduced.

THE AMERICAN REVOLUTION IN THE NEW MAN

There are conservatives, Edmund Burke and Michael Oakeshott among them, to whom the wordiness of the word, the idea-iness of the idea, is a fallacy, and a dangerous one, whether in the Declaration of the Rights of Man, in the Declaration of Independence, or in the Bill of Rights. These are only recipes, they say: people can learn from them only a kind of "do it yourself" technique as if from a manual; the true cook does not learn from a cookbook, he learns by being a sauce boy, from the practice of others and from his own practising; he must be apprenticed. The free man, so their logic runs, must be apprenticed to a tradition; a nation must be made by and must follow a tradition, and it will break with the tradition at its peril. There is something in it all: the call of the Old World, with the encumbrance of its past, its pains and its defeats, its acquaintance with "failure and fear at the heart of the world," it's awareness of the travail of the new.

There is something in it, in particular, if applied to the Old World. The ideas of the French Revolution were poured into an old mould. Frenchmen in this mould were to be taught by prescription to be new men, and the mould both cracked and proved too strong. This is why the French Revolution, compared with the American Revolution which preceded it, is beginning to seem so parochial. We still, in the second century of American time, write our history with Europe at the centre and, from this Eurocentric point of view, what happened in France in 1789 must seem more important than what happened in America in 1776. But, as we move from the Eurocentric view, the French Revolution appears, more and more, in a true light: to have left France and Frenchmen, and Europe and Europeans, much as they were before, the traditions of the centuries still asserting themselves even after the revolution. Moreover, the same can be said of the Russian Revolution, which is also beginning to seem parochial, little more than the substitution of one imperial state for another.

The explanation is simple, and seldom has it been put better than in a most unlikely place: by W. H. Auden in his introduction to an anthology of romantic poetry. The word "revolution," he says, has normally been used to describe the process "by which man transforms himself from one kind of man, living on one kind of society, with one way of looking at the world, into another kind of man, another society, another concept of life." If revolutions are conceived as such, the conservative case against them stands; such a transformation will be achieved, if at all, only at a terrible price, and the price, as we know, will include the perversion and eventual destruction of the revolution itself. In these cases, the warnings of the conservatives were justified. Such revolutions, in the Old World, would crack the old mould, but not break it altogether; and fail to substitute a new one.

But if, continues Auden, the word "revolution" is applied to "what happened in North America between 1776 and 1829"—the dates must be noticed—then it has a special meaning:

> The American case is different; it is not a question of the Old Man transforming himself into the New, but of the New Man becoming alive to the fact that he is new, that he has been transformed already without his having realized it.
>
> The War of Independence was the first step, the leaving of the parental roof in order to find out who one is; the second and more important step, the actual discovery, came with Jackson. It was then that it first became clear . . . that, although the vocabulary of the Constitution may be that of the French Enlightenment, its American meaning is quite distinct.
>
> The American had not intended to become what he was; he had been made so by emigration and the nature of the American continent. An emigrant never knows what he wants, only what he does not want.[1]

Here, in short, was a revolution which was not poured into an old mould, which it could crack but not break, as in France and in Russia and probably, as will be discovered, in China, but prepared in its own mould, realized in the new mould before the new man was aware that it had been realized in him. In this case, the warnings of the conservatives are not relevant; and this is one reason why, among others that will be noticed, conservatism is not intellectually tenable in the United States, since each man is the new man. No transformation was demanded, it had already been accomplished; prescription was not opposed to tradition, they had grown, side by side, in the new country.

To say that America is an idea is, therefore, to say something that is very specific. One is not saying that it is possessed of an idea, or that an idea was imposed on it, or that it manufactured an idea: in all of such cases, again, the warnings of the conservative would apply, and it could be said that America had in the first place, and was henceforth doomed to go only to a cookbook, to learn about freedom only from a recipe, from a table of weights and measures, the checks and balances, as they are supposed to be, of its constitution. But none of that is what happened. The idea was realized in the new man, out of his experience in the new land. That is the importance of the most famous of the early questions which were asked about America, the cry of Crèvecoeur—"Who is the American, this new man?"—as it was the importance of the assertion of Frederick Jackson Turner, which no picking at his thesis can undo —"The fact is that here is a new product that is American."[2] The idea had grown out of an actual experience.

THE COUNTRY THAT MUST CONSTANTLY BE REMADE

But equally one must not forget that, out of their experience, it was an idea which the Americans—the first colonists, the founding fathers, the western pioneers—wrote down on their scraps of paper. They did not write down only their experience; in writing it down, they transformed it into an idea. Seeking to realize what he had become, what had already been realized in him, this new man conceptualized his experience, and so uttered it as an idea, and gave it a meaning that was universal. Conservative historians like to suggest that the American Revolution, at least in its beginning, was little more than the reclaiming of ancient rights and the reestablishing of legal precedents, with which the English crown and parliament had interfered; and much of the Declaration of Independence was couched in these terms. But not—not—in one phrase. The justifications of the rights and precedents, customs and statutes, charters and usages, to which appeal was made, were announced as nothing less than self-evident truths. Since a truth that is self-evident cannot be proved, it is an idea in one of its purest forms; and is likely to travel.

A country which is an idea will be restless. From time to time— at almost, it sometimes seems, regular intervals—it will turn back to the idea, find that it has not been fulfilled, or that it has been perverted; perhaps even that it has been lost. It will then try to recover the idea, or to reinterpret it, and at last to restore it; it will attend once more to the "unfinished business" of the nation, a phrase which could have come out of the political experience of no other country; it must constantly remake itself in order that it may be, as it was bidden in the beginning, a "more perfect union." America can never for long be satisfied with its performance, because the idea always remains to prove the performance inadequate. In 1971, a young and intelligent radical, looking forward to the celebrations in 1976, looked back to the body of ideas to which as an American he believes himself to be heir:

> . . . a set of beliefs that form the revolutionary aspect of the American experience—human equality; respect for the judgment of the common man; distrust of those who command positions of power and privilege; allegiance to freedom of expression and the right to self-determination; cooperative enterprise; government of the people, by the people, for the people; conscience above property and institutions; sympathetic interest in the new, the untried, the unexplored; equality of opportunity; confidence in the ability of the people to create a more just and humane world; faith in the brotherhood of all mankind.[3]

Perhaps no other American would offer exactly the same list, but all Americans could offer some such list: the experience of two hundred years uttered as a set of ideas which command to further exertions.

THE PAST THAT IS PRESENT

There is a further curiosity in this situation: the impulse to move forward is found by looking back, to the idea, translated into a set of other ideas, which governed the nation in the beginning. Richard

Hofstadter, in much of his historical writing, was at pains to demonstrate that progressive movements in the United States have usually looked backwards for inspiration; and his exploration of this curiosity, which he once said had the dimensions of a major paradox, had a profound influence on a whole generation of readers. Even if it was not his intention, one of the effects of his studies, by his continual slighting of the progressive movements, was to supply the historical backbone for the development of what is superficially a kind of intellectual conservatism in the United States during the past quarter of a century. But his thesis was based on almost a majestic misunderstanding of the nature of his own country.

In a country which is an idea, one does not look back, as he puts it, to "bygone institutions and conditions," in the hope of restoring them, although that may seem to be the impulse in the rhetoric. In fact, one does not look back to institutions or conditions at all; but to the living idea, present in the past as it is present in today. The experience of the new man in his new land is seen as one; his past is constantly being rediscovered in order to remake the present. One is no more looking back than when one is curious about the childhood history of a friend. The idea, alive in the present, has a biography; it has had, so to speak, an upbringing. To know about its upbringing is to understand better, and to enjoy more fully, the richness of its life. Just as a friend never ceases to delight by the constant revelation of the many things that he is, so the idea never ceases to astonish by the variety of things that it has been, and therefore that it can be. The living idea is not a dead letter; like the memories of a friend, it is alive and actual now, in the recalling.

This deeply American sense of the past as present, accessible and usable, is one of the most revolutionary aspects of the country's life, of its awareness of itself; and one of the most baffling to the stranger from the Old World. From his earliest days, he has stepped on ruins, travelled among monuments, lived in a museum; the past in Europe is dead, but it is all around him, and he inhabits it; his cradle is a graveyard, and the graveyard is his home. European cities are most lovely, the American artist Georgia O'Keeffe has said, perhaps more lovely than any that will be built again, but they are now no more than conversation pieces. Her observation is acute: with the dead past the European talks, not asking, as

Michael Oakeshott says, that it should make any sense. So he comes to America, and as he makes his first journeys into the country, he asks: What have you done with your past? Lay bare your ruins to me. Show me your monuments. Where do you live when there is no graveyard for you to inhabit? At last the American voice will reach him: We do not inhabit the past, because the past inhabits us. It is not around us, but in us; the past cannot be seen in America, because it is not allowed to die; it cannot be laid out; it is not flat on its back, where you expect to find it, it is upright in front of you, where you cannot recognize it. You say that we constantly remake our present, but that is because we constantly remake our past; every American may not become the President, but every American is a founding father. Where are our ruins to lay bare to you? Why do you think that so eagerly we lay bare ourselves?

Once he has sensed that the past is actual in every American, the stranger finds that what are too facilely called the paradoxes of American life no longer contain the contradictions which are supposed to make them. The radical right, for example, is able to appeal to the same traditions, the same idea, the same words, as the radical left, because the traditions are not handed down, once and for all made, from the past, to be interpreted by a priesthood; the idea is not a once-and-only covenant, preserved and carried around in an ark; the words are not a scripture. They have their existence in every American in the present, there to be remade in whatever manner he will. This may be demonstrable only in the literature and the art, the law and the history, the philosophy and the science, even the sociology, of America, but it is demonstrable in them only because it is true of the whole people.

THE I RELEASED IN THE EN-MASSE

To speak of the country which is an idea is to talk of America as a nation; to speak of the idea which is a country is to talk of America as a democracy. The two cannot be separated. If the land was to become a nation, the experience of the continent translated into an idea, the nation had to become a democracy, the idea of democracy in turn transforming the experience. In the soil from which the nation was made, the seed of democracy was planted; and from that soil, in the generations that followed, harvests have been lifted, American and democratic, which have challenged men everywhere, moved them from their customs, and nourished them. The promise of America has not yet been fulfilled, but it has never for long failed to be fertile. Even in the lean years of the democratic idea, the seed is underground, preparing for a new fruitfulness.

Even if Jefferson had made more use of the nations natural right and the social contract, he would have been appealing to ideas, but to none so sweeping, so purely an idea, as the original idea which he enshrined in the tremendous second sentence: "We hold these truths to be self-evident, that all men are created equal; that they are endowed by their Creator with certain inalienable rights; that among these, are life, liberty, and the pursuit of happiness." The experience of the Americans had issued in an idea; and in the year in which it triumphed, in the memorial that has already been quoted, Thomas Pownall wrote:

> Every inhabitant of America is, *de facto* as well as *de jure,* equal, in his essential inseparable rights of the individual, to any other individual; is, in these rights, independent of any power that any can assume over him, over his labour or his property: This is a Principle in act and deed, and not a mere speculative theory.

He had it right, as he usually did. The idea had issued from the experience of the new man in his own continent, in act and deed, and had not, as the conservatives would have it, sprung in the head of a theorist. The classic work of Bernard Bailyn, *The Ideological Origins of the American Revolution,* should have proved for all time how radical was the transformation of political ideas that had taken place in America before 1776.

In every American the idea pullulates; and, in saying that, one is saying what the idea is. *In every American,* each created equal: not some but all, not only all but each. Not to a caste or a class do the words apply, not to a rank or a degree, not to an order or an estate, not to a category of any kind, but to all and to each; not to the "workers of the world," but to all mankind, each member of it conceived and proclaimed as an individual. That is what Pownall saw in act and deed in the country; that is what Jefferson wrote down in his precise and universal formula; that is what the new country, in the moment of inventing itself from its own experience, proclaimed to the world; that is what the new man, at the moment of his exodus from the Old World, announced himself, on behalf of all men, to be.

It is important to understand what is being said; the sweep of the proclamation in the Declaration of Independence is so great and so awe-inspiring that it is easy to neglect its two-sided exactness. In one and the same document, the United States called the masses to the front of the stage—that is the profound meaning of the assertion that it is from the consent of the governed that the just powers of government are derived—and identified the masses as individuals— each equal, at the hands of his Creator, in his own self. It is in the opening lines of *Leaves of Grass,* which alone would justify its being regarded as the most American of all American literature:

> One's-self I sing, a single separate person,
> Yet utter the word Democratic, the word En-Masse.

It is impossible that a European poet would think that the I and the En-Masse can be sung together, yet this dialectic, between the mass and the individual, which Whitman establishes at the beginning of his poem, is at the core of the Declaration of Independence, and at the heart of the American political experience. It is the seat of all the creative tension in the society, and of all the desperate ambiguity.

In this American dialectic between the I and the En-Masse, the conflict between liberty and equality is, not resolved, but made fruitful. This is what the English Revolution, which was not concerned with equality, and the French Revolution, which was concerned with man as an abstraction but not with men as individuals, and the Russian Revolution, which was not concerned with liberty, all failed to accomplish. This is what Tocqueville did not observe and why, with all its insights, his work lacks sight; he was blind to much of the America even of his own day, receiving only vibrations from it. He might be regarded as the first of the Impressionists, sensitive to the atmosphere, painting the light in which objects are bathed, until the object in the end vanishes, which is what has happened to painting since the Impressionists, and what has happened to the observation of America since Tocqueville.

THE IMAGINATION OF JEFFERSON

To make fruitful the conflict between liberty and equality, so that neither would be destructive of the other: this was a wholly candid preoccupation of the founding fathers. After the death of Jefferson, it was this double concern which Madison noted in him: "an early and uniform devotion to the cause of liberty" *and* "a systematic preference of a form of Government squared in the nicest degree to the equal rights of man." What a care there was in these men that the one should not be destructively advanced at the expense of the other; and what a care especially there was in Jefferson, perhaps not a founding father of his country so much as its founding god-father, bidden to instruct the child-nation in its faith, until it was of age.

What did he know, this man who was to the democracy which was forming what Washington was to the nation? When one has picked over his actions and his utterances, caught him in his contradictions, noticed how nimble he was in moving his ground, there remains the thing that he knew before all men of his time and, one is at last persuaded, before all but a few men of any time. He knew his formula, the theorem which, once it had entered his mind, he could not expel: all men are created equal. But, if that was all that he had known, he would have been only Voltaire, able to envision man as an abstraction, but with no habit among men. What did he import into his formula that was his and was American, that was the American Enlightenment and not the French Enlightenment. In place of wit, he had humour. One can have wit about mankind, but humour can only be about men. Voltaire tried to kill God with his wit, Jefferson was among men with his humour when he said: "It does me no injury for my neighbours to say that there are twenty gods or no god. It neither picks my pocket nor breaks my leg." One has to ask: Did Voltaire ever have a neighbour? He was visited by mankind, and he received it, but did anyone ever ask if he could borrow his lawn mower? Somehow or other, by an act of imagination in which lay his greatness, rather than by personal habit, Jefferson thought, not only of men rather than of man, but of men as neighbours.

Although he was aloof by disposition, there is a friendliness to the world, and to the men and women who are in it, in the words of Jefferson which is nowhere in the words of Voltaire. There was in Voltaire a noble—one cannot deny it—but scorning love of humanity; there was in Jefferson a noble—one cannot deny it—and curious attention to neighbours. Although he disliked familiarity with crowds, even on his hill at Monticello he seems always to have thought of man as men who were day by day on the streets, about their business with their neighbours. One especially has this sense of him in all the reserved and qualified observations which he made about the two unenfranchised human beings who were, in his time, more close than neighbours, but never to be regarded as such: Negroes and women. To have neighbours as slaves, and slaves as neighbours, that puzzled him: he could never be altogether forthright on the matter, but he was not dishonest; he fell back on the formula, the theorem, the idea; it would work itself out.

THE CREATIVE TENSION IN AMERICAN LIFE

The social equality in America can be easily disdained: what significance can it have when the economic inequality is so deep? Yet the stranger, coming from a country of degrees and ranks, where a man will reveal his class in his greeting, cannot help being astounded by the commonness, the universality, of one syllable. He leaves Heathrow Airport at London, with the "Good morning, sir. . . . Have a pleasant flight, sir. . . . Goodbye to you, sir," of the customs officer in his ears; and seven hours later he arrives at Dulles Airport at Washington, hands his passport to the customs officer, who looks at it, discovers his name, and then greets him: "Hi, Henry." Later, he presents himself at the White House for an interview, and is welcomed by Bill Moyers, whom he has not met before: "Hi, Henry." In a few minutes, he is translated to the office of the President of the United States of America, with some of the feelings of a subject who at last finds himself before his emperor, and "Hi, Henry," says Lyndon Johnson, extending the largest fist in Christendom. The word is everywhere. "Hi," says the girl at the checkout counter at the supermarket; "Hi," says the attendant at the gas station; "Hi," says the child playing on the sidewalk as one passes; "Hi," says the suffragan Bishop of Washington as if it were a blessing, and it seems that it is. The word is a democracy, the idea in a syllable. However much the idea is obstructed or distorted or neglected, it is proclaimed day by day in a greeting, a reminder of what the country was meant to be: one in which neighbours could, in equality, raise their hats to each other, and not the many touch their caps to the few.

Equality and individualism; the I and the En-Masse; the masses as each his-self; one's-self as equal to other selves; all selves in a mass of equality: the ambiguity in the idea is desperate, for how can one allow to each individuality the fullest expression of its-self, and yet maintain the equality of all of them? But this is also the source of the tension in the American idea, and therefore in its society, which is so creative. Two hundred million I's released En-Masse to express each his own self, each to realize his own nature: that is the idea which is a country, and the force of it was felt in the world in the 1960s. With all the mischief of the decade, that is what has not been lost. One can hear the tread, the dance of these I's in the En-Masse everywhere about one, asking for some new thing, their "liberation."

This "principle of equality is the heart of the social philosophy contained" in the Declaration of Independence, Adrienne Koch says in her study of the American Enlightenment. But within two pages she has added that those who composed the committee which formulated the Declaration "were *prescribing* the policy that would allow man to realize human nature as fully as possible."[4] The two cannot for long be separated; they are the one idea, the idea of America. No sooner is it proclaimed in the Declaration that all men are created equal, than it is added that each is equal in the rights with which the Creator has endowed him, that these rights are inseparable—inalienable—from him as an individual, and that they include life—one can understand that—and liberty—one can understand that—but also the pursuit of happiness—how can one understand that except in terms of the expression by each of his own nature?

We have to explore the answer, at length and in depth, for the working out of this idea *is* the time in which we live; in the working out of the American idea will be the fulfillment of American time. In passion, it will be done, and in heartbreak; the search for the right path will lead many times in a false direction; in hope the journey will be made, and at risk; each and all, together and alone, the new man must travel to this new discovery of his-self. There is no choice; this is the idea that America in its time is carrying to the world; and perhaps it has never been expressed more clearly than in the sermon of William Ellery Channing, *The Great Purpose of Christianity:*

> I wish to regard myself as belonging not to a sect, but to a community of free minds, of lovers of truth, of followers of Christ both on earth and in heaven. I desire to escape from the narrow walls of a particular Church, and to live under the open sky, in the broad light, looking far and wide, seeing with my own eyes, hearing with my own ears, and following the truth meekly, but resolutely, however arduous or solitary the path in which she leads. I am, then, no organ of a sect, but speak for myself alone. . . .
>
> We must start in religion from our own souls. In these is the function of divine truth. Here is our primitive teacher and light. Let us not disparage it. . . . What but a vague shadow, a sounding name, is the metaphysical Deity, the substance without noise, the being without properties, the naked unity, which performs such a part in our metaphysical systems? The only God whom our thoughts can rest on, and our hearts cling to, and our consciences can recognize, is the God whose image dwells in our own souls. . . . Thus the soul is the spring of our knowledge of God.

Channing had graduated from Harvard in 1798, and his was the voice of the new man at the moment at which he had left, not only the paternal roof, not only an Empire and a Monarch and a Church, but all narrow walls. In every inflection, it could be only American.

CHAPTER 5

The Americanization of the World

The reader may, from time to time, pause at the argument of this book, and wonder whether the American who is being discussed is not so much American as contemporary: specifically, contemporary Western man. Fifty years ago, this was the judgment of Ortega, who did not know the United States, one of his few weaknesses as an observer of the contemporary world:

This fact, that the ordinary level of life today is that of the former minorities, is a new fact in Europe, but in America, the natural, the "constitutional" fact . . . when this psychological condition of the ordinary man appeared in Europe, when the level of his existence rose, the tone and manners of European life in all orders suddenly took on a new appearance which caused many people to say: "Europe is becoming Americanized." . . . This, to my mind, is to trivialize a question which is much more subtle and pregnant with surprise. . . . Europe has not been Americanized; it has received no great influence from America. Possibly both these things are beginning to happen just now; but they did not occur in the recent past of which the present is the flowering. . . . The triumph of the masses and the consequent magnificent uprising of the vital level have come about in Europe for internal reasons. . . . But it so happens that the result coincides with the most marked aspects of American life.[1]

American experience and European experience are, in this view, simply coincidental.

Marías, who did know the United States, also wrote in terms of a coincidence, but he altered the emphasis:

> What happens is that new things usually start in the United States and are more intense and outstanding here. This is why things that often simply belong to the twentieth century seem "American." . . . It is true that in the United States we find the full development of things that elsewhere are unsurely and timidly begun. This is why we can learn so much by observing the United States, and this is why almost nothing of what is happening in the world (and especially what is going to happen) can be understood without watching the United States.[2]

His position is awkward: things happen first, more intensely and more surely, in the United States, yet they are of the twentieth century as such, rather than of the United States. Moreover, he held this view even though he elsewhere wrote that "there is no doubt that the United States stands at the prow of today's world."

The problem has also been addressed by Americans. John Dewey once praised a writer "because he understands by 'American' a type of mind that is developing, from like causes, all over the world, and which would have emerged in time in Europe, even if there were no geographical America, although its development has been accelerated and intensified by the experience of this country."[3] Twenty years later, in *The Lonely Crowd,* David Riesman wrote that "my analysis of the other-directed character is at once an analysis of the American and of contemporary man. Much of the time I find it hard to say where one ends and the other begins."[4] The thing to notice about all these passages, European and American, is their determinism, as if the discovery of America, the experience of the immigrant in his continent, the invention of the United States, the publishing of the Declaration of Independence, the self-discovery of the new man, all in the end did not matter; that what has happened would have happened anyhow in Europe, perhaps not so quickly or so intensely—there is always that qualification to the thesis—but with the same result.

Even on the face of it, this proposition is hard to believe, but the relationship between America and Europe is something of which neither Europeans nor Americans have yet made much sense. It is interesting to put side by side two quotations: one from the American critic Babette Deutsch, who wrote of the "anomalous position of the cultured American, with his double allegiance, to Europe and to his own country,"[5] the other from Karl Jaspers, who was writing as a European when he said: "Every Westerner has, in a sense, two countries: the country of his heart, his origin, his language, his ancestors, and one that is the sure foundation of his political reality. Those fatherlands are many, but this foundation is today only one: the United States of America."[6] These two voices are complementary, echoing the twin fears, of the European that he is being Americanized, and of the American that he will never rid himself of his initial Europeanness.

What is interesting about them is that, if they are true, then there is a falsehood in the position of Ortega and Marías, of Dewey and Riesman, when they argue that the American in reality is only the contemporary, and that it would all have happened in Europe in time, in much the same way, without America. This is not how most Europeans or most Americans in fact feel: the European feels threatened by a future which will make him into an American, there is something specifically American which he wishes to resist; the American feels threatened by a past which will hold him forever a European, there is something specifically European of which he needs to be rid. Both are contemporary, but the past in the one and the future in the other are opposed. In short, the Americanization of Europe is an event: the "double allegiance" to "two countries" tells of a specific new influence in the world.

THE MATERIAL INFLUENCE

What do we mean by the Americanization of the world, for the influence has already travelled much farther than Europe? In answering the question, we must not restrict ourselves to the Cokes (which are everywhere) and the McDonald's (which have reached even the countryside of France), to the supermarket and the packaging, although even these are important. Something is missing in Geoffrey Gorer's description of 1962:

The American entertainment industry and its associated manufacturers have been extraordinarily successful in inventing and exploring adolescent tastes and preferences for leisure amusements, and while doing this have almost inadvertently created one of the first great international communities since the breakup of the medieval Church. Throughout the world, to the best of its ability, urban youth wears the same sort of American-style clothes, listens and dances to the same sort of American-style music, probably drinks American-style soft drinks, goes intellectual in an American-style Beatnik fashion, picks up the same American crazes.[7]

A cultural phenomenon is here discussed only in terms of its material manifestations. It is not even considered that the young in various parts of the world may buy the American products because they are accompanied, and may in fact have been preceded, by an American idea to which the young are responsive. One might as well describe the worldwide reputation and influence of American art in terms only of the dealers, who are quite as skilled in exploring and manipulating the tastes and preferences of adults, and exploiting the products of the artists.

But the material manifestations of American society are themselves significant. One does not, after all, make it possible for the French peasant to buy a hamburger, cooked and wrapped, without altering more than his eating habits; and it was in such terms that some time ago the writer and traveller James (now Jan) Morris noticed how far the Americanization of the French countryside has already gone. Again, in England, the "vogue for more cafés offering the sort of food intended for eating in the hand," which *New Society* noticed in 1971, must mean in time a change of manners; that is, in social relationships. "Dedicated to the American hamburger, they are semantically self-masking: The Great American Disaster, the American Haven, the Load of Bull." Cafés with names such as these are doing more than admitting, with however much backhandedness, the American influence in the food that they serve; they are acknowledging, as they try to mask, a much deeper American influence in English society, and the mockery is as sincere a form of flattery as the imitation.

THINGS AIN'T NECESSARILY SO

There is a meaning in the material progress of America, beyond the physical benefits that it bestows. The gadgetry and the invention, the mass production of the past century and now the technology, may all have had their origin in the peculiar conditions of the American in his new continent, and in his need to adapt to them; but this kind of physical explanation does not really account for the inventive genius of the country, generation after generation. More than imagination and skill and technique have been at work; there has also been an idea, and we ought not to be surprised that it is the idea of the country, in the country that is itself an idea.

The meaning of the invention or the machine is to be found in the assumption that life need not always be like what hitherto it has been. Confronted by their continent, this had of course to be the premise of the Americans from the beginning. They had to do something about it; the land was not already tilled for them, there were no immemorial ways for them to imitate. They were free to adapt and to invent. By the beginning of the seventeenth century, a sawmill had been invented in England, but it was outlawed in case the new technology should cause unemployment among the sawyers. (One may say that this spirit still survives in England.) But labour in America was scarce and expensive; and only thirteen years after the Pilgrims had landed, the settlers had built their first power saw at the Falls of Piscataqua.

They found themselves in a continent with extremes of temperature. For the cold weather, a century later, Franklin had invented his stove, which was remarkable, among other features, because it was prefabricated from cast iron, so making possible its mass production. For the hot weather, yet another hundred years later, an English traveller, Adam Ferguson, reported in 1831 that his hosts in Washington "contrived to preserve untainted their fish and butcher meats" in a household refrigerator, and the New York *Mirror,* as early as 1838, described the refrigerator as an "article of necessity." Almost more remarkable, natural ice was being harvested and transported, distributed and exported, especially from Boston, by the beginning of the nineteenth century, not only to Cincinnati and Charleston, Savannah and New Orleans, but to the Caribbean, to London, and even to China.

But neither the natural conditions of the continent, nor the scarcity and cost of labour, is sufficient as an explanation. The wider meaning of the inventive genius, of the willingness and ability to try new things, is made clear by Daniel Boorstin in his description of another "invention," the establishment of the cow towns of the West:

To build a cow town called for the ability to imagine that things could be very different from the way they were. One who had this imagination in great measure was Joseph G. McCoy. . . . What he imagined was not so much a new trail as a new destination. Why not establish a depot on one of the Northern railroads 'whereat the Southern drover and the Northern buyer would meet upon an equal footing and both be undisturbed by mobs or swindling thieves'?[8]

This is what matters in the invention and the machine: not only that they represent a triumph of man over his environment, but that they are a form of his own reimagining of his estate. "It ain't necessarily so," said the song; and so say the invention and the machine, and even the technology of today. That technology can even be made to correct its own mischiefs.

The people who have made their own country in a new continent, and continued to remake it, still conducting it as an experiment, have taught the peoples of the rest of the world that they too can remake their own lives in their old countries. It is not a matter of revolution, as usually it is understood, or even of ideology; but of experiment and contrivance. Malcolm Bradbury, the English writer, once said that the reason why he was afraid to fly in an American plane was that in mid-flight, twenty thousand feet in the air, some American who was on board would decide to take the plane to pieces, in order to find out how it worked. Under the influence of their experience, of their pragmatism, and now of their sociology, the Americans are always ready to take their own society to pieces, in order to find out how it works, and to try to put it together again in a different way. It is never for long assumed that things must be as they are; that it is necessarily so. This is an American idea and, insofar as it has travelled to the traditional societies of Europe, it has arrived there from America. It is a contemporary notion, of course; but in act and deed, as Pownall put it, it has issued from the mind and the habit of the American.

SOCIOLOGY AND THE REMAKING OF SOCIETY

American sociology is not altogether a bad joke. It has even been known to recall, from time to time, that its subject is people in the daily rounds of their lives, in relationship with other people with whom they share their estate. In spite of many seductions, it has continued, at its best, to bend to its own tradition, which was most firmly established by the "Chicago School" at the beginning of the century: that its most fruitful task is the empirical observation of actually existing societies. Even in this tradition, there have been weaknesses, such as the tendency to observe a society in terms only of what are imagined to be its problems; but this also is a part of the mind of the American. A situation is a problem, to be formulated so that it may be solved, and this also is an idea that has travelled to other countries, itself a form of experiment and contrivance, gadgetry and invention.

The influence of American sociology has been widespread, not least in England, where the subject was established in the universities only in the late 1950s and early 1960s; where the first issue of *Sociology*, the journal of the British Sociological Association, was issued only in 1967; and where the more popular journal, *New Society*, had made its first appearance only five years before. "We are becoming aware that there is a science of society," it proclaimed, at least three quarters of a century after the claim was accepted in the United States. In one of its early issues, Donald Macrae made its obeisance to American sociology, to which he asked "all humane persons" to give two and a half cheers:

American sociology, until recently always good for a comfortable laugh in most British academic or administrative circles, is now an object of pretty solemn and general respect. . . . This is an excellent change: at its frequent best American sociology is today one of the most considerable achievements of the American mind . . . and one of the most fruitful influences of America in a world where increasingly—whether we like it or not—the United States is replacing France as everyman's second fatherland. . . .

I stand by a basic awe and admiration. . . . I can say of American sociology, as Hobbes did of *Leviathan,* there is no power on earth which compares with this. And this is not a tyrannous power.[9]

We ought not lightly to dismiss this hymn. Since the novel has ceased to describe our societies to us, we depend on sociology, and it has not performed at all badly. Its characters may not have names, like those of Dickens or Dostoevski or Joyce, but it has offered us its own kind of characters for our recognition; especially in its more popular forms.

"The tremendous growth of sociology in the United States is one of the manifestations of the continuing efforts of American culture to explore, to cope with, and to control its changing environment. . . . To much of the world today, sociology is practically synonymous with American sociology. . . . Its techniques are everywhere emulated, and its theories shape the terms in which world discussion of sociology is cast, and the issues around which intellectual debate centers."[10] This verdict of the American sociologist Alvin W. Gouldner cannot be denied. But the point will be missed unless it is understood that the influence of American sociology is merely one expression of the influence of an American idea, merely one aspect of the Americanization of the world, now that the United States is the second homeland to everyman.

When the public mind and philosophy of America in the early years of this century were strong and inventive, they were inspired by a living idea: that a society should be experimental and that its politics also should be conducted in the spirit of experiment. At the conclusion of his three-volume history of the American people, Boorstin places an epigraph from Archibald MacLeish: "The American journey has not ended. America is never accomplished, America is always still to build. . . . West is a country in the mind, and so eternal." Whitman is always embarking, forever starting out, to "vast trackless spaces. . . . Ever the dim beginning. . . . Ever the mutable." Beside this continual movement of a society to new frontiers in its mind, the experiment of the Soviet Union is parochial and static.

"In whatever medium he works, the American artist is conscious of being a pioneer," said the English critic Alan Pryce-Jones. "He is out to discover something, to push back a frontier of some kind, even if his act be only one of self-discovery." America must always move on; and with it, now, the world. Having been invented, it can be reinvented, with an intent that is deliberate. "In this country," said Herbert Croly, in his classic work, *The Promise of American Life,* "the solution of social problems demands the substitution of a conscious social ideal for the earlier instinctive homogeneity of the American Nation." This is the idea that travels with its commerce. The idea which is the country is always there, accessible and usable, when the country that is an idea seems to be flagging, or to be facing new problems, or to have lost its way; whenever the nation seems to be ceasing to be a nation, it reaches back to the idea, and remakes itself.

For the once instinctive homogeneity of the old nations needs a replacement now as well. Like the individuals who compose them, they are no longer subject to the physical constrictions of the past. In particular, as Hannah Arendt has said, one of the peculiar conditions of the American Revolution is now a universal condition. Her argument, that the American Revolution has been unique, not only in its concern for freedom, but in the fact that it carried through in conditions that did not include mass poverty, enables her to claim that this is one reason why it is no longer of merely local significance, since the possibility of eliminating mass poverty now exists in other societies in the rest of the world. This is partly what one means by the Americanization of the world: that its idea is becoming, not less, but more relevant; and that its influence is reaching, with its invention and its technology, its Cokes and its McDonald's, its sociology and its art, to the farthest ends of the earth, freeing men from the immemorial ties that have bound them, and from all narrow walls.

EDUCATING THE MANY

But the societies, under the bidding of the American idea, are not merely to be remade; they are to be remade so that within them "the masses" are no longer a lump, but active and assertive, their members more and more differentiated as individuals, each equal in his right to the fullest expression of his nature. Once again, one must observe that this idea cannot be divorced from the invention and the technology, or from the social philosophy that is ready to distribute their benefits to everyone. The genius of Henry Ford—that he would pay his workers high wages, so that they could afford to buy the family car which they produced, so that he could afford to pay them high wages, so that they could afford to buy the family car—was a peculiarly American genius. Mass production in the United States has curiously always been intended for "the masses." The stove of Franklin was intended for every home; the refrigerator, as soon as it was invented, was announced as an article of necessity, and not of luxury.

The intention can sometimes have an element of farce. In the 1950s, Procter and Gamble noticed the "mass" fact that American mothers changed their babies' diapers about twenty-five billion times a year. At once, its research and development teams set about inventing a disposable diaper, and by 1956 Pampers were ready to be marketed, not for the privileged but for the many. Immediately, its sales amounted to tens of millions of dollars a year. There are profound questions that are raised by this equalization of consumption under what is still a capitalist system. But for the moment we may be satisfied to observe that it has been an American idea to regard as necessities for "the masses" what in older societies have, until quite recently, been considered as properly the luxuries of the few. Even today, the average middle-class home in England is a place of inconvenience if contrasted with the average middle-class home in America. As an American sociologist, Howard Higman, put it after a visit to England, its social ideal is "the equal rationing of poverty."

But we must again move from the tangible to the intangible. In England, wrote the English critic John Russell, not long ago, "the undertow has set in toward a higher education more like America's and, with time, toward the kind of democracy in which all the citizens share a common language; and this will be a liberation."[11] In fact, the progress that England in particular, and Europe in general, has made since 1945 toward the provision of higher education to the children of "the masses" has been laggard; but the undertow is there, as Russell said, the influence is at work, and it has travelled from America, and will not in the end be resisted.

Once again, the questions that are raised are profound; higher education in America is itself in a parlous condition. But again we may be satisfied for the moment merely to observe the meaning of the Americanization of the world. It is not only in the numbers of students who are admitted that the influence is felt; more and more, the curricula of even the ancient universities of Europe are resembling those of American universities. As long ago as 1908, the *American Political Science Review* observed: "The day is past when college graduates upon the commencement stage debated such themes as 'whether the going back of the shadow upon the dial of Hezekiel was universal,'" as they did at Harvard University in 1769. "The graduates of today discourse upon primary elections, the restriction of immigration, and the control of trusts." Fifteen years later, H. L. Mencken in *The American Mercury* quoted from a Chicago newspaper: "The Chicago meat-packing industry and the University of Chicago . . . are to be united. Meat packing is to take its place in the curriculum of the university, along with Latin, economics, psychology, and the rest." Such examples are egregious, but they could be multiplied; as in the establishment, for example, when Hollywood was still an empire, of course in cosmetology at the University of California at Los Angeles. Again, the questions that are raised are profound; again, we may be content for the moment merely to observe the influence, as courses that are "relevant" to the many are introduced into the universities of Europe and even of England, replacing the disciplines that for centuries were intended only for the few.

There have been other influences; for example, in the mere concept of the student. Thirty years ago, at Oxford University, there was a considerable hostility to the National Union of Students, because the undergraduates there considered that the student was, at best, a provincial, at worst, an American, phenomenon and category. But in August 1963, *New Society* could report: "The undergraduate is a dying species. Seen only at Oxford and Cambridge, the number of colleges in which he is represented in significant numbers is dwindling. In his place is the student. . . . The replacement of tweeds by jeans is a well-observed phenomenon." One has only to ask: From where came the jeans, the anonymous apparel of the classless student?

But the influence has been still deeper. The English undergraduate, or the continental European student before the Second World War, was an actual or potential member of an elite, and the purpose of the universities was his initiation into the elite by his subjection to its disciplines. "If he is poor," commented Paul Shrecker, who was a refugee from Germany in 1943, "he may be compelled to spend all his spare time in a coffee shop with the classical *café crème,* because the attic where he lives is not heated." But in America, "most students spend almost all of their time on the campus. . . . Most continental students have never seen—let alone used—an institution offering so much comfort."[12] What is the meaning of the difference, for the comfort and convenience of the student have since become a concern in Europe and in England as well? It is that the student is considered, not as a being in limbo, so to speak, who is being prepared for a situation in life in which deference may be paid to him, but as already a being to whom deference is owed. The student has rights, as already a being in himself; and this was the idea that could be seen to have travelled from America in the worldwide character of the "student movement" during the 1960s.

THE CHILD AS REDEEMER

If one goes even deeper, one is here close to another of the influences at work in the Americanization of the world. Not only the student but the adolescent, not only the adolescent but even the child, is to be considered as a person with rights. It may have been Rousseau who wrote *Emile;* but it is in America that Emile has grown up. Perhaps none of our attitudes raises more directly the question, whether what seems to be American is in fact only contemporary, than our worship of childhood, carried then to a worship of adolescence, and then to a worship of "the young," in the sense of the "under-thirties." Until recently, the European scorn of the American child was freely expressed, but was too often only a form of fastidiousness, as in the laments of Henry James, returning to America with his European *persona,* to grieve over the wretched infants as they scampered through the lobby of a hotel late at night. Even today, one may observe, the initial encounter of a stranger from the Old World with an American child is likely to produce in him a considerable alarm and even a ferocious indignation.

After much observation at close quarters, and even more reflection when the children have been removed, one must incline to the view that the emergence of the child as the sovereign of our lives is a working out of the American idea, even if in a form that is banal, which has now travelled to the rest of the world. One is even tempted to call down on the modern child in general, and on the American child who is his prototype, the severe judgment of Jonathan Edwards that, unbaptized and unrepentant as they are, they are "young vipers and infinitely more hateful than vipers"; certainly a correction in the balance of our attitudes is overdue.

Bernard Wishy, in *The Child and the Republic,* has shown how quickly in the United States the idea of the child as born in sin was transformed, first into the optimistic notion of the child as redeemable, and then into the extravagant promise of the child as redeemer. What was interesting in the change was the interchange between two conceptions of the purpose of child rearing. They were both expressed by Lydia H. Sigourney as early as 1838. The mother, with her "mission so sacred," had to make certain that "the harp . . . be so tuned as not to injure its tender and intricate harmony"; and this "greater respect . . . due to children" was also desirable because they were the "ark of the nation." In short, every child is not only Emile; he is also Moses to be rescued from the bullrushes for the sake of his people. Already in the individual soul of every child is the promised saviour of his nation.

It is in this twin concern, with the child as an individual and with him also as the guardian of the future of the Republic, that we know that we are in the United States. The promise was held out that, generation after generation, the individual could be so made that, generation after generation, the Republic would be redeemed. If attention was paid to the "waxen state of children's minds" in the "miniature temple" of their bodies, the future could be deliberately made. No such notion, that the future is plastic as the child is plastic, was held in Europe so strongly or so early.

It was after the Second World War that this idea became a form of national mission, and the literature of Women's Liberation is false in believing that the emphasis that was then placed on motherhood and the family was merely, although it certainly was in part, a device to keep women in the home. The centre of concern was the child. An article, one of hundreds, in *American Family* in 1949, put it clearly: "Parents who make companions of their children, who treat them as equals and friends and who join with them in their enjoyment of life, are amply rewarded in knowing that their children when they leave home are fortified with characters that will stand any test which may be met. . . . Our world and tomorrow's civilization are in the hands of the parent of today's children." The prescription is far-reaching. To read the family magazines of those years is to read of a nation that was confident in its power and its mission in the world, and certain that it could make the future by making its children.

"The travellers agree, we think," wrote the *Edinburgh Review* in 1818, in a notice of four books by English travellers to the United States, "in complaining of the insubordination of American children —and do not much like American ladies." They were, of course, complaining of a kind of freedom that was allowed to women and children in the family, to which they were unaccustomed at home. It is a curiosity of America that, although the idea of the family is nowhere more celebrated, it has always been a more fragile institution than elsewhere. "In America the family tie is weaker," wrote the Italian historian Guglielmo Ferrero in 1910. "Divorce is too easy by far; the women are too emancipated; the children too independent of parental control. In this respect, it has seemed to me that America has reached a limit beyond which really dangerous social disorder lies." The answer that one may expect from an American was given in 1948 by Arthur J. Todd, then the Chairman Emeritus of the Department of Sociology at Northwestern University: "The questioning youth of the twentieth century is the legitimate descendant of those questioning forefathers of the eighteenth century who remade the entire Western world." Back from England in 1961 came the dry observation of the English critic Graham Hough on some lectures of Archibald MacLeish that, "like all American professors and no English ones," he is always telling us "how much he has learnt from his pupils."

When one talks of the Americanization of the world, one cannot dismiss these differences of manners. The opportunities and the mythology of mobility in the United States, social as well as geographical, have had a profound influence on its manners. The young can always move on, the adult can always move out. In an English seminar on "The Family and Its Future," which was held in 1969, this revealing exchange took place between English observers:

Hilde Himmelweit: "Why in the States do the children with problems often run away? In this country they may have the same problems but they don't necessarily run away from home?"

Derek Miller: "I really don't know. But American society has always been highly mobile; movement has been its culture for a long time."

Robin Fox: "There is also somewhere to go now. . . ."

Olive M. Stone: "To run away you need not only somewhere to go but also the means of running away. The typical American adolescent goes outside and drives away in his own or somebody else's car. This is also what happens with matrimonial disputes. English reports of these resound with doors being slammed and locked, American ones with cars being driven furiously a thousand miles or so."[13]

One may call in evidence, again, the claim of Jerry Rubin that the first rebellion of American youth against its parents took place in the 1950s, with the demand to borrow the parents' car, the concession to that demand, and whatever then took place in the back seat to the sound of Elvis Presley on the car radio.

"LIBERATION": A CODED WORD OF OUR TIME

The movement for Women's Liberation, like the "student movement," has travelled to the rest of the world from America. It is an important movement, certainly one of the most important to have come out of the 1960s, and it needs our careful consideration. For the moment, however, we may again be satisfied to offer it as another illustration of what is meant by the Americanization of the world. It is once more an equal right of each individual to the full expression of his own personality that is being claimed: the I released in the En-Masse that is being announced. It is in changes in social attitudes in England, Peter Hall has said, and in the resulting changes in social and political relationships, "that we shall see the greatest Americanization in the next quarter of a century"; and he spoke in particular of the fact that in America "rights of all kinds have become a positive obsession," creating "a sense of serious involvement by large numbers of people," which has made America a "much more genuinely radical country than Britain."[14]

The impact of these participatory movements in the United States has again been widespread. Friends of the Earth was founded in England by Graham Searle after he had spent a period in the United States studying the American organization of the same name; and the Public Interest Research Centre was similarly founded, "very much in the Nader mould," by Charles Medawar after he had spent three months in the United States working with Ralph Nader. But it is the liberation movements which are most characteristic, not only Women's Liberation, but also the Gay Liberation Front, for example, which was already well established in America before it was founded in England in 1971. Indeed, the working out of the American idea in our own time is to be found, at least in part, in the word "liberation," one of the coded words of our time, whose meaning we have yet to decipher. At the beginning of the third century of American time, it is the unravelling of the meaning of this word which will be our preoccupation; and, as we begin to unravel it, we may begin to understand how governing is the idea that America carries with it.

As the meaning of "liberation" becomes clear, it will provoke a reaction; in fact, the reaction is already gathering. In the next quarter of a century, at least, a struggle will be waged in the minds of men between the American idea and its enemies, as the I released in the En-Masse, which can stand as one of the meanings of "liberation," makes its entry. The attack on "the masses," which were brought by America in 1776 to the front of the stage, has already commenced; at the beginning of the attack, what is called "mass society" seems to be almost friendless; even in the United States, men are today no longer hesitant to proclaim themselves an elite, to whom "the masses" ought in reason to condescend. It is the very idea of America that is at stake.

It was Seneca who predicted, almost two thousand years ago, that one day a land would be found beyond the seas and that, when it was found, "the chains of the world will be loosed forever." In the copy of the works of Seneca which belonged to Christopher Columbus, his son wrote that this his father had done in 1492. During the eighteenth century, as we have seen, the *philosophes* were engaged in a profound debate, centred on the question: Was America a mistake? At first, they concluded that it was. But, as the American began to step forth, the new man in his new continent, to claim his own freedom, the New World not only found its defenders in Europe, it was acclaimed as the hope of the human race. "It is not enough," wrote Condorcet, "that the rights of men be written in the tomes of philosophers and in the hearts of virtuous men. The weak and the ignorant must be able to read them in the example of a great nation. America has given that example"; and he was echoed by men as great as Brissot and Gentz and Turgot.

This hope of the rest of the world in America has never quite been lost; backwards and forwards, as has been said, over the generations, the hope is dashed and then returns. Indeed, much of the disillusion of the rest of the world with America, whenever it recurs, is its disillusion with its own high hopes of America. However much the world may resist, it cannot rid itself of the probability that in America its own future can be discerned, and it wishes that future to be good. "Are we becoming too Americanized?" said *New Society* not long ago, "has been one of the recurring questions of the British post-war scene. In a sense, the underlying question is: are we Americanized enough . . . ? There is an attack, an imagination, and a seriousness of purpose about what is going on, in the United States that must at the very least serve as a yardstick for our own efforts."[15] Behind all forms of anti-Americanism, something of this understanding may always be found.

There are those in America today who would shackle the New World again with the chains of the Old World, who would so drain the American idea of its meaning that there would in the end be nothing of America left. But this book is written in the conviction, after several years of observation, that the country which is an idea, and the idea which is a country, are not yet without their resources. Coded in the word "liberation" is already a new life: for America, and its masses; for Europe, and its masses; for the rest of the world, and its masses. In thrusting and reaction, the idea of America is coming to a new fruitfulness; and it would be a tragedy if, in the rage that must be endured, America wearied of its own idea.

CHAPTER 6

The Quest for the Public in America

America is today the only nation in the West that has the opportunity, the incentive, and, above all, the capacity to create a public philosophy which has meaning and is compelling in the private lives of its citizens. At least since the beginning of this century, it has not done so. As the public estate of America has grown, both at home and abroad, the mind and imagination of the country have increasingly disengaged from it, and left it without a public philosophy. By and large, its thinkers and writers, artists and intellectuals, do not inhabit the public sphere. Walled in their universities, preserved in the isinglass of the foundations, clustered like spiders at the centre of the web which they have spun for themselves in New York, alert to the arrival of any newcomer who can be trapped and devoured: even when they are publicists and celebrities, as some of them are, they are not really public men. In fact, one of the strangenesses of the United States is that it sometimes seems to have no public men at all outside its politics, a condition that may reflect the democratic nature of its society. There is certainly no "establishment" in America. One must be a celebrity or a politician, elected in the market place or the ballot box.

The term "a celebrity," used in this concrete way and applied to a person, was still quite new when it was employed by Emerson in 1856. There was no need for such a word—it could have no place —in the aristocratic societies of the past. The members of "The County" in a Trollope novel were not celebrities in their shire, they took precedence by their rank, and it was to their rank that deference was paid. But by the middle of the nineteenth century, with the rise of the middle class and of its newspapers, an altogether different kind of fame could be earned, and it was only seven years after its first recorded use that Emerson wrote in *English Traits* of "one of the celebrities of wealth and fashion"; not of rank, it must be noticed.

The feature about "People" in each issue of *Time* is as good an index as any to the celebrities of the day; but they are not public men. They are not men to whom the society in general looks for instruction and guidance. To take an example for one field. There is today no university president who has the national standing as a public figure that was once held by Nicholas Murray Butler, say, or Robert Hutchins. The public mind of the country, is today influenced only intermittently by its intellectual mind: a fact that is most obvious on television.

From time to time, the thinkers and writers, artists and intellectuals, may foray into the public sphere; but it is nearly always on a political issue, and the political issue is nearly always a presidential policy. In other words, they arrive in the public arena too late, when the mischief against which they wish to protest has already been done. A war has been started; they wish it suddenly, at the lifting of their voices and the raising of their lances, to be stopped; and, when this does not happen, they retire again behind their moats, into their isinglass, back to their webs, there to complain that the public estate is beyond any saving and beneath their attention, until they again sally forth to duel, belatedly and unsuccessfully, with a President.

It is this contraction of the public estate to a political arena, and the political arena to a presidential duel, which is so damaging. The public estate—the place where the public life of the country from day to day endures—has all but vanished from the literature of the United States. This is even true of the work of Norman Mailer which is supposed to be most concerned with public issues. He does not really visit the public estate, but takes himself to the political arena, where there is a happening or, if there is not, he will contrive a happening. Philip Roth arrives from writing *The Breast,* which is his concern, to excoriate a President who was elected in the public estate, even though he has shown in his work only a teetering concern for the health of that estate.

But this has become the stance of writers and artists in America to the public life of their country. It is never presented in their work, if it is presented at all, as continuous, rich in the incident of routine; only as an episode, happening out of nothing, the President and his challengers in an arena which, so they make it seem, can be struck like a set in a studio as soon as the filming has stopped.

THE PUBLIC AND THE PRIVATE IN TENSION

It was not always so, and that it is so now is disturbing. America was invented out of a concern for the *res publica* and, if that concern is diminished in the mind and imagination of the country, it will not live as America. It must be a nation of citizens, or it will be a mere agglomeration of individuals, each pursuing his own interests, and few achieving any measure of contentment in their lives. The strong thread of individualism in its political tradition has often been noted; and the liveliness of that individualism has been reasserted in the past two decades. But the outsider in the United States is constantly aware of the subtle observation of an early visitor to Japan in the nineteenth century: "It is a singular fact that in Japan, where the individual is sacrificed to the community, he should seem perfectly happy and contented, while in America, where exactly the opposite takes place and the community is sacrificed to the individual, the latter is in a perpetual state of uproarious clamour for his rights."[1] It is for this reason that any weakening of the public life of America must seem to threaten its social cohesion.

But at least part of the answer lies in the American idea itself. Much of the writing about the country, especially since Tocqueville, has rested on the notion that it pursues ideas that are irreconcilable: equality *and* liberty, individual achievement *and* democratic opportunity, absolute personal freedom *and* aggressive social regulation, dissent *and* conformity; and the list could be extended. This notion of irreconcilable opposites even entered into the literary criticism of the 1950s, when the American tradition and experience were increasingly presented as finding their truest expression in the melodramatic opposition of irreconcilable contraries. Walt Whitman had proclaimed, "Do I contradict myself?/Very well then I contradict myself," and this attitude was given an almost mythical importance in the interpretation of the American experience.

If America did pursue ideas that are irreconcilable opposites, it would be unbearable. So, in the Americans' own version, it is not denied that the ideas are opposite, or that they are irreconcilable; it is merely held that a devastating conflict between them is avoided because the country swings between them in a regular cycle, in what has been announced as the rhythm of American history and life. The most impressive exposition of the rhythm theory—equilibrium by calisthenics—was given by Herbert Croly; since then, it seems to have become the property of the Schlesingers in perpetuity. But neither the European version of irreconcilable opposites nor the American version of rhythmic adjustment is necessary.

Both of them interpret the American experience in the light of the European experience, American ideas in terms of European ideas. Liberty had grown in Europe, for example, in a way in which it did not grow in America: as a series of inch-by-inch claims made by the three estates on behalf of the comparatively few people who belonged to them. Liberty has always seemed to the European, and to the Englishman in particular, a matter of particular rights, secured by particular groups, as a result of particular concessions, made to particular interests. When liberty is so conceived, equality must be a threat to it. It was with such a preconception that Tocqueville travelled to the United States, with the baggage, as he again and again confessed, of an aristocrat; and from such a preconception that John Stuart Mill believed that he had to choose between liberty and democracy and chose liberty; and it is this preconception that, like a siren, sings still to troubled Americans from across the Atlantic.

But it was not this kind of liberty that had to be won in America; neither was it that manner in which it had to be won. The colonists came to the land with the Magna Carta, and all the other charters that it represented, already in their hands; and then went roaming about their continent, scavenging for land, as Washington urged every settler to do after the expulsion of the French, the liberty which they required being claimed on behalf of individuals and not of an estate. Liberty was claimed in America as individual and therefore as general; and that is why, in the Declaration of Independence, the assertion of equality precedes the right to liberty; it could be given no other base. Equality and liberty, the general and the individual, the public and the private, had grown together and were asserted together; the pole supports the bean, the bean supports the pole.

Personal freedom in America does not exist outside the public estate and, if the public estate is allowed to wither, personal freedom will wither also. In fact, in no other country since antiquity have the public and the private been in so intricate a dependence on each other. The nations of Europe were born out of a medieval society in which the reach of the public power was so limited that the area of private repose had been able to establish itself, in habit and in manner, before the public power had the resources to extend itself. The private in Europe is secured in niches; set back in a wall, as is an effigy in a cathedral. The wall and the effigy are not in tension; and both are very still. The private in Europe is a sanctuary.

But there are no niches in America; the country did not exist, not even the colonies, when the public power was weak; and the public and the private can therefore not be separated. There is no cathedral in America where the American may secure and enjoy his freedom in a sanctuary. His situation is more intricate. Just as equality and individuality, the I and the En-Masse, are not in conflict in the American idea, but are held in tension, as in a rope when it is taking the strain, so the same is true of the public and the private: there are only two ends of a rope and, if one strand is disentangled from the other, both will break. Freedom in America was not secured against the public power; it was bestowed on the individual by the public power, exercised to the full in a national war; the American will not, therefore, secure his personal freedom unless he participates in the exercise of the public power. He is bound, if he is to be free, to act as a citizen of a republic.

THE INDIVIDUAL AS CITIZEN

The American cannot desert the public estate without deserting himself at the very core of his own being; as an individual, he is whole only as a citizen; as a citizen, he must act as an individual. This is one of the acute differences that a traveller from England feels between America and his own country. There is an important sense in which a policy in England is the policy of a government, and the government is the government of a party, and the individual is distanced from the actions that are taken. This is the significance of the fiction that it is "the Crown" that acts in the deeds of the government. The individual citizen may get angry with the policy and with the government and with the party, but there is no reason for him to get angry with himself. He may be personally upset; he does not feel personally responsible. The private and the public are not pole and bean; they are sufficiently poles apart to permit a personal disengagement, even when one is politically active.

But this is not the position in America, where the acts of a President are acts done in one's own name. One does not, as an outsider, have to be in the United States for long to realize that there come moments, and they are not infrequent, when every man and woman sees himself or herself as personally responsible for the country's behaviour. Indeed, it is in America, more than in any country in Europe, that one senses one of the predicaments of the citizen of a democracy: that he feels a sense of moral involvement in, and responsibility for, the deeds (and the misdeeds) of a government which he helped to elect, but over which, for the term of its office, his control is tenuous and indistinct. One was aware of this predicament during the war in Vietnam, and again as the public disquiet grew at the revelations of presidential misconduct in 1973. On both occasions, it almost seemed as if every American had a visiting card, which entitled him or her, even obliged them, to go to the White House, when the occasion made it necessary, and claim the place as their own.

After the fiasco of British arms at Suez, for example, Anthony Eden was replaced as Prime Minister by Harold Macmillan as the result of an internal manoeuvre in the Conservative Party, which was conducted in secret, and in which even the House of Commons, as such, played no part. In the enforced departures of Lyndon Johnson and Richard Nixon, the popular voice in America played a much more positive and direct role. These occasions may seem to be rare, but it is sometimes necessary to pay attention less to the actual working of a political system than to the assumptions that underlie its working, for those assumptions will usually be found to be more active than is often realized. It cannot be denied that the relationship of the private citizen to the exercise of the public power in America is of an exceptional character, the result of its own political tradition.

After all, the private citizen in America *is* always appealing in defence and extension of his private rights to the Constitution, to the Bill of Rights, to the judiciary, in the last resort to the Supreme Court; and these *are* the public power. Moreover this is not all: one of the features of American life that is most noticeable to the outsider is that the dissenter expects to enjoy the freedom to dissent, not only from within the established society, but with the support and the encouragement of that society, even of its guarantee. It is this notion that has given to "dissent" in the past two decades in America a new meaning and a new force, so that it has, like "liberation," become a coded word of our time.

RETREAT TO THE PRIVATE

The American cannot live unless the public philosophy is in some sort of correspondence with his private philosophy. There have been times, in the history of his country, when this correspondence has existed, and been vital; and they have been times of confidence and fulfillment, for the nation and the individual. They have been times when there were no émigrés from America, neither émigrés abroad nor the internal émigrés, malcontent with their own country, who nevertheless do not leave it. At these moments of correspondence, America may always be seen to be pulling itself away, once more, from Europe and turning a deaf ear to its sirens; certain that it can find itself only in its own experience, it has again been certain of its own design and its own vision. This was true of the remarkable group of diverse figures at the beginning of this century, who included such men as William James and John Dewey, Charles Beard and James Harvey Robinson, Oliver Wendell Holmes, Jr., and Thorstein Veblen. Diverse they might be, but their views cohered. They worked on a public philosophy, almost explicitly, for the public estate, explicit also in their Americanness, in their awareness that America had come into being in a different time from Europe; and it was the working out of their ideas in the public arena that helped to create the confident American of the mid-century.

Nothing is more necessary, if America is to recover a sense of its public estate and re-create a public philosophy, than that it should recover this awareness. As has been said, much of the thought and the literature of Europe, for more than a hundred years, has been the thought and literature of decline and dissolution and decay; and the reasons are not hard to understand. It is not merely that power has gone from Europe—even from a wealthy and united Europe, as was shown during the Middle East crisis in 1973—but that its reason for being has gone. The death of God meant the collapse of Christendom; the collapse of Christendom ment the end of the West as it had been conceived for a thousand years; the end of the West in these terms meant the dissolution of Europe. The public estate of Europe no longer has a vital existence; it requires only bureaucrats to maintain it, and it can live by dead forms. It is no wonder, therefore, that so much of its thought and its literature has been one of anguish at the life sapping from its public estate; and of a retreat into private worlds, each in himself to discover his-self, and play with his toes.

But the United States was created in a different time. We have already said that it never existed when the public power was weak; equally it has never existed when God was alive. It has never been a part of Christendom; it has never had to feel that it is the heir to Rome, to nourish itself, deliciously but futilely, on the dream of the Holy Roman Empire. The public estate in the United States has never rested on these ruins. There is no reason why the individual American should either feel anguish at their dissolution, or retreat from their melancholy spectacle into his private consciousness. Yet it is precisely the mind and the imagination of Europe in decline that has tempted, one cannot believe that it has actually seduced, the mind and imagination of America during the past quarter of a century; and it is to the nature of the temptation, and to the response which, from its history, one would expect America to make, that we are about to turn.

A TENACIOUS REGARD FOR THE COMMON WELFARE

For the moment, it is enough to say that, in its mind and imagination, America needs to go again in quest of the public. As a result of the relics of feudalism, Erich Fromm once wrote, individualism for the majority of people in Europe "was not much more than a façade behind which was hidden the failure to acquire an individual sense of identity."[2] Thirty years ago, Dewey made the point clearly: "The prized and vaunted individuality of European culture that is threatened by the leveling standardization of the American type was a very limited affair. . . . How much share in it was had by the peasant and proletariat?"[3] This kind of limitation has never for long been tolerable to the American idea. The individualism that is claimed, is claimed for all, whatever their situation or condition: the I is released, not as the eccentricity of an aristocracy, but in the En-Masse.

But the claims of this extreme individualism are themselves not tolerable unless they are anchored to a public philosophy. "Something very important has been lost sight of in the American quest,"[4] wrote George Norlin, one of the more creative presidents of a state university in the history of the United States, before he died in 1942. "It has had little regard for the common welfare." This persistent tendency in America, to pull on one strand of the rope but not on the other, has always to be guarded against. The individualism that is claimed for all can degenerate all too easily into the claim of William Graham Sumner, which was also the claim of Richard Nixon in his Second Inaugural address: "Every man and woman in society has one big duty. That is, to take care of his or her own self. This is a social duty. . . . Let every man be happy in his own way."[5] Precisely because the release of the I in the En-Masse is so tremendous an experiment, the protection of the En-Masse in its common estate, a tenacious regard for the common welfare, must be a primary concern of the American.

"Our presumption is," wrote Ezra Pound of his own country in 1913, "that those things are right which give the greatest opportunity for individual development to the individual of whatever age or sex or condition."[6] The presumption must be for all, or it can be for none. "American society," said Arthur Mizener in 1962, "offers the individual every encouragement to develop his natural perceptions to the limits, according to his lights."[7] The encouragement must be to all, or it can be to none. There can be no other foundation for the claim to individual liberty in a country that has none of the relics of a feudal society.

But the guarantee of that equal claim to freedom can be given only in the public estate; from year to year, there are corrections to be made, extensions of the claim to be won. The process of redefinition is continual: of the kind of liberty to which the individual is entitled, of the kind of individuals who are entitled to enjoy it. In the past twenty years, the United States has been engaged in a more vigorous redefinition than at perhaps any other time in its history, at least since the beginning of the nineteenth century. Seldom have the ideas of equality and individuality been more creatively in tension; seldom has the strain on the two ends of the rope been so strong. The years have been tumultuous; they could not be other. But the danger is that, given the carelessness for the public that is also one of the marks of the time, the "liberation" that is won will be only personal, and the common welfare will be disregarded.

When he was still able to think and feel as an American—and how much better, one may say in passing, his poetry might have been if he had continued to think and feel as an American—Pound wrote of "the uprights, or, so to speak, the piles that are driven deep, and through the floating bog of our national consciousness." All that has been attempted so far in the argument is, amid the bog, to try to recognize some of the uprights, and take hold of some of the piles. At first, the outsider as he journeys into America is aware only of the bog; but at last he finds that the uprights are there, where he had been told he would find them, driven as they were driven at the beginning, so that they do not shift.

PART III

The Human Estate

"One day the boy saw his mother planting an apple tree. 'Why do you work so hard, Mother?' he asked.

"'I may never see the tree in bearing,' she replied, 'but someone will.'"

—A story of GEORGE NORRIS, as told by ERIC GOLDMAN[1]

CHAPTER 7

In Praise of Survivors

The human estate is being neglected. In the imagination of our time, and therefore in our practice, we have grown careless of it.

To talk of the human estate is to speak of what we ourselves have made. It is our artifice. Because it is artificial, it is that part of our reality which is most directly accessible to us, in which and on which we may act with our wills; which we may choose to preserve or neglect, to improve or let decay. We may prosper in it if we will, or by impoverishing it make paupers of ourselves. Our estate is not the human condition in which we are placed, of which we hear so much; it is the human place which we have made, in which we may modify our condition. It is that which is un-natural, which we have made un-natural; fenced and hedged, tilled and gardened, to separate it and ourselves from nature. Our human nature is not only our *nature,* it is also our *manners;* and the human estate is the place where we are mannered, where what we are and cannot help being is informed and altered, enriched and complicated, by what we have learned; by what we have learned, above all, to make of ourselves.

The human estate is the field of our cultivated behaviour; and it at least, whatever in our condition may seem to be, is not absurd. We can make sense of it and, within it, sense of our lives.

We have grown careless of our estate in our imaginations, but the truth may be harder than that. It sometimes seems that we can no longer imagine what it is to be human and, if we cease to be able to imagine our humanity, it will fall away from us; we will shed it, until all that we can find of it are the dead leaves of what once, in the past, men were able to imagine it to be. The human estate, for all its solidity and worldliness, has itself to be imagined. We can continue to be human, at ease in our estate, only if we can continue to imagine for ourselves what it is to be human. The task which confronts us is to reimagine the place which we have made, so that we may then reimagine ourselves within it.

THE ARENA OF THE INDIVIDUAL

It is characteristic of our time that we have simultaneously two popular literatures: one which invites us to sink ourselves in our animal natures—we are no more than naked apes; and another which invites us to elevate and then to submerge ourselves in a transcendent consciousness—we are actually to extinguish ourselves in a hallucinated godhead. By the first, man is placed below his estate; by the second, set beyond it. By both of them, he is separated from the home which he has made, either unfit to inhabit it or unable to be content within it.

A third popular literature has the appearance of being more humanist; it invites us to find our-selves inside ourselves. The objection to this imagining of our humanity is its limitations. If man is not an ape, and he is not an angel, it is equally clear that he is not alone. To be a human being is to be a public being, in a way in which it is impossible for an animal, and would be inappropriate for an angel, to be public. If one is going to find one's-self in oneself, one is well advised, before beginning the search in earnest, to make sure that one has put something inside which has made one's-self worth the discovering. The self can be nourished in this way only by its contact with—its action on, its reaction to, its interaction with—what is other than it. To consider man in his estate is to consider him as public.

Much of the worry about personal relationships which nags at so many people today—a fourth popular literature—springs from the failure to understand that, even in these relationships, man is public: that by entering into a personal relationship he assists in creating a public, each in the relationship becoming public to the other. His behaviour in such a relationship is un-natural—mannered, learned, cultivated—and even the spontaneity and authenticity which he seeks within it are the attributes of its public character. Even two people, together in the intimacy of their love, are a public; they are public to each other, in their approach, in their awareness, in their apprehensions; each is actor, each is audience.

Even the hermit, conscious that he is a hermit, conscious of the plot which he has chosen for his life, is public to himself; he has an audience, however diminished; from day to day, he discovers himself, not so much in himself as to himself. Even he is acting out his life, as we say; he does not cease to have a public, he merely reduces his public to one. That is why we regard his life as inhuman; not because he is alone, but because he is alone with himself; still an actor, he is implausibly his own audience.

To be human is to have a narrative, a plot to one's life, a dramatic route which it follows, and these are public, enacted among others. Even a gaze exchanged in passing with a stranger on the street can be immediately endowed with an "imaginative narrative thread," a plot of what might have been; and the plot remains with us, we never wholly forget the occasion or the face or the exchange of a glance. In contrast, a dog that meets another dog on the street must do or not do whatever by a dog is done or not done on a street; but the thing, done or not done, is then over. Neither of the dogs remembers—reimagines—the plot which either happened or might have happened. But human beings imagine and reimagine such encounters and exchanges; they are the source of each individual's knowledge of himself, and they are public. They occur in an arena, the human estate.

Man is not born, in nature and under god, into a place which is not defined. He may be born from eternity, but into a time which has a limit; he may be born from space, but into a place which has a hedge. In this "now" and this "here," he has his life. He may not be able to order his birth or his death, but the life which intervenes is his to order, in the company and with the co-operation of others who are "now" and "here" with him. He is born not only into his condition, which may be absurd, but into his estate, which is sensible. He may be able to do nothing about his condition, except try to defy it, but he may with others do what he will about his estate.

"A CERTAIN PRIDE TO BEING HUMAN"

The importance of the human estate is that it stands against the human condition; it is the *theatrum mundi* whose worth to man (and therefore to god) the theologian used to proclaim. In *La Condition*

Humaine—translated as *Man's Fate* in the American edition—the characters of André Malraux pit themselves against the human condition, but do not reach for what is to hand for them in the human estate, which already stands against it. This is why they are not only unsuccessful as revolutionaries but at odds with the revolutionary committees whose interest is that the revolution should succeed. It is difficult to grant that they are even heroic, because they throw themselves against an adversary against which nothing but heroism is possible; and to put oneself into a situation in which there can be no recourse but to heroism is to deny oneself the choice of being heroic, especially in any particular act to any particular end. This is why the act to them is itself the measure of its own value, for what is its own justification not only requires no further justification but in fact cannot otherwise be judged. But in the human estate the act is measured by its consequences, by what it does to the actor himself and to others on whom the act impinges, and not least by what it does to the estate in which all must live. In standing against the human condition, the human estate stands also against the self-sufficing act of the solitary will, and invites men to discover themselves in plainer ways.

"It is no small thing to feel the blood in our veins and to be warmed by the sun," wrote Lionel Trilling in 1939. "Common human life, neither ascetic nor hedonistic nor given to much thought, may bring contentment"[2]; and we know at once that with such words we are in our estate. It is, to use the language of a sociologist, "the small primary personal relationships of society . . . the small areas of membership and association in which human values are made meaningful and compelling to human beings."[3] In contrast, those who are concerned overmuch with the human condition seem not to be interested in human values at all, but in values which are other than human, and in the inability of men to find accommodation for them.

Man "cannot live without happiness altogether." Marías has said, "and we must understand that he can find happiness even in the direst straits. In contrast to the thoughtless cult of anguish, bleakness and nausea, I find the truly human qualities, qualities that lend a certain pride to being human, in man's marvelous capacity to discover delight amid pain, suffering, misery and fear; and in his ability to see humor even in his own misfortune."[4] That is a voice from our estate; we have only to hear it, and we know that in our estate it is true. We have only to mend its fences, till its fields, clean its ditches, keep its roofs in repair, and we may enjoy in our estate a human measure of happiness, and even recover the "certain pride to being human" which we today so conspicuously lack, and are therefore in all ages conspicuous for our anxiety and despair.

Man needs, in his mind and imagination, his literature and his art, to come home. The homelessness of man is one of the images of those who are concerned with his condition. But, if he is homeless, it is not for a cause about which he can do nothing, it is because he has left his home, neglected it, and no longer is familiar in it; and to cease to be homeless, he has but to return to it, relearn his way about it, and care for it. He is not just set on this earth, he is domiciled in it, and building that domicile has been the work of his civilizations. He is not doomed to wander between a nature from which he is separated and a god who is dead, unable to discover himself in either of them; he has a place of his own, and his own place in it.

There he will find himself; and there he may dwell. On any estate, especially in England but not only in England, there is what is called a home meadow. It lies beyond the house and its garden, but before the fields are reached, and the fields then give way to nature. It is a pasture, green and lush, shaded by great trees which an earlier generation in its care planted; its fences in order, its hedges in trim, its gates that open and shut on their hinges. It is protected and is kept; the health in it is secured. There the cow may be brought to calf, the ewe to lamb, the horse to rest, so that they may be watched. It is not nature, for it has been tended; and it has not been tended by a god. Even to our city-bound minds, the image can speak; even in our cities, there are places that we may secure and keep, and there succour with our fellows the health that we may discover in us.

THE SHEER ENDURANCE OF HUMAN SOCIETY

To some extent, the argument of this book is concerned with the way in which we have allowed the words that we use, the systems that we build, the models that we construct, the art that we make, the literature that we write, to get in our way of noticing and understanding our actual situations, from day to day, in the societies in which we live. Nothing that is said is meant to disparage any of these.

If our minds and imaginations did not roam far into the past and deep into the future, if we did not inquire into being and nothingness, we would not be men. But all of them are our manufactures. They are not our reality, but ways of imagining and trying to order our reality. To confuse what is real in our situations with what we imagine to be the reality of our condition is an invitation to sterility in both fields.

Although the beliefs of primitive peoples, John Plamenatz has said, are uninfluenced by theory, "popular ideas and sentiments in advanced and literate societies are deeply, even though indirectly, influenced by it." It is illuminating, for example, how such an abstract notion as "alienation" will today travel into the popular mind, there to be taken, not as the conceit which it is, but as a literal description of our condition; or how the idea of ego identity leaves the psychologist's study and journeys into the excitable mind of the adolescent, there to be indulged by him as a literal description of his insecurities. When a student once said to Erik Erikson that he seemed unable to find his identity, the propagator of the idea asked him curtly if he was making a complaint or a boast; and we ought to ask the same of many of our laments, whether they are at our age, at our societies, or at ourselves. It sometimes seems that we are not complaining but boasting of our wretchedness, and this is itself a form of arrogance; only we, it is implied, are capable of being wretched.

A book such as this has an origin. A journalist is a layman in everything. He gathers his material from the doings and utterances of others. He is a jackdaw, whose industry in collecting material for its nest is, according to the encyclopaedia, "as marvellous as often it is futile," although it has sometimes been known to build a nest as much as twelve feet high. After observing the affairs of twenty-two countries, during the past quarter of a century, one has gathered many loose sticks, but now and then it seems that one has also made a nest. What has been most striking, in a time of upheaval, has been to observe close at hand the sheer endurance of human society, the mere living of the human beings who inhabit them. They have been promised earths and heavens beyond their dreams; but when the disappointment comes, as come it must, they can still be seen, attending to the hour that is present, with reward to themselves and to others, with a measure of grace, and above all with the humour that Marías asked us to notice. It is not only their tenacity that is to be remarked, but what they make by their tenacity.

One has been in England when it stood alone against Hitler, when its cities were bombed and burned, when crisis has followed crisis even in the victory and the peace that it had earned, when it was torn by the adventure into Suez; in Algeria when the colonized had risen in savage rebellion against *les colons,* and *les colons* tried as savagely to hold down the colonized, and in France when it had itself been reduced by the bitterness of this conflict to a state almost of civil war, and it called back de Gaulle to be its saviour; in Berlin when the wall was being built; in Yugoslavia when its people were being asked to make yet another adjustment in their imagining of their society, of their place in it, and of its place in the world; in Greece when it was fatefully divided; in the Sudan when its people in the north had recommenced their agelong effort to enslave or exterminate its people in the south; in Ethiopia during a time of determined repression after an attempt to usurp the throne of the Lion of Judah; in Kenya after the Mau Mau and before it had been granted its independence; in Uganda and Tanganyika and Northern Rhodesia and Southern Rhodesia and Nyasaland, as the struggle between the natives and the settlers was joined; in South Africa when it was simmering with racial conflict; and so on. Above all, perhaps, one has been in the United States when its people have been subjected to an almost endless series of provocations.

One does not, after such experiences, emerge with an easy optimism about the human estate, and our age indeed seems to be monstrous, although one may doubt that it is more monstrous than any other. Yet it is a picture of the human estate that remains uppermost in one's mind; and the realization that the estate is common even to peoples who are so diverse. Even during the savagery, wonderfully the societies held together, and within them the majority of human beings still tried to bear themselves as if to make some explicit statement of their humanity. Returning after the savagery, it could be seen that the keeping of the estate had been worthwhile, that something of value had been preserved in which men might prosper in a human degree. One was grateful to the survivors.

THE ASSURANCE OF THE FAMILIAR

It is the survival of men that needs to be celebrated; and by their survival one does not mean a listless dragging of the feet from day to day, but an affirmation that the day can itself be so made that it will be good. Men rest much on their affections, rather than on their loves, and their affections are the gift of their estate, made and sustained by that part of their behaviour that is mannered. When one recalls the societies of men that one has observed, usually in circumstances that are trying, one remembers most what today seems to be most forgotten: the insistent willingness, one might even say their determination, of men to correct themselves in their mannered behaviour, to be instructed by it in how to be human; to avoid the hurt that can be avoided, manage the smile that can be managed, proffer the caress that is needed. All of this one can observe from day to day; all of it we have been taught to disregard.

The majority of men do not waken each morning to visions either of a utopia or of the apocalypse. They waken to the assurance of the familiar, and it is the familiar that the human estate can guard for them. This is true even of those whose lives we have allowed to remain so impoverished that the estate has little to offer to them; the familiar is still to them a resource on which they can rely. The familiar has for a long time been disdained by our thought and our art and our literature; these have called men from their estate, and made him homeless. It is in the mind and imagination of our time that the individual in his-self has been separated from the individual in his society, so that they live almost separate lives, the one regarded as authentic, the other as simulation. The solitary individual has been placed in opposition to his fellow men with whom he shares a common situation, and who ought to be his companions.

There is no need why we should imagine our condition in this way, but that is how we have been instructed by our thought and our art and our literature. We have been persuaded to take the worlds that they have created as more real than the actual world in which we live, their imagining of ourselves to be more accurate than our own perceptions of our day-to-day lives. Even our sociology has been deeply influenced by what essentially are literary ideas, in such a way that much of it seems to be a commentary, not on the actual state of society, but on how it has been imagined by artists and writers. The reputation of the commonplace, of what we share of our common humanity in our estate, has never been lower. It needs to be restored, and it ought to be restored by the country in which the phrase "the public domain" once had, not only a particular meaning, but a proud meaning in its public philosophy.

PART IV

The Rebellion of the Self

To separate himself from the society of which he was born a member will lead the revolutionary, not to life but to death, unless in his revolt, he is driven by a love of what seemingly must be rejected, and, therefore, at the profoundest level, remains faithful to that society.

—DAG HAMMARSKJÖLD, in *Markings*[1]

CHAPTER 8

The Do-It-Yourself God Kit

The neglect of the human estate has many causes, but it is hard to understand why some of them should have had this effect. One would have thought, for example, that the death of god, although it at first might be regarded as a tragedy, and one difficult to bear, would in the end persuade man to pay more attention to his place on this earth, there to better his lot, to find contentment and meaning in his life, and to discover the human values by which to judge himself: "to construct at last a human justice, the contribution of our star." But the opposite has happened, or at least it seems to have happened. Instead of settling to care for his estate, man has gone incorrigibly in search of god, or of a replacement. All of this, one must insist, is surprising. After all, the wonder had been, not that god had created man, but that man had created god, this was the conception that was miraculous; and again one would have thought that, when god had died, man would have been satisfied that he had once wrought so well, that his work had endured for so long, and that there had flowed from it apprehensions of life and of himself which he might otherwise not have contrived, and that he would have then sought to work as well again without the benefit of an idea which he no longer found useful.

THE MAGNITUDE OF THE DEATH OF GOD

Man began to put god to rest a long time ago, long before Nietzsche, or the romantic before him, chose to make such a song and dance about the interment. Paul Hazard, in *The European Mind, 1680–1715,* has shown that, during those years, not just a few intellectuals, but a significant number of the intellectual leaders of European society, had openly rejected the Christian faith: not just some part of the Christian doctrine, but the Christian faith in its own God, and even, so tenuous was the theism that remained, of all faith in any god. This was the secularization to which Voltaire and the *philosophes* were heir. But, in spite of this inheritance, the philosophers of the Enlightenment did not succeed in toppling the "heavenly city" even in their minds. From that day to this, in spite of the dust which each generation has shaken over the place where god is buried, man has been reluctant to let go the awareness of himself which he achieved when god was still alive, in him and to him.

One of the reasons why the eighteenth-century philosophers did not succeed in doing away with god was that they had a very limited and, indeed, bland conception of the awfulness of what they proposed. God may only have been an idea, created in the minds of men, of which men at their will could dispose. But he was an idea without which men had not before tried to live; even the Greeks had invented gods in order to enable them to postpone some of the more awkward questions about life. God had been meaning and purpose and hope; he had been the Incarnation, born among men, the Cross, dying among men, and the Resurrection, among men victorious over death; he had been Father and Son and Holy Ghost. "I am the Resurrection and the Life"—and abruptly, as if the trick could be worked in an encyclopaedia, man was to live without it all. One of the severe criticisms which must be made of the shallowness of the Enlightenment philosophers was that they never stood affrighted at what they proposed. For this reason, they neither achieved, in their own minds, what they purposed; nor prepared the minds of other men to anticipate the nausea which they would feel at the emptiness within, when they realised the magnitude of what had been attempted.

THE FALLACY OF THE ROMANTIC RESPONSE

The romantic mind did stand affrighted. It is one of the secrets of the romantic, like the emigrant that he is, that he does not know what he wants, but he knows what he does not want. His characteristic state of mind is to be interested, not in what is, but in what is not. A god who *is* would have bored him; but he is fascinated and appalled by a god who *is not*. He would have seen no light round the throne of god, but in the darkness of his grave there is effulgence. The response of the romantic to the death of god at least has grandeur. But in that response—in his obsession with what is not, in place of an interest in what is—we can find at least a part of the reason for the neglect of our estate in the imagination of our time.

The genius of the romantic was that he grasped the tragedy in the death of god; his grandeur that, at least in the beginning, he made a tremendous affirmation of man's soul left alone in the universe; its corruption, that he remains absorbed in the tragedy. He will not look at what remains, man as he is, but only at man as he could and must aspire to be; in other words, at what man is not. This is his affliction, and it is one of the afflictions of our age. As has often been said, life to the romantic is a desire, not a reality. There is nothing that he does not wish, or believe that he has the power, to experience; yet the experience not only will not satisfy him, he will not even accept it. He cannot say, for more than a moment, "Stay! Thou art so beautiful," because if it stayed he would have to concern himself with what is; and he must travel to another what is not.

The images in which his states of mind are revealed, as Eric Newton says, seem to be designed to obscure things as they are: in the moonlight, we cannot tell whether what is before us is a tree stump or a man; what is real in the mountains is always beyond the gorge or beneath the precipice, where we cannot see; love does not hold to a course to which a fulfilling end can be predicted, it is always running into trouble, and has the chart of a fever. With what is mysterious, what is abnormal, what is untamable, with what cannot be known, what cannot be predicted, what cannot be controlled, he dooms himself to live. He can "imagine all things as they could be"; but he cannot turn his gaze on what they are and call them to stay.

Such a man will never feel at home in the human estate, since it is things as they are, and man as he is, that are its concern, and to which it bids its welcome. Indeed, the more it feels like home, the more determined he must be to leave. He must be homeless. He must emigrate. He must go where he may create, not only what has never been but what will never be. Although he can imagine all things as other than they are, if he should ever create what he imagines, it will *be;* and in its being it will not satisfy, it will in fact offend and not even be acceptable; if necessary, he will destroy it. God is dead; his death is a tragedy; as a result of his death, man must be his own creator. But if man were to create what is good and *will be,* what is true and lovely and of good report, and will last, where is the tragedy in the death of god, where is the what is not, on which the romantic in his imagination must lean? So he must create what can never be created, what is completed only in its death. He will create his-self. By his individual and solitary will or his individual or solitary imagination, he will work in his individual and solitary self his individual and solitary creation; and then he will turn round, as the romantics have in fact turned round to us, and say: Look, there is nothing there, man the creator and the self-creator is as dead as god. The problem which the nineteenth century had to confront, said Malraux, was the death of god; and he asked, is not the problem that faces us the death of man?

To go through such anguish in order to discover, what many could have told the romantics over breakfast, that man is not divine is perverse. But it is perhaps even more perverse to say that, because man is not divine and because he cannot create himself as divine in the way in which he once created god to his satisfaction, he therefore does not create. After all, not only did he create the idea of the creator, when he needed it, he then created a world, and a place for himself in it, in which the idea of the creator was no longer necessary to him. To accuse man of not being divine when it was he who created the idea of divinity is as absurd as to accuse him of not being a creator because he has had the good humour and the common sense not to imagine himself as divine.

Among the theologians who are still to be found—some of them, as journals such as the *Harvard Theological Review* and *Concilium* illustrate, of honest purpose and unusual intelligence—the phrase "the death of god" is now old hat. It has ceased to be adequate to them, in their effort to confront the problem; as a statement, it has too blunt an edge. Yet it must suffice. God has died in our civilization. There is nothing in it that we can, or even need to, explain by his presence or his intervention; we neither fear him, nor hope in him. The attempts to recover his name and put it to work to describe what is other than god are misleading.

"I shall suggest that God was (or is) a single perfect transcendent non-representable and necessarily real object of attention," says Iris Murdoch; "and I shall go on to suggest that moral philosophy should attempt to retain a central concept which has all these characteristics."[2] One can understand, and even agree with, what she says— one may even be ready, in some moods, to agree with the young Coleridge that the lower world of meaner powers and secondary things that we inhabit is like a cloud which veils an effulgent reality that blazes beyond—and still object that the name of god is unsuitable, and is not even necessary, for either the concept of the one or the image of the other; and that it can only confuse the minds of ordinary people to whom the idea of god means more than an *object* of attention, but a supernatural power which is capable of intervening in the natural world, by his own will and to his own ends, as our civilization has taught.

THE IDEA OF THE HOMELESSNESS OF MAN

The theme of the homelessness of man, since the death of god, is so seductive, its imagery so powerful, that it is sometimes necessary to meet it with a curt common sense, if only because "home" is one of the few words in our vocabulary that has the simplicity of our affections, and it ought not to be carried into the emptiness of space or the universe, in order to demonstrate that we have none. Most of us are able to observe, at the end of a day, that the majority of people make their way to a house which they can find, put a key into a lock which it fits, walk into a place that they can recognize, are greeted by the familiar, and say with confidence and usually with relief: "I am home." We do not ask a stranger, Where are you homeless? We ask, Where is your home? He has a roof, a *domus,* a domicile, an address; that is what we mean.

If there are people who are homeless, it is because we have neglected them in our estate, and not made homes for them, or enabled them to make homes for themselves; because we have left the poor on the streets, the sick in institutions, the aged to be lonely. But if we are all of us homeless, why care about the man whose actual home in this world is wretched, or who has no home at all? The complaint which lay against god when he was alive was that, in his name, men were persuaded to postpone to the hope of the next world their expectations of a life of dignity and convenience in this one.

The same trick is now being worked in reverse: since there is no hope of a next world, how trivial are their complaints in this one.

The rich man in his castle is no better off than the poor man at his gate, it used to be said, because both might enter the kingdom of heaven, the poor even more easily than the rich; he is now no better off, it is said, because there is nowhere that anyone is going anyhow. The house of the poor man is damp, its windows do not close, rats are his visitors: if he cries out against this condition, how trifling is his complaint, for we are all homeless. But is not the home of the rich man at least warm and light? It is an illusion, he like the rest of us lives in the cold and dark of a universe which has become empty and silent.

This is what one means by the neglect of the human estate in the imagination of our time. As early as 1790, the German romantic Jean Paul proclaimed to the sun: "Wherever you go with your planets, in the whole of your course you will find no trace of God . . . of the God who was painted as a glittering eye, there is nothing now left but a black socket"; and he cried to men:

> *Dieu est mort! Le ciel est vide! . . .*
> *Picturez enfants, vous n'avez plus de père!*

"The first conception of this piece," he wrote, "was terrifying to my soul, and I trembled as I wrote it." Even if one allows the romantic his description, need we feel bound to tremble with him? Cannot our earth be enough for our imaginings? Cannot it be the focus of our care? "The heavens remain black, and God does not reply," exclaimed de Vigny. But the earth is green, and there are men with whom we share it who will speak to us.

The idea of the homelessness of man and the meaninglessness of his life has travelled into our popular literature. On this "lousy earth"—Joseph Heller in *Catch-22*—where our lives make no sense, we live in "a motley, mindless world"—John Barth in *The Sot-Weed Factor*—where man is only a "mayfly flitting down the winds of Chaos," in which all we can do is forage in the "rathouse of history's rags and straws"—Thomas Pynchon in *V*—or in "any yearly Almanac, under 'Disasters'"; and always it is to the neglect of our estate, always to an affirmation that is purely selfish: "I've been fighting all along to save my country. Now I'm going to fight a little to save myself." With what, one may ask; and for what? All of this we read with a complacency of temper that itself is revealing, for what is there in it but a sentimentality of self-indulgence by which even an adolescent might be irked.

This misplaced emphasis on the homelessness of man will lead always to a reliance that is no less misplaced on an utter selfhood, and to a disdain for the commonplace world, and for the everyday lives by which ordinary men and women contrive to make something of it and of themselves. The ordinary man is despised because he has been abandoned by his god, and crawls the earth, puny and abject, born to no purpose, living to no purpose, and dying to no purpose. He is despised because he is supposed to be not even aware of his own wretchedness; since his consciousness is not unhappy, it must mean either that he has no consciousness, or that it is false. He is despised because he is not an artist, and only the artist can create; in particular, only the artist can create his-self as a work of art. He is not a genius, he is not Prometheus, he is not a god; and, if he is none of these, of what worth is his living? He does not defy either the indifference of the universe or the oppression of his society; of what value, then, is his witness?

That he reverences life, his own and that of other men, and does so by making possible its continuance from day to day, this is not allowed to his credit; on the contrary, it is his damnation. One often wonders where, in the romantic vision, there is an honourable place for the nurse. Modern humanism, Gilbert Murray once remarked, resembles the Stoic view: *Deus est mortali iuvare mortalem;* god is the helping of man by man.[3] There is something of an echo of this in the affirmation of the Christian humanist W. H. Auden that god is "he who confers dignity and freedom on his creatures." Certainly these two humanist statements, from an agnostic and a Christian, come nearer to what of god we ought to remember than we are likely to find by searching in the emptiness and silence of the universe for an answer that we know is not there.

A PRESCRIPTION FOR WAYWARDNESS

In all of his attitudes to men, the romantic is concerned more with what is different between one individual and another than with what is common to them all. This is a severe break with both Christianity and the Enlightenment, for the emphasis in each of them was on the common element which distinguished all men in their common humanity: in Christianity, the common fatherhood of god; in the Enlightenment, the common possession of reason. In contrast, the romantic concept has not been concerned with any such common element; far from being interested in what distinguishes all men in their common humanity, it has been interested only in what distinguishes each man in his individual personality. Moreover, it does not, so to speak, do this politely. It does not, as both Christianity and the Enlightenment took the trouble to do, allow men both their individual personality and their common humanity as of equal worth in them. Christianity did not cry down the individual soul, or the Enlightenment the individual reason; far from it, in both cases. But whatever the romantic finds to be common to all men, he finds to be banal and pitiful and wretched.

The humbling and attrition of itself which the individual personality feels today cannot be met by yet another romantic assertion of its own solitary worth; it can be met only in the human estate, where we may relearn the common worth of our humanity. "The authentic romantic earns his vision by looking hard at the real world and by acknowledging that world's resistance to the imagination of crisis and transformation. The visionary assertions of such a writer have force only in so far as they have been wrested from a genuine confrontation with the toughness, the recalcitrance, of the ordinary universe."[4] To these words of David Thorburn, addressed to the romantic of our time, may be added the earlier words of Wallace Stevens, addressed to all romantics: "The romantic is to the imagination, what sentimentality is to feeling." Sentimentality is feeling that is uninformed by any sense of what is real, not least of what is real in the object of the feeling; and the imagination of the romantic is also confined in the end by his lack of care for what is. This is what is damnable in his discovery, as Ortega puts it, "that life is not reality which encounters a greater or lesser number of problems, but that it consists exclusively in the problem of itself"[5]; which is the false cry of the existentialist.

Why should we, then, be concerned with the problems of our estate, and try to solve them? What we are being given is a prescription for waywardness; and the waywardness, in particular, of the self in its-self, preoccupied only with the problem of its own life. We have talked already of the weakened imagination of our time, and this after more than a century and a half during which the imagination has been celebrated more than at any other time in history. Our imagination today has no nerve; it will not dispute with the real, it flees from it; it makes no effort to reimagine the actual so that we see it differently, find in it a new enjoyment, or change it if we will. "I will astound Paris with an apple," said Cézanne, and with an apple he did, and the apple was never mislaid. Our imagination needs again this kind of anchorage; the romantic as much as the rest of us needs to come home.

THE DEATH OF GOD AND THE DEATH OF EUROPE

In God We Trust. The unexpected legend on the back of the dollar bill is a matter of incontinent amusement; but it is fitting. It is an echo of the sprightly assertion of Jefferson that it did not matter to him if his neighbour believed in one god or in twenty, since it neither broke his leg nor picked his pocket. The casualness and civility of his remark were possible only because the death of god had already been accomplished; as we have already noticed, the United States never existed when God was alive.

It is essential to understand the meaning of this. When he was a young man, W. E. Gladstone went on the grand tour of Europe, arrived at last in Rome, and entered St. Peter's. He was there, as he recorded in his journal, struck by a revelation of "the pain and shame of the schism in the body of Christ's Church," as a result of the Reformation. It was this revelation that altered the man, so that he ceased to be merely the spokesman of the new commercial class in England, from which he had sprung, and became one of the last great statesmen of Europe, trying to re-create the system of Europe, to reimagine Christendom itself, in a secular age. From this one man, from this single moment in his life when he stood in St. Peter's, the liberalism of Europe, and through it of America, was to draw much of the inspiration which widened its horizons, and made it generous and internationalist in spirit.

The schism in Christ's Church had already occurred when the first colonists arrived on the shores of America; and the English colonists were, in fact, the descendants of those who had caused the division. However much the Puritans believed in their god, they did not believe in the one God, of the one Church, of the one

Christendom, of the one Europe. The revelation to Gladstone was as political as it was spiritual. The schism in the Church was a division in the body of Europe. Every nation in Europe, even those that maintained themselves as Catholic, came into being in part as the result of a violent assertion of itself in the long dispute over the oneness of Europe, which was the oneness of Christendom, which was the oneness of the body of Christ's Church, which represented the oneness of the one God. The anguish of Europe in the modern age has been the guilt and despair of understanding that, in killing this one God of its creation, it killed itself, its own vital existence. When Jacques Maritain spoke of "the miserable state of the modern world, the corpse of the Christian world,"[6] he was talking of Europe.

The death of god was an event in history. It occurred in a particular place at a particular time: in Europe before the calling into existence of America. The responses in Europe have been numerous, but in all of them has been the dread suspicion that there may be truth in the assertion of Romano Guardini: "Europe will be Christian or it will not exist at all." The fate of the one has never really been separated from the fate of the other, not even in Sartre, who has never believed that god existed except in man's imagination; even he is aware that, by his denial, he is depriving European man of a grace which needs to be replaced. In fact, the argument could be reversed. "If Europe suffers cultural death," said A. V. Demant, "it is doubtful whether Christendom will arise anywhere else." In short, not only did the death of god mean the death of Europe, the death of Europe meant the death of God.

This has been the burden of European literature for a century and a half. This has been the wasteland, out of which Eliot could extricate himself only by asserting that we must "have God (and he is a jealous God), or perish in the spirit." This has been the source of the equation, made by Lamenmais and de Maistre at the beginning, between a dying Christianity and a dying social order, each reinforcing the other. This has been the cause of the desperate cry of a Maurras, who did not believe in god, and a Toynbee, who can hardly be counted as a man of faith, that a restoration of Christianity is needed to save the civilization of the West.

But why should all this matter to the American, to whom it did not matter that his neighbour might have twenty gods or one? For this phrase of Jefferson was soon to be translated into a fact, in the two hundred and fifty sects—the estimate is conservative—which have together composed the religious history of the United States. Nothing is more inexplicable to the outsider than the readiness of the American to be carried away by the literature of the dissolution and decay which reaches him from Europe. It is as if he must suck the corruption of Europe—which he had once expelled from himself, as he had already expelled himself from it—back into his veins, and drink to the dregs the poisons of a dying body which is not even his own. Unless he is a necrophile, there is something out of place in an American who pores over Nietzsche, and imagines that he is reading about himself.

In arguing the exceptionalism of the United States, its non-European character, one is not proclaiming a manifest destiny for it, which is the most obvious form that the idea has taken. One is saying no more than that the country and its mind were created in a place, at a time, and out of an experience, different from those from which emerged any country or the mind of Europe. Thirty years ago, this would hardly have been disputed. But when one gazes on the career of existentialism into the public mind of America, on the deference that was paid to Jaspers and to Heidegger, on the popularity today of, say, Harvey Cox and notices how deeply his own theology, if one may call it such, has been influenced by the theology of a dying Europe in the works of such men as Bonhoeffer and Tillich, then one is forced as an outsider to inquire if the American's sense of his own time has evaporated.

REINHOLD NIEBUHR AND CHRISTIAN PESSIMISM

It is worth taking an example from the immediate past, whose effects in the intervening years we can trace. One would have thought that, by the middle of this century, America would have had done with such a notion as Original Sin; but, no! In the second quarter of the century, it was sedulously spatchcocked into the public mind of the country by Reinhold Niebuhr, and by others who were generously lumped under the curious label of the "neo-orthodoxy"; in particular, it was spatchcocked into its liberal mind, which was then, of course, its ruling mind. By 1927, he was "criticizing 'modern religious liberalism' for its 'sentimental optimism' which still spoke of 'the essential goodness of men without realizing how evil good men can be.'" By 1932, he had issued "a somber and powerful rejection of the Social Gospel–Dewey analogue, with its faith in the politics of love and reason. Individual egoism, he asserted, was not being progressively checked by either 'the development of rationality or the growth of religiously inspired goodwill.'" Both of these summaries of his views are taken from Arthur Schlesinger's essay on him[7]: a fact of some significance, since Schlesinger wrote elsewhere that "no one has preached more effectively to this generation of the reality of human imperfection than the liberal (in politics, at least) Reinhold Niebuhr"[8]; and this was, indeed, his influence on the public mind.

By 1952, Niebuhr was saying that the "perennial moral predicaments of human history have caught up with a culture which knew nothing of sin or guilt," which was an amazing statement to make about a country in which the puritan influence was so strong; that "man cannot rise to a simple triumph over historical fate"; and, indeed, that "nothing that is worth doing can be achieved in our lifetime," which the intellectual historian Morton White has described as a "monstrous falsehood." But perhaps Niebuhr's most direct influence was to establish the idea that, as a result of the picture which he gave of man's nature, the realm of love was separate from the realm of power: "Better to accept a frank dualism in morals than to attempt a harmony between the two methods which threatens the effectiveness of both." It was exactly this moral "realism" or "dualism" that was the undoing of American liberalism in the 1960s.

One has immediately to say that, not only did it have little to do with liberalism, which is ambitious to "make the best" of human nature, even to the extent of trying to improve it, but that it had equally little to do with America. An Old World theology of man in his relationship to god was reintroduced to subdue a New World concept of man in his relationship to society. One need not inquire of the philosophers or the theologians to give the answer to Niebuhr. It was given by George Washington himself, when he wrote in 1783 to the governors of the states:

The foundation of our Empire was not laid in the gloomy age of ignorance and superstition, but at an Epoch when the rights of mankind were better understood and more clearly defined than at any former period; the researches of the human mind after social happiness, have been carried to a great extent, the treasures of knowledge, acquired by the labours of Philosophers, Sages and legislators, through a long succession of years, are laid open for our use, and their collected wisdom may be happily applied in the establishment of our forms of Government. . . . At this auspicious period the United States came into existence as a Nation, and if their Citizens should not be completely free and happy, the fault will be intirely their own.

One may hesitate at the final flourish; and yet allow it to stand. At least it proclaimed that the United States had been created at a time when men could claim to have their fate in their own hands and, by their reason and their science, try to direct it. God was not there; he was not even given a mention.

The example of Niebuhr is telling because his theology was the underpinning of his views on politics and society. He might claim that, "in my view, adequate spiritual guidance can come only through more radical political orientation and more conservative religious convictions than are comprehended in the culture of our era"; but the truth was that his own "radical political orientation"— which meant that he became a member of the Americans for Democratic Action—was profoundly distorted by his own "conservative religious convictions." The essence of radicalism, as Judith Shklar says, "is the idea that man can do with himself and with his society whatever he wished . . . the belief that people can control and improve themselves and, collectively, their social environment."[9] Niebuhr looked for a political radicalism which would enable man to improve his social environment, but wished it to rest on a religious conviction which denied that man could improve himself; this is a fractured foundation on which to build.

One is not denying that the pessimistic view of human nature which he offered has had its echoes in American history from the beginning, but its consequences have seldom been attractive. Equally, one is not saying that Niebuhr was alone in this pessimistic view during the second quarter of this century. In various ways, it was common to all who were included in the "neo-orthodoxy," and it drew from Robert M. Hutchins, robust as ever in his Americanness, the retort that they were carrying and relishing "the good news of damnation." It was at this time that American intellectuals, not least the literary critics, discovered, and claimed that America itself had discovered, a "tragic view of life," and the theology was made secular, as by Schlesinger:

> . . . history is not a redeemer, promising to solve all human problems in time; nor is man capable of transcending the limitations of his being. Man generally is entangled in insoluble problems; history is consequently a tragedy in which we are all involved, whose keynote is anxiety and frustration, not progress and fulfillment.[10]

All of which is a European conservative view.

THE ESSENTIAL OPTIMISM OF THE AMERICAN IDEA

It is often pointed out, especially by conservatives, that the founding fathers had an unillusioned view of human nature, and this is true. But it was unillusioned, and not pessimistic; and one of the reasons why it was not pessimistic was that they fixed men in their human estate. It was in this civil society that man might pursue his "social happiness," there to realize his own nature, there to improve his condition or not, the choice was "intirely his own." Man was not to pursue his happiness as an isolated individual, or in a state of nature, or even under "nature's God," except in a polite way. The founding fathers had no need of theologies to explain their design. Jefferson and Madison and Monroe might be seen conversing on the green outside the parish church at Charlottesville after divine service; one thing we can be sure they were not discussing was the divinity.

"There has been, I suggest, an end to innocence," says George Middleby in Richard Chase's symposium, *Democratic Vista,* which so neatly caught the intellectual climate in the United States in the 1950s. What was substituted was the tragic view of life, as in the writings of Max Ascoli, the founder and editor of *The Reporter,* one of the most influential journals of the 1950s, who in his own book, *The Power of Freedom,* emphasized the limitations of human nature and the illusion of all utopias. Ascoli was one of the three hundred and more brilliant refugees who came from Central Europe after the rise of Hitler, almost immediately to occupy three hundred and more dominating positions in American life and culture. They had a profound sense of the failure of their beloved Weimar. "The excitement that characterized Weimar Culture," it has been said, "stemmed in part from exuberant creativity and experimentation; but much of it was anxiety, fear, a rising sense of doom." We cannot ignore the influence of these refugees on the mind and imagination of America; and we will indeed have to return to it.

A tragic view of life can be just as enfeebling a form of sentimentality as the idea of innocence; it is also alien to the only kind of public philosophy which in America can be made satisfying and compelling. The outsider cannot live in the United States for long without acknowledging that the essence of the American view of man is optimistic, or it is nothing; of his view of society, that it is experimental; of his view of politics, that they must be radical, in the sense that has been given, that men can remake their societies to their will; and that their view of the state and temper of mind in which all of these ought to be considered is that it should be pragmatic. "There is still time to make a new beginning on what the world used to call 'the American experiment,'" cried a recent editorial in a radical journal.[11] It was right; and it is evidence of the American experiment, of the willingness and confidence of the American people to continue it, which the world is missing. The last thing that the Old World needs from the United States is that its own worn theologies should be recycled and returned to it; America has another story to tell.

THE PROLIFERATION OF CULTS IN AMERICA

The proliferation of contemporary cults in the United States, like the proliferation of sects in the past, is a reminder that the United States is an irreligious country. Only a people who do not take god seriously could permit him to be sought and worshipped and proclaimed by any person who takes it into his head to do so; for any reason, in any manner, to any purpose, for any satisfaction. As long as men took seriously the idea of god, they believed precisely that he could pick their pockets or break their legs, and that if they transgressed his commandments he would; but it is exactly this, given the time when the country came into existence, which has never been believed in America; at least, not in general, and not for long. To imagine a god who does not intervene in this world, at his will and to his purpose, with punishment as well as reward, is to imagine no god at all.

But his name is powerful, it is of value as a concealment of fraud; and if one does not believe that he will punish—that he is jealous—it can be appropriated with no fear of penalty, in particular of hell fire. "God" in the United States has usually been a form of packaging for what is not god; and what is not god can be as legion as the goods in a supermarket, and the promise is usually the same. God will mop up your heart at the same time as he mops up your underarms. He comes in powder, and in liquid, and in spray; whichever is your preference. Try our god, say the cults and the sects; spray our god into your left ventricle, and any other leading god into your right ventricle, and we know that in your heart you will find that our god is right. Personal religions, like the popular revivals that are an expression of them, are a perpetual threat to an irreligious country such as the United States.

It used to be the habit, in an established church, to dress the young as choirboys, forcibly persuade them to participate in divine service, and then trust, usually with some justification, that they would thereafter be immune to the excesses of religious fervour. It is not the cynic or the *philosophe,* but the truly religious man, who has cried with most earnestness down the ages, *Pas de zèle!* Fanaticism and personal inspiration and sentimentality have always been recognized as the emotions, in the individual or in the mass, that are most destructive of religion, and of genuine religious feeling. There was much, as Bernard Shaw acknowledged in *St. Joan,* to be said for the Inquisition; it at least stopped a lot of deluded individuals from imagining that the bells in their heads were the voice of god, vouchsafed to them alone, and bidding them to take up the sword in his name.

It has sometimes seemed in recent years that almost everyone who is around, on the streets and in the marketplace, not only has bells in his head, but is persuaded that they are the voice of god. Some of the young in particular, but not only the young, appear to be under the misapprehension that they may find, embalmed in themselves, the corpse of god; bring him to life with no more than a say-so; utter him forth, decorated with beads and embroidered with flowers; chant to him with a mindlessness that one ought not to expect god to have to endure in his eternity; then to proclaim that they have found salvation for themselves, and will lead us to it, either for a fee, or for the even stiffer penalty of patting them on their heads, giving them our blessing, and never asking them for their credentials.

Of all the movements that have originated in the United States during the past two decades and spread to Europe, there to be imitated, although less intensely, none has been more characteristically American than the proliferation of cults by which people aspire to reach a personal heaven of their own. To use the vocabulary of one of the traditional forms of a motion for debate, it needs to be said that the influence of personal religions in the United States has increased, is increasing, and ought to be diminished.

Perhaps we ought not to be too fascinated by the cults; very few of them are individually of much interest. There is something that is tedious about the lack of discrimination in it all. When one inquires into any of them, all that one finds is a kind of dis-grace, of the feelings, of the mind, and of the spirit; pitiful ignorance and intellectual frivolity, emotional shallowness and spiritual disorder.

Of what serious concern can it be to us that a girl by the name of Wanda Moore, the mascot of a motorcycle gang in California, took it into her head one day to transform herself into an apostle of hard rock, only then to transform herself again, beckoned by fashion, into the Aquarian Child, with her own pathetic rosary of putty beads, made of whatever she had collected of spiritualism and Oriental mysticism and reincarnation? How much attention ought we to give to the growth in the United States of the Japanese sect of Suka Gakka, of which *Time* reported: "One San Francisco hippie who joined the sect prayed for—and got—'a pocketful of drugs,' then tried for something harder, a girl named Sue. 'That week,' he disclosed in an English monthly published by the sect, 'I met five girls named Sue' "[12]—which is five more, one must admit, than the Pope would have found for him.

That the contemporary cults have an American character hardly needs to be demonstrated. Winthrop S. Hudson has summarized it sufficiently in his scholarly work, *Religion in America:*

The pursuit of the occult—a mélange of astrology, spiritualism, psychic prediction, numerology, and a mixed-bag of prescriptions for almost every personal need, intermingled with notions of reincarnation and astral projection (out-of-body travel) —was an old enterprise in America. The psychedelic and drug-induced mind-blowing (consciousness-expanding) experiments also had a long history which Aldous Huxley exploited. Witchcraft, as a nature religion and fertility cult, had ancient rootage, while the quite different Satanism had antecedents stretching back at least to the seventeenth century. Even the Scientology of L. Ron Hubbard ("the bridge to total freedom and total power") had connections with mental healing fads of the nineteenth century. And the influence of Oriental religion had been introduced to the American public in a significant way at the World's Parliament of Religions in 1893.[13]

One need add only that the evangelism of Billy Graham, with which he invaded England as early as 1954 (the same year, one may point out, in which "Rock Around the Clock" went to the top of the pop charts in England), the sentimentality of the "Jesus Cult," and the unexpected development by which Pentecostalism has been transformed from a sect of the disinherited into a sect of the at least moderately well-off, have all grown from an American stock of proved if intermittent vigour.

THE FLIGHT TO MYSTICISM

What concerns us here is that most of these cults and sects, each in its own way, are forms of retreat from the estate, and that the forms, by and large, fall into two categories: an effort at self-discovery which all too easily turns into self-abnegation, or an effort at transcendence of the commonplace world which leads all too easily either to passivity or to an apocalyptic vision.

Ralph Headstrong, another of Richard Chase's characters in his symposium, noticed fifteen years ago, during the down-to-earth years of Dwight Eisenhower, "the search for a mystic center which will alleviate and annihilate the conscious self, thus quelling the self's spirit of adventure and the pain and travail of the self as it seeks to work out its destiny in an intractable world. . . . I am not prepared for the release of the self into the Unknown; I like to be encompassed by reality. I quake at the modern will to self-annihilation—immersion in the destructive element, as Conrad says."[14] He would have quaked even more, ten years later, when this will to self-annihilation, for which art and literature had prepared the way, was celebrated in the young.

"When mystical *theories* are fashionable," wrote Auden in his essay on the Protestant mystics, "talked about at parties by people who have no intention of submitting themselves to the arduous discipline required for *practice,* society is probably not in a very healthy state."[15] It has happened before. The period following the Peloponnesian Wars, wrote Gilbert Murray, was one.

> based on the consciousness of manifold failure, and consequently touched both with morbidity and with that spiritual exaltation which is so often the companion of morbidity. . . . This sense of failure, this progressive loss of hope in the world, threw the later Greek back upon his own soul, upon the pursuit of personal holiness, upon emotions, mysteries and revelations, upon the comparative neglect of this transitory and imperfect world for the sake of some dream world far off which shall subsist without sin or corruption, the same yesterday, today, and forever.[16]

This sense of the manifold failure of our civilization is again the justification for the retreat into a mystic center to be found within the self; and both the diagnosis and the remedy are delusions.

What we are confronted by, as so often in our time, is the idea of the self contained in its-self, there to expand into a godhead or an eternity that is, in one way or another, hallucinated or contrived; the spirit is free to roam, not into the past or the future, but only into the flicker of the now made eternal, with the promise of oblivion in the *Hansa Upanishad:*

> The Migratory Bird
> enters into every creature
> and becomes present in them
> like fire in sticks rubbed together:
> Knowing this is to conquer death.

Perhaps one may be allowed to give way to one's irritation at the passivity of the religions of the East, and say that, if one wishes to make fire by rubbing two sticks together, which seems a rather banal way of imagining the human spirit, it might be better not to rely on the arrival of the Migratory Bird, but instead to call in a Boy Scout.

If we need the goadings or the consolations of religion, we ought to stay with our own god, who does not just exist, like the *brahman*, but acts; who acts in time and not only in eternity; who released man into history, leading him on the great exodus from the cosmologies of the East; who grants us a narrative, whether the story of a people in the Old Testament, or in the New Testament the story of his own life, born as man; who is not incommunicable, as is the *brahman*, but was incarnated a child, to speak to us in our own language, with parables drawn from our everyday lives; and whom we can conceptualize to each other in a theology that is subject to our reason.

"A revolution in religion is occurring," said Ninian Smart in 1961, "though it is not everywhere obvious. Thanks to the work of Western orientalists and Eastern exponents, we now have the means to a proper and sympathetic understanding of the great non-Christian religions."[17] This is an important point. The expansion of Western civilization during the past five centuries, but during the past century and a half in particular, has brought all the societies and cultures and religions of the world into close contact with each other; and there is much for us to absorb. Even by 1939, a standard bibliography of Buddhism alone, which was published in the United States, listed more than two thousand works in the English language. But a proper and sympathetic understanding by which we may profit is one thing; a facile imitation is quite another.

It is worth recalling the ancient Hindu thinker who had persuaded himself of the unreality of the world of physical phenomena, and so taught the "fourfold nothingness" in the text: "I am nowhere anything for anybody, nor is anybody anywhere anything for me." There is no possible way of combining such an attitude with the mind and feeling and temper of the Judaeo-Christian religion that is at the foundation of our own civilization. "Religion in the West is but one of the moods of man," said Salvador de Madariaga, an observation to which we desperately need to attend. "So that the God of the Westerner seems always to be an external notion rather than the sea of spirit in the immensity of which the Easterner feels but as a drop."[18] We cannot move at will from one to the other, picking from each what suits our fancy, and then try to patch them together, although it was this "large and loose impartiality" which the *Times Literary Supplement* observed in Vachel Lindsay as a characteristic mark of the American spirit, and which we may today observe, as loose even if not as large, in Allen Ginsberg.

There may indeed be a point here with which America itself has yet to come to terms, because the further that one travels to the west in the country the more surely one must come to the point where there is nowhere left to gaze but still westward across the ocean to the East. The poem "The Wedding of the Rose and the Lotus," which Lindsay wrote to celebrate the opening of the Panama Canal, and read before the cabinet of Woodrow Wilson, was not successful; but his drawing "The Rose and the Lotus" is like an emblem of the underground of the United States, telling of something that the taloned eagle does not know. All the myriad cults of Southern California today were jam-packed, tooting and garish, then as now, longing and urgent, in his verses fifty years ago; and we cannot ignore the possibility that the American, standing on his continent, separated only by a sea from Europe, and from Asia only by another sea, has a destiny to fulfill, of which the impartiality of his cults and his sects is only an omen, only the beginning of the exploration.

But, if the Rose is to wed the Lotus, it must keep its thorns. It is the thorns that prick, as they do in so many other of his judgments, in the words of Ozenfant:

For I am of the Occident. It is impossible for me to lay down, or not to act or think. . . . Oriental wisdom is the sense of the uselessness of everything, and of Idleness. Action has always made the Occident. The greatest, indeed, have always seen the vanity of acts, measured in relation to the Infinite and the "Unknowable," and they have seen it just as well as the most passionate of Oriental sages: but they have understood the relative grandeur of Action in face of man's incapacity.[19]

Quoting the lines of Goethe,

I, I confess, am of the race of those
Who from the dark aspire to clarity . . .

Ortega added: "Europe and America mean the attempt to live by clear ideas not myths"; and it is time perhaps that America recovered at least some of the prickliness of Santayana when he declared: ". . . mysticism is the most primitive of feelings and only visits formed minds in moments of intellectual arrest and dissolution."[20]

THE CULT OF VIOLENCE

The trouble with transcendence, it was once well said, is that it may lead in the direction either of trans-ascendence or trans-descendence; and there seems to be little more to be said. It may lead some to the stars; it is more likely to lead most back to the mire. We need to ask those who today seek to transcend the commonplace world by what standards we are to measure their claims, and by what standards they themselves are able to judge that they are not merely indulging whatever, at best idle, at worst malevolent, whim may have seized them. Perhaps we ought not to take too seriously the dabblings in the occult, and in witchcraft and in satanism, but there is the odour of trans-descendence about them; and it is hard not to associate them, and the tolerance that is allowed to them, with the cult of violence in our contemporary societies.

It is not physical violence, as such, that is at the core of these attitudes, although they may lead to that. For example, the physical violence in the film *A Clockwork Orange* was comparatively slight, and so stylized that it might have occurred in a pantomime or a Punch and Judy show. What was degrading about the film—the book had a wit and a complication, both of which were invitations to dissociation—was that, with the exception of the drunken bum who was beaten up at the beginning, none of the characters, predator or victim, had a single feature that was redeeming, or that suggested that he was redeemable. We were presented with a world from which the possibility of redemption and the opportunity of grace were excluded.

But from where does this violent imagining of our world come? Surely it is from what Richard Chase once called our "glib familiarity with doom." We are no longer able to manage the utopian vision, although we yearn for it, as in the feeble-minded effort of the "counterculture" to achieve that "qualitative transformation" for which Bakunin looked, "a new living, a life-giving revelation, a new heaven, a new earth, a young and mighty world." Instead of the utopian vision, we contrive the apocalyptic vision, which then too easily issues in the kind of self-satisfied complacency of Gore Vidal, a characteristic dabbler in the modern sensibility, when he remarked, from his position of advantage and privilege, that the end of the human race would be preferable to the present existence that we have to endure. Was ever a bed of nails so velvet?

THE DELIRIUM OF THE APOCALYPSE

The apocalyptic vision, Martin Buber said, was a decadent form of the prophetic tradition; and it has never been more decadent, in any of its frequent reappearances in the Western imagination, than in the current representation of the apocalypse, not as an event that will occur in history and will bring history to an end, that will happen to man, but as an event that has occurred already in man himself. The beasts of the apocalypse are in ourselves; it is the condition of our natures. We do not have to wait for the end, it has already been accomplished in us; we are literally the end, with no chance of salvation. This trivially—and, in the end, comfortable—romantic view of ourselves is a conceit: we are to think and feel our own disease, to live our death, because only we are capable of this imagination.

We are our illness, it is claimed, not our health. We are our madness, as that monger of visions R. D. Laing would have us believe, not our reason. This is a recurrence of the darkest side of the Christian understanding of man, without the benefit of the Christian doctrine of grace. To celebrate our psychopathology, the abnormal as the normal, the mad as the sane, the schizophrenic as whole, gets us no further than the loathing of our humanity with which a St. Augustine began, that we are conceived and born *inter faeces et urinam:* to translate it bluntly, between our shit and our piss.

None of us in fact thinks of either our conception or our birth in this way, any more than we imagine with St. Bernard that man is "vile as a dunghill" and woman "the opening to hell." But at least the Christian fathers believed in the possibility of grace, of our redemption from our squalid and mortal condition, whereas the secular prophets of our time have no such hope to offer. Since they must peddle some hope, since they can imagine the apocalypse only with sentimentality, they must present what is most hateful in us as what we ought most to cherish. We are reduced to nothing more than the disordered private experiences of our innermost selves, which are ultimately no more than what we are born with; and, in our expression of these, finding significance in nothing but our "natural instincts," we exhibit our health.

It is because of this reduction that so much of our literature seems to be able to represent the human situation only in terms of madness. Man is imagined only in isolation from his society, removed from it and the reality that it represents, standing in opposition to them with only himself as an ally. This is a prescription for hysteria; and a justification of hysteria as the only expression that is authentic. "All walking, or wandering," says Norman O. Brown, "is from mother, to mother, in mother; it gets us nowhere"; and the young for a time were seduced by his artfulness. If this is how he imagines the variety of the activities and the experiences that are available to us in our societies, it is no wonder that the alternative which he proposes is a form of delirium. The delirium is in fact celebrated as the poise with which we can hope best to encounter our lives; in our madness we will have repose.

In this manner we are to encounter, not only our own lives, but the cataclysm which is imminent, for the more traditional forms of the apocalyptic vision are still retained, so that, in what John Barth calls "an age of ultimacies and 'final solutions'—at least *felt* ultimacies," it is only in ultimacies that we trade, the utter and the extreme. If we have choice, it is to walk a line, as one critic of this vision has said, "between . . . the 'orbiting ecstasy of a true paranoia' and the terrible blankness of the quotidian, between the imagination of disaster and no imagination at all." It is on this hairsbreadth that we are to quiver, always to be presented with choices that are so extreme that neither our daily lives nor even our imaginations can embrace them without the vocabulary of violence to assist us.

We can trace the causes of these attitudes in our literature and our thought. "Has man ever found himself in so tragic a moral situation?" asked Ozenfant.[21] "Every belief has been bled white or abolished, and we are left stewing in our own skins." This was the cry of Jimmy Porter in *Look Back in Anger,* of course, and it has a perfect expression in the fable of Georg Büchner in *Woyzeck:*

Once upon a time there was a poor little girl who had no father or mother because everyone was dead and there was no one left in the whole world. Everyone was dead, and she went off and kept looking for someone night and day. And since there was no one on earth, she thought she would go to heaven. The moon looked at her so friendly, but when she got to it, it was just a piece of rotten wood. So she went to the sun, and when she got there, it was just a dried-up sunflower. And when she got to the stars, they were just gold flies stuck up there as if they'd been caught in a spider web. And when she thought she'd go back to earth, it was just an upside-down pot. And she was all alone. And so she sat down and cried. And she's still sitting there alone.[22]

All these years after Jean Paul first cried that the heavens were empty, that there was only a black socket in place of the glittering eye, we are still to manage only the same complaint.

Disabused of his belief in god, man is then taught that he has no control over his own world. "Today's citizen is not sure," as Merleau-Ponty has said, "whether the human world is possible."[23] There is a widespread feeling among men, according to Robert Birley, "that they have lost control of their destinies."[24] Of what significance is anything that we accomplish, since "our little experiment in modern development," as Ralph Hendricke says, "is but a millisecond of time in human evolution"?[25] Taught only the vocabulary of this nihilism, why should we be surprised that we descend, as Lionel Abel said, in a review of *The Naked Lunch,* to "the need for utterness in some form, however degraded, painful, spasmodic, or obscene, utterness as a sign, at least, of something more real than the things we are normally in contact with"?[26]

William Burroughs was explicit in *Nova Express.* The only recourse for the writer, he said, might be to take "orgasm noises . . . and cut them in with torture and accident groans and screams . . . and operating-room jokes . . . and flicker sex and torture film right with it." The voice is all too familiar to us, and what is most treacherous in it is the self-pity, and the communication of this self-pity from one generation to another, from minds to minds which are taught in youth, as Lionel Trilling has said, "to accept these sad conditions of ours as ineluctable, and as the only right object of contemplation."

Not only are there other objects of attention, but even if our condition is as sad as we are persuaded, there are other responses that we could make. The strenuous Christian answer was given by Simone Weil: "You could not have wished to be born at a better time than this, when everything has been lost"[27]; and she was always far distanced, however deep she struck, from an apocalyptic vision. If we feel that we do not control our destinies, then perhaps the reason is, not that we are in a worse condition than were our ancestors, but that we have a new awareness: "It is not new for men to be cogs in the machine," as Birley said; "it is new for them to be frustrated by the fact"; and that we ought to be able to count a gain, and from our frustration go on to build. If man now "finds himself compelled," as Ortega put it, "to take his stand on the only thing left to him, his disillusioned life," there to confront "himself as reality," at least he could be taught to understand that this means confronting himself "as history," forced for the first time "to a concern with his past . . . because it is all he has,"[28] and so learn from his narrative, and determine to continue it as his own plot.

But this is not how we have been taught; and it is certainly not the response of the cults and the sects that now infest our lives. Wherever we gaze—on the power of positive thinking, revived as profitably as before under the name of transcendental meditation; on the chants of the saffron monks of our supermarkets; on the therapies of yoga or the satori of Zen; on the candy floss of *Jesus Christ Superstar* or on the sugar candy of *Godspell;* on the fascination with the occult— we can find no idea or spiritual experience or feeling—even if they endured, which is unlikely—which bends our attention to our estate, persuades us that we may remake it to our reward and our satisfaction, or promises to diminish the injustices of this world, or to succour one other individual who is suffering. Here and there, a commune, fleeting in its life; but that is all.

CHRISTIAN HUMANISM IN *LUMEN GENTIUM*

Let us set against these cults, before we go any further, another standard, that of the Roman Catholic Church itself, as it was set out in the remarkable statement, *Lumen Gentium,* which accompanied Vatican II:

In every group or nation, there is an ever-increasing number of men and women who are conscious that they themselves are the artisans and authors of their culture and their community. Throughout the world there is a similar growth in the combined sense of independence and responsibility. Such a development is of permanent importance for the spiritual and moral authority of the human race. This truth grows clearer if we consider how the world is becoming united and how we have the duty to build a better world based on truth and justice. Thus we are witnesses of the birth of a new humanism, one in which man is defined first of all by his responsibility towards his brothers and towards history.

What is remarkable in this passage is that the Church here associates itself with the new humanism; what is put first, commented one theologian, "is man's commitment to life: it is here that the divine mystery offers itself. . . . God is the redemptive mystery in human life and revealed in Jesus Christ, which forces men from the bondage of the superficial and the self-centred, which enables men to discern and wrestle with the destructive powers in human life, and which opens men to the healing and elevating of life that continues to be offered to them in history."[29] In contemporary theology this is now a familiar perspective.

It is a much mightier voice, and one that speaks much more clearly to our needs, than that of any of the contemporary cults, which are themselves, and invite their disciples to be, "in bondage to the superficial and the self-centred," and almost all of which cannot discern, and many of which are not inclined to wrestle with, "the destructive powers in human life." Some of the "Jesus groups," for example, like the Children of God, demand a complete separation from the world which is about to perish: a forsaking of the world which—it is the point, one would have thought, of his story—Jesus did not forsake. Above all, man is placed in history, where he will work out his redemption: in short, in opposition to the fatalism of a Niebuhr, history is a redeemer.

There is much in the "radical theology" of the past few years which has been slipshod, which fights the wrong fights, which is impatient with forms whose virtue lies in the patience with which they survive to be used to new purposes. But at its best—in the pages, for example, of *Concilium*—it has been honest and searching and effective; its influence on *Lumen Gentium* was obvious. "A faith in God," another of the *Concilium* theologians has proclaimed, "which justifies suffering and injustice in the world and does not protest against it is inhuman and even satanic in its effects."[30] It is beside this voice that one must set the promise of the Maharishi that, by practising "transcendental meditation" twice daily for thirty minutes, one may achieve "cosmic consciousness" and with it instant serenity, while continuing to lead whatever life one has chosen; no wonder he has attracted the Beatles and the Rolling Stones, Mia Farrow and Shirley Maclaine. The neglect of the human estate is vindicated, and salvation is painless.

THE LITTLE COSMOS OF THE SELF AND COSMIC CONSCIOUSNESS

If we need a god at all, he must be the God of our civilization, revealed in history, the mystery of his redemptive power at work in our society; and he must be a god whom we can think with our minds, instructed by a systematic theology that we cannot imagine him at our whim. This rigour and this discrimination are lacking in the contemporary cults in America, as they will commonly be found to be lacking in all personal religions; and it is when this lack is lent authority from no less an institution than the Divinity School at no less a place than Harvard University that one's irritation gives way to contempt. No man in recent years, confessing that he does not believe in the god of our theology, has nevertheless gone round so assiduously spraying god over the United States from his aerosol containers as Harvey Cox. He wants, and he wants us, to be able to talk about god; "To Speak in a Secular Fashion of God" is how he first put it in *The Secular City*. This book was derivative and commonplace in its ideas, even quaint and old-fashioned, as he acknowledged when he quickly abandoned the entire thesis, to speak of god in another *fashion;* it is not hard to lean on the word. He must baptize us and himself, in the name of the god whom he imagines; and it is not baptism by the Sign of the Cross on the forehead, or baptism by immersion which he experienced as a child, but baptism by aerosol. Let us spray! At least the Chinese general who baptized his army with a hose had a concrete purpose: he wanted it to win a battle for him. But in Cox it is hard to find any purpose, except to spray a little god, lemon-freshened, about the place.

The Secular City at least had a coherence of argument, even though it is hard to understand why, if we live in a secular city in which god cannot intervene at his will and to his own ends, there is any need to continue to try to talk of him. (This is a question which can also be addressed to a much more serious man, Gordon D. Kaufman, at the Divinity School at Harvard University again, and his much more serious book, *God the Problem.*) There is much truth in John Henry Newman's observation that one can no more *argue* than one can *force* people into a belief in god; and, if the arguer has no faith other than that bred of his fancy, what tale does he have to tell? In the case of Cox, the answer has been made clear by his succeeding books. The god of whom he wishes to talk is the god of the Sunday school and the kindergarten: a god of simple reassurance and undemanding solace, who is always there to hold one's hand, and conduct one safely across the traffic lights to a lollipop stall. In this mood, whatever may happen in our societies, Cox will find grace in it. God is always there, a happening in the happening, improbably revealed in workaday heroes, John F. Kennedy in *The Secular City,* Emiliano Zapata in *The Seduction of the Spirit.*

His theme from one book to the next is the same: if only we will look no deeper than the surface in our society, we can always find signs that are comforting. Anything can be included, everything can be connected:

> So folk religion and popular religion are finding each other. The evidence for the convergence is considerable: the use of dance, masks, exorcisms and other "primitive" elements in the new liturgies, the popularity of folk hymns like "Amazing Grace," the use of new instruments and pop tunes by older groups, and the incorporation of the drums and sitars of other cultures into contemporary liturgies. The result of this confluence will be enormously significant not just for religion but for American society as a whole. It augurs the breakdown of barriers that have separated the youth-hippie-rock culture from the rural-pietistic-gospel song culture as each discovers its kinship with the other and with the ethnics, rednecks, Indians, black militants and other marginated groups who have retained a sense of joy and resistance in face of the homogenizing pressures of the larger society.[31]

This is a loose impartiality with a vengeance.

On the outskirts of Denver is a shopping centre, said to be the second largest in the world, with the interesting name of Cinderella City. There, among its fountains and its malls and its Muzak, everyone and everything is transformed, until the clock strikes. All that is ugly in the world, it can take and absorb, soften and glamourize; nothing need be very troubling. Harvey Cox is the supplier of religion to Cinderella City. He is the teller of bedtime stories to the suburbs. In his last book, the stories are spun, like floss, out of his own life, and one knows the purpose: he must explain, to himself and to us, why everything can be relevant to him, and he can be relevant to everything. The whole world is an encounter group. He must touch it all, and it all must touch him. In this avarice, the church

must be truly universal. It must somehow, like Noah's sagging ark, find room for all the aardvarks, gnus, and three-toed sloths. I am combining the chanted Mass with the gospel hymn, the planetary scope of St. Peter with the congregational freedom of Roger Williams. The religious community we need now must be both intensely local and inclusively universal. I think I see it coming. . . . It will include in its roster of saints and range of rites much more scope than any Catholic Church does today.[32]

Of course he sees it coming! One thing which he has demonstrated is that there is nothing that he cannot see coming, if he wishes to see it. No pumpkin will not glitter for him like a glass coach. What amazing grace!

Cox addresses the I in the En-Masse and, with all the truth and promise in the concept, we may here see its danger. The fate of the mass man is in the care of the United States; and it will be at its peril, and at the peril of the world, if he is allowed to maunder after false gods, capriciously searching for personal heavens. He must constantly, by the repeated exertion of its public philosophy, be brought back to the civil society where he may find his real measure. It was to this, in the "golden age" of its philosophy, that the mind of America gave its attention.

We ought not to rely, said Charles S. Peirce, on either personal insights or established authorities; instead our belief should have a public character, being the result of subjecting our thinking to a public standard, "which itself remains unaffected by that thinking." Josiah Royce refused to allow that religion was supportable without it being given a strict expression in philosophy and theology. These were inquiring American minds, severe in their American accents, which refused to assist in what Ernest Hocking once called "the retirement of the intellect" in our time. They would not entertain the possibility of "wisdom without thesis," as Isaac Rosenfeld has named our temptation.

It does not matter whether the invitation is to turn outward to a cosmic consciousness, in a moment of transcendence that is hallucinated or contrived; or to turn inward to the self in its little cosmos, there to follow each whim as an authentic expression of the self in its-self; or sentimentally to imagine that all that happens in our societies can be avariciously enjoyed as a variety of religious experience, to recall the seductive title of the work of William James: in each case, the rigour and discrimination of the mind are absent, and not least the inspiration of the public philosophy of America as once it was proclaimed.

The rejection of the mind is far too common an occurrence in America for any example of it to be tolerated; no country needs to hold philosophy in a stricter regard, to make more certain that its wisdom is sustained by thesis; and this is why one must protest, not only against the sects and the cults, against the trans-descendence and the utter selfhood, but even more fiercely when there comes from the Divinity School at Harvard University a mountebank, a man of beads and baubles and banjo strings, to tell a people that they need no longer think, to offer, not a foundation for hope, but an excuse for optimism, the mere working of an interior facility, for which no particular fitness is required.

As was made clear in *Lumen Gentium,* it is the capacity of men to control their societies, to reimagine and remake their estate, that needs to be taken into account if we are still to call on the name of god. This was not the understanding in the earlier encyclical, *Rerum Novarum,* which accepted the basis of society as it was, in which god had created rich and poor, "while taking a mite more from the first and offering the second the consolations of the after-life." But ours is a time, as one theologian has said, "in which men realize that they have real power over the very structures of their social existence"; and any sect or cult, any bidding to utterness, which neglects this opportunity is engaged in political reaction.

CHAPTER 9

Making a Fool of Nature

We are persuaded to neglect our estate, our concern with man to be translated out of our own domain, by many kinds of people. Those who used to be known as nature lovers were always chatterboxes. It was as if they had spent all their day talking to things that would not talk back to them, so that in the evening, lonely after their vigil, they must corner a human being, in order to reward his patience by telling him that only man is vile. They were in fact the living proof that in man's use of language lies the sharpest distinction between him and the animals, the bees and the birds and the butterflies; but they were not at home talking of men.

One is speaking of those who were known as nature lovers, a distinct species. Most of those whom one has known to enjoy nature, and to enjoy it with astonishment rather than with reverence, are usually silent about it. If they go for a walk, they return and say that they have been—for a walk. One may notice a wildflower in their hands, they may mention a sunset, they may observe in passing that the crows are gathering in the tall elms again, not that the leaves have fallen, but there is not much talk about it. It is as if they sensed that there is little that anyone can say about nature, unless one is a botanist, perhaps, or a poet.

The ecologist and the environmentalist whom one is apt to meet today are of the same species as the nature lover. One is not talking of the true scientist. As anyone may discover by reading almost any issue of *Scientific American,* the man who has spent the best part of his life recording the mating song of the willow warbler has secrets to tell that are as entertaining as gossip, and the observation is as minute. "Do you know what the female then replies?"; and one willingly bends one's ear. But these do not talk about *nature*. For one thing, it would destroy the intimacy, even the voyeurism, which there is in observing the love play of a duck, and which forms so great a part of the enchantment of their conversation, and even of their most scientific writing. Nature is too loose an idea for them to handle, even for the true ecologist. No; one is speaking of those who call themselves ecologists and environmentalists because these represent "a cause." They usually join the large organizations, like Friends of the Earth, with vague aims and passing enthusiasm; they are rarely members of the Jersey Wildlife Preservation Trust.

They talk a lot about nature, and they are very tedious. Ask them how they know that there is such a thing as nature, and what it is, and they are silent. "Nature" is, after all, only another word which man has given to another of his ideas; to what did he give it? There are streams and trees, of course, beasts and flowers; but in what sense do we imagine them as one, each a part of a nature that is single, and what does it mean to say that they are? Is man a part of nature? Enthusiastically they say that he is, and that it is his membership of nature that he has mislaid. But if man is a part of nature, how can he separate himself from it as no other part can, be conscious of it, give it a name, alter it and know that he can alter it?

The chipmunk does not brood on the fate of the beaver. The giraffe does not hold conferences, under the chairmanship of whatever to giraffes is the equivalent of the Duke of Edinburgh, on the conservation of foliage in East Africa. The tiger in Bengal does not organize an expedition to save the bison in America. If nature, as we are told, preserves its own balance, it is not by nature, or any part of nature other than man, being aware of it, or doing anything about it. Nature is passive and dumb, neutral and indifferent, stupid and brutal. How many of the eggs in the spawn will become a tadpole; how many tadpoles will not become a frog? We know the answers; and we are separated from this world.

The point is that there cannot be such a person as an ecologist who does not acknowledge, not only the separation of man from nature, but even his dominion over it. He may say that man must stop his wanton destruction of nature, and help to restore the balance which he has rapaciously and ignorantly disturbed. But in saying that, he is asserting that—for worse (in the past) or for better (in the future)—man can and does act, and has no choice but to act, apart from and on nature. Even if man were to choose not to intervene with the course of nature, re-creating himself as exclusively a natural being, he would still, by that choice, be acting apart from and on nature. The withdrawal of his interference would still be an interference. The refusal to exercise one's dominion is still an assertion that one has dominion, and that its exercise is at one's will. Non-intervention is a word, as Talleyrand said, that means much the same as intervention.

THE AVARICE OF THE ROMANTIC

To interfere or not to interfere is a choice that is available only to man, and not to acknowledge that in this choice he has the dominion is to make a fool of nature; and that is exactly what many of the nature lovers—the naïve term is used deliberately—succeed in doing. The romantic, we can hardly be surprised, makes a fool of nature, as Nietzsche pointed out: "Here we should note that this harmony which is contemplated with such longing by modern man, in fact, this oneness of man with nature (for which Schiller introduced the technical term 'naïve'), is by no means a simple condition that comes into being naturally and as if inevitably. It is not a condition that, like a terrestrial paradise, *must* necessarily be found at the gate of every culture. Only a romantic could believe this, an age which conceived of the artist in terms of Rousseau's *Emile,* and imagined that in Homer it had found such an artist Emile, reared at the bosom of nature."[1] The romantic, in fact, debases nature: avid for experience that is subjective, he finds in nature a looking glass for man; seeking to expand his-self beyond all limits, he multiplies the reflections of it in the exterior world, his is the voice, nature is the echo; his is the image, nature is the mirror in which he may gaze.

It is, in fact, the avarice of the romantic imagination, rather than the rapacity of the technological mind, which is most at fault in the American attitude to nature. "Henry talks of Nature," said an acquaintance of Thoreau, "as if she had been born and bred at Concord," and there was much of this in Emerson as well, as there was not, for example, in that truest of American naturalists, John Burroughs. In all of them there was a tendency to use nature as a kind of therapy. The natural world, and all that was in it, was an encounter group, as in Emerson:

In the presence of nature a wild delight runs through the man, in spite of real sorrows. Nature says—he is my creature, and maugre at his impertinent griefs, he shall be glad with me. . . . There I Feel that nothing can befall me—no disgrace, no calamity (leaving me my eyes), which nature cannot repair.

Nature will make one well; and keep one young. "In the woods, too, a man casts off his years, as the snake his slough, and at what period soever of life is always a child. In the woods is perpetual youth."

To lose oneself in nature, as was their avowal, and is again the avowal of nature lovers today, is in fact a way of finding oneself in nature, greater than one is and nowhere else will seem. The self is annihilated in order to be exalted. In nature, proclaims Emerson, "I am not alone and unacknowledged," and he proceeds:

Standing on the bare ground—my head bathed by the blithe air, and uplifted into infinite space—all mean egotism vanishes. I become a transparent eyeball; I am nothing; I see all; the currents of the Universal Being circulate through me; I am part and parcel of God. . . . I am alone the lover of uncontained and immortal beauty.

This is an exploitation of nature. "In the woods we return to reason and faith."[2] In the woods we do not; reason and faith are things that we contrive in our estate; and the woods, and all that is in them, we might leave to be themselves.

There is something that is false in the life which Thoreau tells us he lived. He was a citizen of Concord, a member of its civil society. In spite of his non-domesticity that was as professional as it was advertised, in spite of his elaborate but tentative adoptions of primitive methods of self-support and nourishment, he remained close to the precincts of the serene village and its community life. He went into nature to bring it back and make it prove what he wished it to prove. "Never does he rest," said a critic in 1908, "until he has transferred the experience won on one plane of being—the earth plane—to that other plane of existence—the mind plane—where he analyzes each sensation and resolves the material into the intellectual. . . . He represents, not the few whom nature imperatively calls to her, but the many who call nature to themselves"[3]; and it is all too greedy; all too desirous of life that is not one's own.

No exposure of the flaw in Thoreau in recent years has been more penetrating than that of Stephen Railton.[4] "I would be as clean as ye, O woods," Thoreau wrote in his journals. "I shall not rest till I be as innocent as you. I know that I shall sooner or later attain to an unspotted innocence." His goal was to purify himself, and this meant, as Railton points out, not least his body: "The whole duty of man may be expressed in one line—to make yourself a perfect body." What he sought in nature must be pure and chaste, and if it proved not to be, he was repelled. "Nature imitates all things in flowers. They are at once the most beautiful and the ugliest of objects, the most fragrant and the most offensive to the nostrils, etc., etc. . . . Nature is even perhaps unchaste herself. . . . For what purpose has nature made a flower to fill the lowlands with the odor of carrion? . . . What mean these orange-colored toadstools that cumber the ground and the citron-colored (ice-cream-like) fungus? Is the earth in her monthly courses? . . . They impress me like humors or pimples on the face of the earth, toddy-blossoms, by which it gets rid of its corrupt blood. . . . A sort of excrement they are."

The violence of this distaste, expressed in terms of menstruation and corruption and excrement, is revealing and significant; and all of it is in his journals, none of it in *Walden,* which Railton describes as not only a "skillfully edited version" of the journals but a "carefully censored one." *Walden* in fact is yet another way of making a fool of nature. It is not to be seen, not to be known, not to be understood, not to be enjoyed as it is. It is to be exalted as chaste, in order to be made an object of prey. What we find in Thoreau's attitude to nature is the double standard of the male chauvinist: nature ought to be virgin, she is not, we must insist that virgin she shall be.

MAN'S REMOVAL FROM THE NATURAL CYCLE

Even if it is not its intention, every false representation of nature is certain to issue in a false representation of man. Only man kills his own species, only he kills for other reasons than his physical survival: we have become used again to these partial truths. There is in fact wanton killing in nature; and nature kills all species wantonly. The woods that are so innocent to Thoreau let fall each year a multitude of acorns that will never come to life, and not bear. But even in the partial truths there are misconceptions which lead to a misrepresentation of the nature of man. It is true, for example, that animals are not cruel. They cannot be cruel; if we say that they are being cruel, we mean only that they are being savage, whether to survive or simply to triumph. They cannot be cruel because they cannot associate themselves with the feelings of their victims, and even their own feelings are those only of enjoyment, if there is enjoyment at all, of their own power. A man is cruel, on the other hand, and is rightly said to be being cruel, when he is associating himself with the feelings of his victims, when he is enjoying, not only his own power, but the suffering of another.

What we are saying, in short, is that man is a moral being, who sometimes acts immorally, while nature is amoral or morally neutral. When man dropped an atom bomb on Hiroshima, he acted as a moral being, whether one judges the act to have been moral or immoral. But when Krakatau Island was almost destroyed in 1883 by a volcanic eruption which, scientists have estimated, had the force of a million hydrogen bombs, it was not an act but an event, neither moral nor immoral. As a result of the eruption, ash and gases rose fifty miles into the sky, and dust persisted in the atmosphere for two years. But there was no one to blame. At the profoundest level, this is what Paul Valéry meant when he said: "There are no problems in nature, there are only solutions."

There is no problem for the crocodile which waits at the edge of a river, to pull a doe beneath the water and stuff it under the bank until its flesh has rotted: that is merely its solution to what is not a problem to it, its need to survive. But when man goes to war, or herds cattle into the slaughterhouse, or shoots a pheasant, there is a problem for him, however he may resolve it. Therefore, to try to explain the cruelty or evil of men in terms of our animal natures is to misconceive our situations; or, as Auden put it:

Those who run to apes to explain our behaviour are
                                        chuckle-
-heads too dumb to know their arse from a hole in the ground.[5]

It is not true, for example, that an Israeli kills an Egyptian merely in response to a "territorial imperative"; to pretend so is to banalize the problem, and make it more difficult to understand.

There is no moral agent in nature; and there is no act in its cycle, but only a recurrence of events. "I don't really feel that nature is all that good in itself," the American poet Richard Bogart has said. "All it can do is go through the cycle." In this cycle, there are not even birth and death as we understand them. Without a world of their own—which they have made, removed from nature—men would not be born and die, as Hannah Arendt puts it, "single individuals, unique, unexchangeable, unrepeatable entities. . . . there would be nothing but changeless eternal recurrence, the deathless everlastingness of the human as of all other animal species."[6] This is not our condition in our estate.

At some mysterious point, about which we can only speculate, man took himself out of the natural cycle; he became a being who can bestow meanings on things and events in the external world. Water is not only a need to him, which he can scent in the breeze; he can freely and arbitrarily find other meanings in it, whether as holy water or as H_2O. A tree can be the tree of knowledge, or the tree of life, or the Cross. These are symbols, and we articulate them in speech; and between our articulated speech and the coded instructions of the animals, there is an impassable distance. Scientists have with skill and patience been breaking some of the codes of particular birds and beasts—their love songs and their dance rituals—but the coded meanings do not make them language. *The* love song of the willow warbler is not *a* love song of a particular warbler. There is not a Marvell or a Donne among them.

One of the most massive of the symbols by which man extricated himself from the natural cycle is that of nature itself. The nature that is diverse and manifold, he has unified in his visions: whether in the great myths of creation or in general theories of science. There is no reason why we should disdain either; in fact, we probably need them both. But that they are both products of the human mind, and only of that mind, is a fact that makes any talk of "the naked ape" a foolish trivialization. The present estimate is that the human egg, to make possible the man whom it will become, and all that he will think and do, contains 10^{12}—in other words, 1,000,000,000,000— pieces of information. It is not a fact with which to trifle.

THE GENETIC EXPLANATION OF HUMAN BEHAVIOUR

Not to acknowledge that the evolution of man in nature at some point involved the removal of himself from nature is a denial of our humanity; and it will always result in attitudes and policies that diminish, if not our view of other men, certainly our view of human nature. This was true of the Puritanism of New England which, insofar as it regarded human nature as only a part of nature, denounced it as unredeemable. "No carrion in a ditch," thundered one preacher, "smells more loathsome in the nostrils of man than a natural man's works in the nostrils of the Almighty"; and from this it followed that only a chosen few, an elect, are snatched from the divine wrath by God's grace. In the Social Darwinism of William Graham Sumner, the struggle for existence was transferred from the condition of nature to the conditions of human society: "The competition of life is the rivalry, antagonism, and mutual displacement in which the individual is involved with other organisms by his efforts to carry on the struggle for existence for himself. . . . Our civilization ordinarily veils from us the fact that we are rivals and enemies to each other in the competition of life."[7] Speculations such as these are not idle: they take hold of us, and make us act as otherwise we might not do.

At this moment, a genetic—that is, a natural—explanation of individual intelligence is being developed and, if it is allowed to go unchallenged, it will directly affect social policies: the things that we do as societies of men to other men. Some of the particular flaws in the explanation will be discussed later. But the most fundamental flaw is its stubborn neglect of the fact that, by the removal of himself from nature, man became a historical and a cultural being: that, in all of his aspects that are most interesting and most significant, what counts in the individual is what he has learned and not what he has inherited.

Moreover, it is depressing that the genetic explanation of intelligence should be refurbished at a time when biological determinants are elsewhere being discarded. Psychoanalytic theory, for example, was explicitly founded on biological considerations but it has begun, if not to abandon, at least to loosen its biological anchorage, and in particular to question the analogies that are drawn from the instinctual behaviour of animals. Erik Erikson may say that "I do not think that psychoanalysis can remain a worthwhile study of inquiry without its basic biological formulations, much as they may need periodic reconsideration," but part of the significance of his "ego psychology" is in his firm distinction between the instinctual behaviour of animals and the learned behaviour of humans: "The drives man is born with are not instincts, nor are his mother's complementary drives entirely instinctive in nature. Neither carry in themselves the patterns of completion, of self-preservation, of interaction with any segment of nature; tradition and conscience must organize them." And he concludes emphatically, "As an animal, man is nothing."[8]

It is significant that the most thoughtful of today's feminists have realized that they must pit themselves against the natural explanations of human behaviour. Of studies such as *The Naked Ape,* Judith Hole and Ellen Levine have accurately written: "Language used to describe human behavior is applied to primate behavior, and from that behavior in turn are 'deduced' patterns which describe human relationships."[9] The point is rubbed home by Shulamith Firestone: ". . . the 'natural' is not necessarily a 'human' value. Humanity has begun to outgrow nature; we can no longer justify the maintenance of a discriminatory sex class system on grounds of its origin in Nature."[10] This is the fundamental point which is made by Women's Liberation: that what is most significant and most interesting in women as in men is, not their biological equipment, not their inherited traits, but their learned behaviour, and *that can be changed.* This is the supreme truth that lies in the "liberation" movements that are all around us.

NATURE'S IGNORANCE OF INDIVIDUAL RIGHTS

There are no rights in nature; there is not even the right to live, but only the instinct to survive, and that is the instinct of the species, present in every member of it, but in none differentiated as individual. "It would make perfectly good sense to say that the cheetah was faster than the gazelle before men could possibly have known the fact," says John Rees, "whereas it would make no sense at all to say that there were rights and privileges before there was a human society."[11] Nature does not, in short, know the individual, and this is one reason why the effort, romantic or otherwise, to find oneself in nature all too easily becomes an effort to lose oneself in it, so that the exaltation and the abnegation of the self are twin.

This was true not only in Thoreau and Emerson but in Whitman. They all exalted the self, and they were all driven to the search for some counterpoise to this self-attention, to find some counter to the unbalanced passions of the self in its-self," and they found it in nature. It was true even of Burroughs, who turned to nature, as he said in his essay "Touches of Nature," "to let down our metropolitan pride, and grasp that man is the outcome of nature, and not the reverse." His expression is misleading. Man may be the outcome of nature, but in the course of his coming out of it, the dissociation of himself from nature was so radical, so irreversible, that his separation from it now is of much more significance than his origin in it.

If we do not accept this, the separation which we have accomplished will seem to us instead an alienation that is unbearable, and we will again disdain the place that we have made for ourselves. A critic once wrote of:

. . . a common and consistent principle . . . a conviction that the dissociation of mankind from the earth-life of creation is at the root of many a mortal malady; at the root of the acrid and unsatisfied cravings, the morbid excitements and, in these later times, the nerve exhaustion to which youth and manhood alike fall prey.[12]

That was in 1908. Almost three quarters of a century later, the American imagination is still tempted, still too easily given to the same mortal malady of unsatisfied cravings, whenever it leaves its estate to contemplate the natural world.

CHAPTER 10

The Exhaustion of the Self

God is a construct of our minds and imaginations, and we may, at any time we choose, surrender to him. Nature is a construct of our minds and imaginations, and we may, at any time we choose, retreat to it. What is not so clearly understood is that the self is a construct of our minds and imaginations, and we may equally, at any time we choose, submit ourselves to it. No one doubts that the self is a modern invention—it is also a local invention in Western culture—and this ought to remind us that it is not an authentic reality which was always there, waiting to be discovered, but that it is another of our artifices, another of the products of learned or cultivated behaviour. The self is as cultured as a mushroom that is grown in a cellar. It does not grow in the fields; it is not wild, it is not untamed; it is our manufacture. If it has got out of hand—and one can hardly deny that it has—it is because we have chosen to let it get out of hand. We may find it difficult to put back in a bottle; but it is not a genie.

CHILDHOOD AND ADOLESCENCE AS INVENTIONS

The invention of the self at a particular moment in our history is one reminder that it is manufactured; the nature of our childhood is another. The extended period—stretching from birth, through infancy, through childhood, into adolescence—during which the human child is dependent on other humans is a period of intense socialization, but also of no less intense individualization. In fact, the growing length of the child's dependence must have been one of the most significant occurrences in the radical disjuncture between men and the animals. It is in the long period of his socialization that the child is formed as an individual; and the adolescence over which we now hover is merely the time when the individual who has been so formed must make his own terms with the society that has formed him.

A newborn giraffe is already long in its legs, long in its neck, long in its tongue, and it quickly is able to use them all. Apart from a brief period to find its strength and learn a few habits, it is born a giraffe with all that it needs to be a giraffe; and that is all that it will ever be, its giraffeness. But it is not only Thursday's child who has far to go, before either his humanness, as a member of the species, or his uniqueness, as an individual, is realized. If, during this period, he is taught to be aware of the self in one way and not in another, then the self is being invented as a symbol in the same manner as any symbol; and by this symbolizing he will know himself.

The point is underlined, again, by the fact that just as the self, as we are aware of it, is an invention of the modern age, so is childhood and, even more recently, so is adolescence. Philippe Ariès, in *Centuries of Childhood,* has demonstrated that medieval art until about the twelfth century "did not know childhood or did not attempt to portray it," and that in Romanesque art until the end of the thirteenth century "there are no children characterized by a special expression but only men on a reduced scale." Since this neglect was obviously not due to incompetence, it suggests that the men of that age "did not dwell on the image of childhood, and that that image had neither interest nor even reality for them. It suggests too that, in the realm of real life, and not simply in that of aesthetic transposition, childhood was a period of transition which passed quickly and was just as quickly forgotten."[1] Childhood had to be imagined, as Rousseau well knew. To reimagine childhood in this manner, and invest it with a new significance, is a way of reimagining and giving a new significance to the self.

Like "childhood" at the beginning of the modern age, "adolescence" had to be invented at the beginning of our century. G. Stanley Hall, the American pioneer in experimental psychology, published his two-volume *Adolescence* in 1904. He not only summarized the work of other pioneers in the psychology of adolescence; by his own interpretations, he was virtually the inventor of the concept, and he was certainly its impresario. (One year later, in his *Three Essays on Sexuality,* Freud spoke of "transformations of puberty," but he did not talk of adolescence.) What concerns us at the moment is that both "childhood" and "adolescence" are important, not as names for a period of life, but as new ways of imagining our natures: what we are, and can be, and ought to be enabled to become. The child and the adolescent are regarded as being already persons in themselves.

It should not surprise us, therefore, that, at the gateway to the modern age, where he may always be found, Luther was one of the first to stress the division in man between the individual and unique self, on the one hand, and the general and socialized member of his species, on the other, the *homo internus* and the *homo externus:* "Each individual human being has on earth two personalities: one for himself, bound to nobody but God alone, but also a worldly personality, through which he is bound to other people." It is only the *homo internus,* the religious man, who is free; and from this it is only a small step, made by the romantics into a giant step for mankind, to define him alone as authentic, and *homo externus* as alienated:

> Luther's *homo internus* is essentially free from social responsibility. He is responsible to God alone, but when the God concept is secularized he will easily become self-centred and ego-directed. Responsibility is then left to *homo externus* and bears the stigma of inauthenticity and alienation.[2]

This division of the self was a heresy; today it is an orthodoxy.

FALSE SELF-CONSCIOUSNESS

When we talk of the self today, therefore, we are talking of our own acutely self-conscious awareness of the self, something that we have invented. His self-consciousness is, of course, a part of man's condition. It is recognized in myth: "I heard thy voice in the garden," said Adam, "and I was afraid, because I was naked; and I hid myself"; and god inquired of him, "Who told thee that thou wast naked?" It was enjoined by the Delphic oracle, "know thyself," and pursued by Socrates; it might even be said to be the purpose of philosophy and, in some sense, of all human life. One is no more denying that this self-consciousness is a part of our humanity than one is denying that there is in each of us a self of which the self which we imagine is a symbol; that each of us is a unique person "with a unique perspective on the universe, the exact like of which has never existed before nor will again"; that each of us can say *I*. But the self-consciousness that is so wearying the self in our time is not this correct understanding; it is a limited understanding that restricts our self-knowledge to a pinpoint of self-intimacy.

" 'Self-knowledge,' in the sense of a minute understanding of one's own machinery, seems to me, except at a fairly simple level, a delusion,"[3] says Iris Murdoch in the down-to-earth manner in which—at least in the exposition of her philosophy—she explores sensitively the human situation; and we may take from Lionel Trilling two quotations which are a warning:

> What a concord is proposed—between me and my own self; were ever two beings better suited to each other? . . . But it is not easy. "Why is it," Charles Dickens wrote in a letter at the height of his career, "that a sense comes always crushing on me now, when I fall into low spirits, as of one happiness I have missed in life, and one friend and companion I have never made?" We know who that unattained friend and companion is. We understand with Matthew Arnold how hard it is to discern one's own self in order to reach it and be true to it.

> > Below the surface-stream, shallow and light,
> > Of what we *say* we feel—below the stream,
> > As light, of what we *think* we feel, there flows
> > With noiseless current strong, obscure and deep,
> > The central stream of what we feel indeed.[4]

We are taunted by the longing for this kind of self-knowledge, and haunted by our inability to attain it; but there is another way.

We must return to the romantic, for it is his own weak imagination which has been most responsible for the weakened imagination of our time: to his insistence on what distinguishes us from each other as individuals, rather than on what is common to us in our humanity; to his preference for the extraordinary. One of the results of this attitude is that there is always something of an exhibitionist in the self as we now imagine it; and that also helps to explain its exhaustion. Always to turn inward to feed only on one's-self, then to turn outward and to have only one's-self which one must exhibit: this is a recipe for weariness.

One may notice it all around. Those who most insist to us on their sincerity, most underline to us their authenticity, most emphasize to us their spontaneity, are always the most exhibitionist, and they are always the most quickly exhausted, as if the pinpoint of their-selves cannot bear the weight of the angels that are asked to dance on it. They are people who need help; but they refuse the help which is available to them, for they can find no reflection of themselves in the society that they know. They will not be reassured by the fact that others see as they see, think as they think, feel as they feel, not all of the time, but at least some of it. Indeed, if this were true, they would take it as evidence of their unindividuality, inauthenticity, insincerity, and unspontaneousness.

ISOLATION OF THE SELF FROM SOCIETY

But there is yet another reason for the exhaustion of the self. When men were told that the reason why they were not free was that they were subject to oppressors who were external to them—superstitions and witch doctors, religions and popes, absolutisms and monarchs—they could engage themselves by exact means to an exact purpose, and the most important of these means was the acquisition and use of knowledge of the external world, so that they might master it. But when they are told that the reason why they are not free is internal to them, that the oppressive forces are inside themselves, they can engage themselves by no exact means to no exact purpose, for the self-knowledge which they need is not attainable, and they therefore weary themselves in the effort, even when Freud has told them that none is any longer the master in his own house.

Liberation is to be found, not in self-intimacy, but in self-mastery, and self-mastery is to be won only from outside. The true explanation of "inner-direction" and "other-direction"—the rather simplified categories with which David Riesman distracted an entire generation—is that the individuality of the "inner-directed" man was the result of a self-mastery that was achieved by drawing on re-sources outside the self, while the conformity of the "other-directed" man is the result of the failure to achieve self-mastery by drawing only on the resources inside the self, leaving no alternative but to admit that the unmastered self is useless to one, and that there is nothing to do but conform. John Dewey, as he often did, had the point: "Conformity is a name for the absence of vital inter-play: the arrest and benumbing of communication."[5]

It is one of the tritest of observations that the individual, if he is isolated, will in the end conform. There is a moment, as Malcolm Cowley wrote, "when individualism becomes a uniform in spite of itself"[6]; and we have had only to look around us in recent years to see how the desire of the young, especially, each to express his-self, all too easily becomes a uniform expression of undifferentiated tastes. This reinforcement of one's-self in the company of one's peers is, in the case of the young, a result of the discovery that there is not much inside their-selves that is yet worth expressing. Facts are like sacks, it has been said, they will not stand up until one has put something into them; and the same, perhaps fortunately, is true of human beings.

The adolescent is, in this respect, wholly a character of our time. What happens in adolescence is not conceived as a social event, the first and normal encounter of the grown child with his society as a responsible being; it is something that occurs *inside* the individual. It is there that he must discover his "identity," solitary in himself, as if his case is different from that of any other, and from that of any generation that has gone before. This burden of self-discovery is imposed on the individual when he has had little time to put into himself anything on which he can draw as a resource, so he flaps and he flops and he flips. Aware that we have weighed him with this load, we have no recourse in our guilt but to be tender at his affliction, to tolerate with equanimity both his "egoism and altruism, pettiness and generosity, sociability and loneliness, cheerfulness and sadness, silly jocularity and over-seriousness, intense loves and sud-den abandonment of these loves, submission and rebellion, materi-alism and idealism, rudeness and tender consideration."[7]

Pushed away from his society into himself, it is not surprising that the adolescent then imagines that his society is hostile to him, and that he returns the hostility. But this perception is not necessary. He can be taught to regard his society as a nourisher of his life, because it can most effectively bring him into contact with the real nature of things, and help him to separate the reality of the world from his own fantasies. Not to be made to encounter life-as-it-is can only be a deprival: not only of the company of others, with whose personalities one must negotiate with one's own personality, but of the self-discovery which is the reward of these negotiations. To find the intransigence of the world, that people and things will not all respond to one's desires, is not to find an enemy, but to find something else that is reliable and has familiarity. Reality itself is the most constant of companions.

One can ask questions of it, and it will reply, even if no answer now comes from the god of de Vigny. If one does not ask one's questions of the actual world, where does one make one's inquiries? The answer is that one takes them to art and to literature, and that is why the young, not only today but in all times, read all literature, from nursery tales to love poems, with the magical sense, which we can all remember, that they are more true than life itself. The love poem is for a time one's love life. Not all of this should be shed as we grow, certainly not as much as our civilization in the past has asked us to shed. But we have reached the point at which much of our literature not only supplies us with a created world in which we can delight but deliberately sets out to present this fictional world as more actual than reality itself; in fact, more true than life.

THE SPOILED AND THE DESPOILER

During the past thirty years, the child's world has itself been pictured as more real than the adult's world; and it is not unfair to say that Truman Capote, for example, in such a novel as *The Grass Harp* is a child novelist, which some would say he has remained, until the advancing years have withered the inspiration where it was once deliberately arrested, like a bud that does not open, and as a bud is sere. Just as the art that is so constricted does not issue in bloom, neither does the life that is so taught, as is demonstrated in *Rabbit, Run,* by John Updike. At the age of twenty-six, Rabbit runs away from the grubby little life that he has made, and he whines: "I once played a game real well, I really did." (He had been a basketball star at high school.) "And after you're first-rate at something, no matter what, it kind of takes the kick out of being second-rate. And that little thing Janice and I had going, boy it was really second-rate." He runs away from another girl, returns to his wife, runs away from her again, at which she gets drunk and drowns their second child in a bath, runs away from the child's funeral, runs away from the second girl when he learns that she also is pregnant, at last only to run.

As far as one knows, Rabbit has never been celebrated as a hero, or even as an antihero, but the callow adolescent out of which he developed was exquisitely celebrated by J. D. Salinger. Here indeed was the child brought forth as redeemer: the prescriptions of *American Family* in the 1940s pursued to their logical conclusion in the self-centred smart-ass Holden Caulfield, the artless child as the artful dodger. "Salinger has a remarkable gift for recording stupid speech," said Robert M. Adams[8]; "I read somewhere that Salinger spent ten years writing *The Catcher in the Rye;* that was eight years too long,"[9] scoffed Mary McCarthy; Salinger was usually unable "to write of adolescence without disappearing into it," declared Leslie Fiedler, placing him in a group of "teen-age impersonators," among whom he included Kerouac and Mailer and Burroughs,[10] and at the top of the list we may put today the name of Kurt Vonnegut. At this level of adult intelligence, Salinger was rejected, but his dreadful creation was to become the folk hero of the young, and especially the educated young, of the American middle-class family, and especially the educated middle-class family, in America. What most matters in the career of Holden Caulfield is not that Jerry Rubin says: "I dug *Catcher in the Rye. . . .* Holden Caulfield is a yippie,"[11] for that is an influence one would expect. What matters is that he had an adult audience as well, he was tenderly appreciated even by adult sensibilities, and given by them a palm.

The persistent accusation of hypocrisy against the adult world which is made by Holden Caulfield was accepted by the adults themselves, as they again accepted it when he issued in real life as Jerry Rubin; and again we ought not to be surprised when we consider what the adults had been taught, by their own literature, that spontaneity and authenticity are to be found only in the self, untouched and unguarded, in other words in the child. It is not only childhood and adolescence that we have reimagined, but our own natures as human beings, ourselves in our-selves, each to gladden itself in terms only of an utter selfhood.

Foretold by Ortega, the spoiled child is now sovereign in our Western societies, bent on discovering his-self only in himself, asking to be judged only by what is unqualified in him, untutored and undeveloped, his sincerity and his authenticity; distraught by his spontaneity, the immediate expression of what he conceives to be his vital desires; given to the exploitation of his-self in any god of his imaginings; finding in nature any reassurance that he requires, whether of his godlikeness or his beastliness; reducing the whole of life to the pinpoint of the self, yet demanding of it the gratification of all his appetites, only to complain, when they are refused, of his alienation. This is not the I released in the En-Masse, where it may find the company of others, its obligations as well as its consolations; it is the I enclosed in its-self. If this man is not persuaded to grow, to take himself out of his-self, as the adolescent must so often be urged, he will become the despoiler of his estate, and his life will indeed be as meaningless and insupportable as he now fancies in his idleness.

We should not be surprised to find this spoiled child most fancifully represented in our images of our movie stars, in a Marilyn Monroe as once in a Brigitte Bardot. "If, as a symbol, she stands for anything in our times," it was solemnly said of Bardot, later to be repeated with as much solemnity of Monroe, "she stands for the absurd, for a view of life characterized by profound, sad, dizzy, gay meaninglessness. As she herself said at Androvet, the cheese restaurant, 'If life is not a slice of cheese, what is it?' "[12] It is to this idiocy that the philosophies of the contingent and the absurd are in the end reduced. But the maundering of the movie star, whom one may expect to be idiotic, is no more trifling than that of a writer such as John Barth, who is taken to be serious: ". . . reality is a nice place to visit, but you wouldn't want to live there." It is the sentimentality, perhaps even more than the lie, that is offensive; and the cheapness of the effect.

The reality that he disdains is the society of other people, who present themselves to us with the manners that we share as human beings, in the estate that is the field of our common and cultivated behaviour. It is in our encounters in this society that we discover both the complexity of our lives and the means with which to cope with that complexity. "I still care about people, but it would be so much easier not to care," Andy Warhol once said. "It's too hard to care. I don't want to get too involved in other people's lives. . . . I don't want to get too close. . . . I don't like to touch things. . . . That's why my work is so distant from myself."[13] It is also why his work is so simple, and could not develop. "Friendship is an education in complexity," said Hilaire Belloc; and it is true, even if less intensely, of all the society we keep.

SELF-INTIMACY THAT LEADS TO SELF-ANNIHILATION

The only course, the only solution, for the man who will only visit reality, who withdraws from his society because it is easier not to care, is to push to an extremity within his-self, and this was indeed advocated in 1968, not only in art but in life as well, by A. Alvarez, later the author of one of the slighter books on suicide, *The Savage God*. The artist who today is significant, he said, is one who "pursues his insights to the edge of breakdown and then beyond it," into insanity and violence, and even to self-destruction, over the precipice until "mania, depression, paranoia and the hallucination that come in psychosis and are induced by drugs become as urgent and as commonplace as Beauty, Nature and the Soul were to the Romantics."[14] This is as much a proclamation against art as it is a heresy against man; in another time, the Church would have known it as the voice of the devil.

We have been told by Anne Sexton that when she met Sylvia Plath in 1958, they then made a ritual of going once a week in Boston to the Ritz Hotel, in the company of George Starbuck, to recall their attempted suicides over martinis in the cocktail lounge: "Poems left behind were technique—lasting, but, actually, over. We talked of death and this was life for us, lasting in spite of us, or better, because of us." But for Plath it did not prove to be life: from her last attempt at suicide, which it is agreed by her friends was intended only to be an attempt, she was not rescued, as she expected to be rescued as so often before; and in spite of her jauntiness it does not seem to have proved to be life for Sexton either.

This jauntiness, which at least was left by Plath in the cocktail lounge, was carried by Sexton into her poetry, pale in its images, not even black in its despair, with no more obvious respect for her art than for life, as she wrote of potties and orifices and bedpans and urine and stools and enemas. This was not how Plath made her poems; and it is time that we recognized that, in the genuine poetry of a Plath, the drive to order and form, the willingness to exercise and drill, were a part of her statement, inseparably linked with the subject matter, an avowal of existence, of a possible order that can be imposed on our unordered experience in our-selves.

She did not, in the description which Robert Lowell once gave of Beat poetry at its worst, present us with "raw, huge, blood-dripping gobbets of unseasoned experiences dished up for the midnight listener." She did not throw her-self onto the paper, "the demonic, fearlessly casual, fiercely candid Sylvia Unbound (but psychoneurotic and suicidal)," as Pamela Smith has described the image of her that we are asked to celebrate.[15] She could be startled, the poet and the woman, by the beauty which presented itself to her in her life; she could build, as if with bricks in a nursery, image upon image of her affection in her poem to her unborn child; and she could cry at a memory of poppies, in a field of cornflowers. How she called us to live; and it is we who put the suicide back into her poetry, where she tried to subdue it, to stand bleakly as her only affirmation, where she surrounded it with the colour of life.

But the difficulty that one has with her poetry is still that it issues too exclusively only from her own self-intimacy; and this celebration of the self, as we have already observed in another context, all too easily converts itself into self-abnegation or even self-destruction. No poet in our time has performed so acrobatically, or danced so tediously, on the pinpoint of self-intimacy than e. e. cummings. He appears to celebrate the I in its own now, discovering and even inventing its-self in the local and the particular of its own life, but in the end these are annihilated, and the self which can meditate on a leaf is surrendered to the leaf: in fact, he says, "canceled" by it. To the leaf, that is blind and deaf and dumb, the man or woman, who is seeing and hearing and speaking, is to surrender his or her particularity, his or her own way of feeling and meditation and articulacy.

THE LONELINESS THAT HAS BEEN TAUGHT

The loneliness of modern man of which we hear so much complaint is subjective, a state of feeling that he has been taught to find in himself, and not an objective fact to be found in the condition of present-day society. If he is lonely, it is because he believes that he ought to be lonely, because he understands no other way of imagining his-self except in its loneliness, because he lives, as Susan Sontag has said, "with an increasing burden of subjectivity, at the expense of his sense of the reality of the world."

The truth is that each of us in his own unordered world of his personal experience must be lonely; in its details it is unique, and cannot in its particularities be communicated; indeed we communicate what is going on inside each of us largely by signals, an exchange of guesses and intuitions. We try to transcend this isolation in two ways. We invent all kinds of constructs, with our science and our art, by which we hope to represent at least a portion of our reality to each other, and so to share a common understanding of at least that portion, not only making it intelligible, but making ourselves intelligible to each other. But we also have another way. Beside the created world of our constructs, there is also the actual world of our estate; and our shared activities in our estate are quite as important a method of making our lives intelligible, and ourselves intelligible to each other.

It is our estate, the place that we have made for ourselves, that has been banished from our art and our literature. Novels used to present a picture of society at work, and of the negotiations of the individual with it; but they have now lost almost all interest in the social. In short, an idiom of our literature—what it chooses to talk about in the voice in which it chooses to talk—has been allowed to oust the idiom of our everyday lives—what we in fact talk about, in the voice in which we actually talk. We imagine our commonplace world as if it is as empty and meaningless as it is represented in our literature. It is extraordinary that in our actual existences we have been willing to capitulate to an artistic idiom, that we have allowed what has happened in the novel to happen in our lives, and perhaps the explanation is not only there.

During one of his visits to the United States, Marías said that "the writer who can re-create daily life is not 'ordinary' but extraordinary. It disturbs me that American literature does not lead the way in imagining, re-creating, exalting and expanding the limits of real life, with a view to the unreal and the unrealizable."[16] There is indeed nothing of this in the contemporary American novelists who were mentioned earlier, and who manage only an apocalyptic vision of human life, and a cheapened one at that. The human estate is left in disrepair, while those who could find contentment in it are tempted only to efforts at personal salvation in a world with which they are ceasing to be familiar.

The twin vision of Henry Miller in *Tropic of Cancer* is now commonplace and facile. American society means to him "The ubiquitous bathtub, the five-and-ten-cent-store bric-a-brac, the bustle, the efficiency, the machinery, the high wages, the free libraries, etc. etc." Against this he sets what? "I made up my mind that I would hold on to nothing, that henceforth I would live as an animal, a beast of prey, a rover, a plunderer"; and in all this he would find "above all, ecstasy." As long as this remains the voice of so much of our art and literature, we cannot look to it for help in reimagining our estate, and the relationships of our-selves in it. We are given a picture of ourselves that is like C. M. Doughty's of the Semites who, he said, "are like to a man sitting on a cloaca to the eyes, and whose brows touch the heavens." In short, animal and divine, but denied our humanity, although it is in our common humanity that we are not alone.

There is an urgent need for our culture, and for American culture in particular, to return from myth to actuality, from a concern with ultimacies and extremities to a care for the daily round and things as they are, from the self in its-self to the individual in his society, from an obsessive interest in personal relationships to a decent curiosity about social relationships. That the need is felt is clear, not only from the popularity of "pop" sociology, but from the engagement of a novelist such as Truman Capote in what has been called the "new journalism," and in the audiences for the serialization on television of a novelist such as Galsworthy, whose interest was in the relationship between the individual and his society. It is the novelists who are keeping themselves in the world of myth and symbol.

Their influence is evident. "I am a myth," cried Free as a spokesman of "The Movement." "Symbols and myths is what it's all about," echoed Abbie Hoffman. "Our myths are greater than we are," declared Jerry Rubin, adding that "the myth is real if it builds a stage for people to play out their own dreams and fantasies,"[17] and the cry is still rehearsed, even though it is now to ends that are less political and more personalized. Yet we know from our experience of a movement such as surrealism how alike and conventional our unconscious lives prove to be. Held to be the most personal thing about us, they turn out to be of such a sameness that they are almost anonymous. The unconscious is universal rather than individual and, when people dip into their unconscious minds, they fish out of themselves images that are so lacking in any particularity that their lives seem to have no secret gardens at all, nothing that they themselves have grown.

THE SELF AS PARASITE

We are again returned to the child, who has not yet grown, whose personality has not yet been formed by what it has learned, who is in fact not yet very adept at learning, who acts on the world only irregularly and to no certain purpose, and whose discourse with the world is intermittent and limited. Not only is this child still outside the world to which it is being introduced, it also has little sense of any reality beyond the still narrow boundaries of its own life. The success of its growth will depend in large measure on the extent to which it is encouraged and even compelled to confront the stubborn reality of what is other than itself; if it is not so encouraged, it will be spoiled; it will remain outside.

One often gazes on the child who has been spoiled, and wonders at his slyness. Because he has never been brought face to face with reality, he is fearful of it, and believes that it may be overcome only by dodging. Because he has been given everything for no reason that even his intelligence can make obvious, he believes that he has won everything, and that everything must be won, by artifice and guile. If life and our natures were simple, one might expect the spoiled child, warmed by so much attention and expanded by so much freedom, to be warm and open to the world; but he is not, he is the opposite. He has never encountered the world, or anything or anybody who is other than himself. If he feels anger, he has never seen anyone else angry; if he is afraid, he has never seen anyone else who was willing to exhibit fear lest it disturb him; if he wishes to be selfish, he imagines that he alone, embraced by such givingness, bears such a guilt. Cooped in his-self, he is chicken; and of all the people that one meets, it is his neck that one wishes to wring.

The spoiled child is lonely for the same reason that he is selfish:

that he has never been presented with reality in any continuous way in which he cannot evade it, but must confront it, and in his encounters and negotiations with it find some company. Throughout this century, it is to this self-centred loneliness that our literature has tempted us; and to the parasitism that is its consequence. The bidding of e. e. cummings—that our art should express "a minute bit of personal feeling"—has been taken as a bidding to our actual lives. Stripped of our learning and our culture and our manners, stripped of our society and its company, we are addressed as the child, spoiled as the child; and, remaining the child, we become a parasite on our society.

There is another way, full of complication and therefore of regard for the adult; and, although it is not only an American answer, it is very much an American one. "Originality and uniqueness are not opposed to social nurture," said Dewey; "they are saved by it from eccentricity and escape." He did not doubt that there is a real problem in the contemporary world: "The problem of constructing a new individuality consonant with the objective conditions under which we live is the deepest problem of our times." But he was clear that the new individuality could discover itself only in the human estate: "Assured and integrated individuality is the product of definite social relationships and publicly acknowledged functions. . . . human nature is self-possessed only as it has objects to which it can attach itself." Where today is there a voice of such levelheadedness?

Elaborated from page to page in *Individualism Old and New*—try to find a copy of it today in a bookstore on a campus, as one runs one's thumb along the bookshelves from Castaneda to Kierkegaard—he offered the prescription which it is in part the purpose of this book to revive and redefine, so that it again may be available to us in our estate:

Individuals will refind themselves only as their ideas and ideals are brought into harmony with the realities of the age in which they act. . . . the mental and moral structures of individuals, the patterns of their desires and purposes, change with every great change in social constitution. . . . There is an undoubted vicious circle. But it is a vicious circle only in so far as one declines to accept the realities of the social estate. . . . A new individualism can be achieved only through the resources of science and technology.

One may hesitate at the *only;* but for the moment let it be. He concludes: "If, in the long run, an individual remains wholly depressed, it is because he has chosen the easy course of parasitism."[18]

We need to return, from god, from nature, from the self, to our estate; from the unknown, which they all are, to what we can know, and use. As we gaze and reflect on the society of the spoiled child, it seems indeed to have realized the description that Georg Lukács gave of existentialism, especially that of Sartre, that it was a "permanent carnival of fetishized inwardness"; and we ought not to be surprised that, isolated in "the emotional abodes of his subjectivity," searching only there "for absolute meaning, absolute freedom, and utter reality," the individual has achieved the opposite of what was promised, not the realization of the self, but its palsy.

CHAPTER 11

"The Movement": Trying to Turn the Inside Out

It is worth paddling for a moment in shallow waters: in the history of "The Movement," a brief five years, if as long, of the late 1960s. It is hard to believe that it was so celebrated at the time, not only by itself, but by its opponents; not only by youth, but by its elders; not only by *Time,* but by the New York *Times*. From time to time, today, we read in these same journals and newspapers how its leaders have left the streets, and gone in search of personal heavens, or simply of personal pleasures; or even more simply have gone home to Kansas. (Winthrop Hudson has acutely said that, for many of the young, the "Jesus cult" is a stage on the way home.) Why should one be surprised? The leaders of "The Movement"—one does not mean, of course, the Students for a Democratic Society in its beginning, or the intellectual New Left—never presented themselves as more than a "happening" in the now. To have a thesis or a plan or a strategy, this was never their boast.

Yet, now that "The Movement" has evaporated, and god and nature and the self have taken the place of revolution, one cannot help being struck by one aspect of it, and by its particular failure in that respect. It was an attempt to take the pinpoint of the self, discovered in its-self, where our culture has for a century and a half been telling us it is to be discovered, and to turn it from the inside out to the world, and there to try to affect and to change the external reality. The failure of the attempt was predictable, but it is interesting and even a kind of justification. In its failure to change the world in any significant way, "The Movement" demonstrated how false have been the prophets from which it drew its inspiration; and, when the walls of Jericho did not fall at the first tootle on their pipes, the prophets had left them with nowhere to go, but back to god, to nature, and to the self in its-self, or simply home to Kansas—to make what of their own children? In a sense, they were not to be blamed, the fault lay in their parents and in their elders. "They don't know anything," said Paul Goodman, who can hardly be regarded as an unsympathetic witness, "because we have not taught them anything."[1]

THE TANTRUM OF THE SPOILED CHILD

"The Movement" was a Little League outing of spoiled children; and all of them would get to bat. In a sense, this was obvious. "Many of the affluent children who often lead the protest movements at colleges," said David Riesman in 1969, "seem persuaded that the society is fully abundant and that nothing really costs anything."[2] (The sense of reality that comes with adulthood is that everything has its price.) This was true of those who were elected to the National Executive Committee of the SDS at its Port Huron, Michigan, meeting in 1962, where its first manifesto was drafted. All but five of its members had already graduated from college, and of those five all but one were still going to college; only one of the whole number had attended or was attending a college west of the Mississippi. It was true of the hippies, thus dictating their concerns, as Fred Davis boasted in an article in 1967:

> Hippies, originating mainly in the middle classes, . . . proclaim that happiness and meaningful life are not to be found in things, but in the cultivation of self, and by an intensive exploration of super-sensibilities with like-minded others.[3]

It remains true of some sects of Women's Liberation, a movement of much more consequence than "The Movement" out of which it came.

But there was a more serious sense in which "The Movement" was one of spoiled children. If one exalts the self in its-self, then the self must exist already in the child, to be reverenced, to be liberated, to be given the opportunity of free expression. This has been the mythology in many modern, and especially in many American, methods of child rearing, as we have noticed; and it was hardly surprising when the children who had been so reared took it into their heads to act as they had been encouraged.

"The Movement" was the celebration of the self, assumed to be already formed in the child and, indeed, to exist truly only in the child. Jerry Rubin had no doubt on this point, and ecstatically proclaimed:

Everything the yippies do is aimed at three-to-seven-year-olds. . . .

We're the child molesters. . . .

Our message: Don't grow up. Growing up means giving up your dreams. . . .

The revolution toppled the high schools in 1958. Soon it will go to the junior high schools, and then to the grade schools. . . .

The leaders of the revolution are seven-year-olds. . . .

It was wholly in character for him to say: "The yippies will consider the left serious when it starts printing comic books"[4]; and the influence of this voice in fact had a tragic effect on the New Left.

Although much innocence was being claimed in all this—childhood was joy and love, play and freedom—there was a reverse side to the innocence, as St. Augustine could have warned, and Erik Erikson and Jean Piaget could have explained. "Too much of this passion," said Edmund D. Pellegrino in a commencement address in 1972, when it was all over, "has been a tantrum, begging for attention and losing itself in masochistic and self-pitying excesses. It has been a form of singeing the ideas it hoped to nourish, blistering the innocent, and searing the many men of goodwill who also hope for reform."[5] A tantrum, it was. "We want the world—and we want it *now!*" was one of the slogans on the walls of the London School of Economics at the time; and that is the cry of a child in a tantrum. Temper, and sullenness of temper, were both given rein. The militancy of many of the rock songs at the time, with their vocabulary of violence and burning, chaos and anarchy, were little more than the longings of the child in a mood of angry defiance at its own limitations in a world that is intractable. Even now one aches at the infantilism.

This vision of the child is the paradigm, as we have said, of the self as complete in its-self. Everything that presents itself to the consciousness of the child is equally real and belongs to the same world. "Everything was *real* and *unreal*," said Rubin, which is exactly what Erikson and Piaget would have expected him to say if he had been a two-year-old. "Only by breaking rules do we discover who we are," he said again,[6] which is exactly what Erikson and Piaget would have expected him to say if he had been a three-year-old. That the child has to establish its own identity by testing the boundaries between it and the external world is a commonplace, and hardly as novel an idea as some child psychologists have seemed to think. But it is when the self, even as it grows, is nourished to believe that it can only be its-self if it stands in opposition to the external world, instead of finding out how it may co-operate in and with it, that the permanent damage is done.

THE CHILD SET AGAINST HISTORY AND REALITY

The child, and the self when it is imagined only in its-self, have no history, and no sense of history apart from themselves. The idea of "relevance," so important to "The Movement," was examined by C. Vann Woodward in his presidential address to the American Historical Association in 1969:

> Highly subjective and capable of as many meanings as it has users, the term "relevance" seems to express an inarticulate existentialism, a headlong immediatism of the "here" and "now," that is impatient with any "there" or "then" that do not have an obvious bearing on present preoccupations or personal problems. . . . The "Now Generation" is not without authentic antecedents. It would be possible to follow the theme of indifference and hostility toward the past through the corpus of American literature.[7]

Above the door of one university library in the United States is the inscription: "Who Knows Only His Own Generation Remains Forever a Child." One used to ponder it, from time to time, as "The Movement" swirled around; and pass inside.

Rubin was explicit in most of his attitudes, and his books will remain as documents: "Age—what's age?—we don't even carry a watch. . . . We live *now*. . . . When you're high on pot you enjoy only one thing—the moment. . . . The revolution is *now*. We created the revolution by living it."[8] Fred Davis claimed that the hippies were achieving "a radical shift in time-perspective . . . a lust to extract from the living moment its full sensory and emotional potential. For if the present is no longer to be held hostage to the future, what other course than to ravish it at the very instant of its apprehension."[9] (It is not irrelevant to point out that exactly the same words could be used to justify a rape or any other abuse of another person in order to gratify a momentary desire.) It all, said Michael E. Brown, amounted to "a profoundly mobilizing idea: Quality resides in the present. The allocation of reality to the past and future is rejected."[10]

In this view, history is no more than what one is oneself at the moment in the process of doing. "Historical experience," claims Rubin again, "is not an intellectual experience. The mind is lost in a spiritual orgasm, adventure: *becoming a revolutionary is like falling in love.*" Orgasm, of course, always that, and a dream: "Making history is like living a dream."[11] A tragic result of this attitude in "The Movement" was that it divorced itself, and succeeded in divorcing the New Left, from the heritage in American history on which it could have drawn. Jeremy Rifkin, a young and intelligent radical, looked back on "The Movement" in 1971: "A feeling of powerlessness and isolation began to engulf the movement. The New Left broke entirely with its American heritage because it failed to grasp a basic historical contradiction—that the American ideology is at once both revolutionary and reactionary. . . . What started as a movement to make institutions live up to the revolutionary part of the American dream transformed itself into a rejection of the dream itself." In particular, he commented, "its non-American style and rhetoric offer a perfect target for the forces of reaction."[12] It was on the basis of its rejection of history that "The Movement" created the mythology of "Amerika," and so finally separated itself from the actual America that it wished to influence.

POLITICS AS THEATRE

Thus the child, and the self imagined only in its-self, is set against reality and history. Where is there for him and for it to go, in order to act in the external world? To the theatre and, in particular, to the happening. Here one may see exactly where a vulgarized existentialism is certain to lead; and does not existentialism lend itself to vulgarization, since any self, however unqualified, may lend an ear to its enticements? Here also one may see the corruption that lies at the heart of the exaltation of sincerity and authenticity and spontaneity.

The closest to an intellectual justification of politics as theatre was given by Arthur Lothenstein, an apologist for the New Left after it had lost, under the influence of "The Movement," its intellectual coherence:

> Committed to the world of process, the politics of the New Left is perforce experimental and open-ended. It is continually subject to radical redefinition in the light of developing social realities and immediately perceived needs. Thus the new politics is as radically contingent as life itself.[13]

This is the vocabulary of existentialism, never very rigorous even in the mouths of its philosophers, turned into pulp. The emphasis of the New Left, he added, is "on existential commitment and the will to act."

"Find out where you are, what you want to do and go out and do it," said Abbie Hoffman.[14] "Act first. Analyze later," echoed Rubin. "Turn every event into historic and mythic significance. Make yourself a symbol."[15] It was all to be theatre, a scenario of happenings. "Many acts of rebellion . . . and countless scenes of insurgency," gurgled Andrew Kopkind in 1969; ". . . the genius of the Movement so far has been its ability to imagine its conceptions."[16] This was the point, it would write its own script, as it went along; each person would write his own script; it would all be contingent and existential. "There are no ideological requirements to be a yippie," said Rubin. "Write your own slogan. Protest your own issue. Each man his own yippie."[17] By 1968, the leader of the SDS at Columbia University, Mark Rudd, could say:

> Let me tell you. We manufacture the issues. The Institute of Defense Analysis is nothing at Columbia. Just three professors. And the gym issue is bull. It doesn't mean anything to anybody. I had never been near the gym site before the demonstration began. I didn't even know how to get there.[18]

What was expected of it all? Rubin had the answer. "History could be changed in a day. An hour. A second. By the right action at the right time." But how trivial the acts were, contrasted with this aim. They added to no more than his own description of the yippie: "A longhaired, bearded, crazy motherfucker whose life is theater, every moment creating the new society as he destroys the old."[19] This is what Kopkind could describe as "the central existential agony at the core of the Movement of this generation,"[20] and one marvels at the idiocy of his remark.

"The roots of the new politics are located in the instinctual life, in lived immediacy, in gut moral feeling,"[21] said Lothenstein, losing his poise as always. "The sources and manifestations of the revolution lie elsewhere," exclaimed Martin Duberman in the New York *Times Book Review* of all places; "in a bewildering grab bag that includes hallucinatory drugs, bisexuality, communal pads, dashikis and blue jeans, rock and soul, Eastern mystics, scientology, encounter groups, macrobiotic foods, astrology, street theaters and food stores."[22] There it was: every little place into which the self had retreated to find its-self was turned from the inside out to the world, and found to be only theatre and costume. It might also be therapy, as Allen Ginsberg, who was in attendance, said in his siren voice: "A demonstration is a theatrical production. The life style, energy and joy of the demonstration can be made into an exemplary spectacle of how to handle situations of anxiety and fear/threat."[23]

Just as the leaders of "The Movement" had learned much of their language of childhood from the child psychologists, so they had learned much of their language of theatre from the role theorists in sociology. They never denied—in fact, they boasted—that they were actors playing roles. "We played out our fantasies like children," Rubin said of a "Human Be-In" in San Francisco. "We were kids playing 'grown-up games.' You can be whatever you want to be when you're a kid. We were cowboys and Indians, pirates, kings, gypsies and Greeks."[24] Their justification was that everyone in his public behaviour, at least, is playing roles; and this is one of the weaknesses in the role theory of a sociologist such as Erving Goffman, that the self when it presents itself in public is made to seem inauthentic, as it is a flaw in the whole concept of sincerity and authenticity, that it is difficult to perceive how one can be sincere and authentic in one's behaviour to anyone else if by bringing the self into public one compromises its sincerity and authenticity.

This is one of the interests of the sexual metaphors which were used by "The Movement." A "lust to extract from the living moment its full sensory and emotional potential," as we have seen that Davis put it; "to ravish it at the very instant of its apprehension." The intention was not merely to shock; the sexual metaphor could only be an orgasmic metaphor, because that was how they perceived the self in its relations to others. "From New York to Berkeley, everyone got ready for the simultaneous orgasm,"[25] exclaimed Rubin. "Joy is doing what you want to do," said Hoffman, and he meant it; this was the sincerity that was sought. So—why not?—"Love is doing what you want to do, it's not all that give-and-take bullshit we were taught to believe."[26] In short, the self in its-self, authentic and sincere, is reduced to the selfish gratification of its own immediate desires.

We are not to inquire into either the nature of the behaviour or its consequences, either for the self or for the other self on which it acts. This was one reason why the film *Bonnie and Clyde* was a kind of scripture to them. "I'm laughing away, dreaming of the house getting blown to Cuba with the floor shaking like a son-of-a-bitch," said Free in *Revolution for the Hell of It*. " 'The Revolution is On!' I scream and grab a cap pistol, preparing to shoot the first cop that comes along. My wife joins in the game and we have this whole *Bonnie and Clyde* thing going. It's all hilarious, really. One big revolution for the hell of it"[27]; and Rubin echoed: "Bonnie Parker and Clyde Barrow are the leaders of the New Left."[28] They in fact had some justification; the film had made the evil of Bonnie and Clyde seem hilarious.

That they reached to these images of the popular culture was significant. "One practices by acting," said Free again. "Billy the Kid strides with 6 guns blazing, receding into his inner space. What does he find? Another Billy the Kid striding with 6 guns blazing, receding into his inner space. There are no rules, only images." Drawing on their own culture—the messages of the high culture, as we remarked at the beginning, more rapidly transmitted to the popular culture than ever before—they facilely managed an apocalyptic vision of earnest unseriousness:

Revolution for the hell of it? Why not? It's all a bunch of phony words anyway. Once one has experienced LSD, existential revolution, fought the intellectual game-playing of the individual in society, of one's identity, one realizes that action is the only reality: not only reality, but morality as well. One learns reality on a subjective experience. It exists in my head. I am the Revolution.

This is a child's collection of the cultural messages of the past fifty years. They were not looking at the society for which they pretended a concern, but only at its art, and listening only to its literature.

THE RETREAT INTO PRIVATE GRATIFICATION

Even as political-minded a leader of the SDS as Tom Hayden had written in *The Activist,* as early as 1961, of "the decision to disengage oneself entirely from the system being confronted." From this disengagement from the estate, there grew the myth that a cultural revolution could achieve what no political revolution had ever accomplished. "And perhaps more than anything else," says Kirkpatrick Sale in his extended account of the SDS, it "touched the lives of millions of young men and women, both formal members and many more on the fringes, teaching them a new way of regarding their nation and its heritage, penetrating for them the myths and illusions of American society, providing for them (for the first time in the history of the American left) a new vision of personal, social, and cultural relations—in short, *radicalizing* them."[29] The claim was absurd at the time; it is even more absurd to make it today, when there is not a scrap of evidence that a generation was radicalized by "The Movement" in general, or by the SDS in particular.

Out of an imagined revolution in their sensibilities or their consciousnesses, they trivially imagined that they would revolutionize their societies with a shake of their fists, if they were militant, or of their tambourines, if they were only beautiful: in both cases, with a wave of the not exactly golden locks of their youth. At the end of it all, their achievement could be observed: Richard Nixon in power in the United States, Georges Pompidou in power in France,

Edward Heath in power in Britain, Willy Brandt in power in West Germany. So they have retreated even further into their-selves, into even more personal longings, ever more private gratifications, and left the estate to deteriorate.

The modern idea of the self, sincere and authentic in its-self, is at the heart of the problem. "I am reluctant," says Ronald Atkinson in *Sexual Morality,* "to attach a high value to emotional sincerity in the absence of any idea of the sort of behaviour it might be expected to lead to."[30] Confessing that he is not "very sure of my own, or anybody's, capacity to distinguish between mutual sexual desire and love, or between enjoying others and enjoying oneself through them," he concludes that "the new morality of emotional sincerity is perhaps not wholly proof against self-deception." To carry the understanding into our everyday lives, at every level, that "self-realization is not possible," as Derek Miller has written, "without important emotional connexions with other people"[31] might enable us to recover the human sympathy of which John Dewey spoke: "For sympathy as a desirable quality is something more than feeling; it is a cultivated imagination for what men have in common and a rebellion at whatever unnecessarily divides them."[32] With an increase of that sympathy, we might cease to neglect the human estate and learn to live appropriately in it again.

PART V

The Fiction of the Masses

From today forward, we are all to be plain men to-gether. Here and everywhere we are witnessing the advent to power of the masses of the people.

—Front-page article, *Times Literary Supplement,* January 2, 1920[1]

CHAPTER 12

The Fiction of the Masses

The masses do not exist. But the idea of "the masses," although it is a fiction, the invention of a few minds, dominates the way in which we think of our societies and even of ourselves. It helps to nourish both the rebellion of the self and the revolt of the privileged, since everyone would like to distinguish himself from "the masses." None of us believes that he is a mass man, and we do not think of those whom we meet as mass men. We live by anecdote, and anecdotes are about what is particular, an individual or an occasion. We do not say in the evening, "I met a mass man today, called Petermass, and he was exactly like Philipmass, the mass man whom I was telling you about yesterday." If that was all that we had to say, we would have nothing to tell; we would have no anecdote.

We can test this from our own experiences. We all have a story to tell about the conversation of an Italian taxi driver who has just driven us from La Guardia Airport to the centre of Manhattan. No story is ever quite the same; the words of the Italian taxi driver which we report this evening are not the same as the words of the Italian taxi driver who drove us on that evening a week ago. Others interrupt with their own stories of Italian taxi drivers; and, although there is something common to them all, which is a part of their point, they are also all different, which is why we tell them. Again, we notice when one mailman is replaced by another. He performs for us the same service, at about the same time each day, in approximately the same way, as did his predecessor; and we are grateful that he does, it is not eccentricity that we expect of him. But we also notice that there is something different about him, and it is this we mention to our neighbours: "I wish we had the old mailman back, he always had time for a chat." . . . "Thank goodness the old mailman's gone, he always wanted to talk when I was busy."

This is how people talk. They have been touched by individuals during the day, whom they have observed as individuals, and on whose individuality they report in the evening with a story. We call our buses "mass transit"; but we get on a bus in the rush hour, and the driver is either welcoming or he does not have the time of day for us. "He's a sourpuss," we say as we take our seats, and stick out our tongues behind his back. We do not lament, "Alas and alack! Mass man is driving us today." We know that the next morning the driver may be Irish, with a "top of the morning" for us. In the common situations that we share from day to day, we notice individuals who behave in their own ways, not as a mass.

Unless we are from day to day aware of this—how each retains his individuality, not in the isolation of his-self, but in his dealings with others in our estate—we will again be persuaded that as a social being he is inauthentic. We will learn to think of our companions in the estate only as "the masses," and the estate itself only as "mass society." The rebellion of the self will be justified by what we have been taught is the condition of our society. We must be ready to go out each morning, and return each evening, and ask ourselves in our ordinary encounters whom we met during the day who was a mass man, who was less of an individual than ourselves; against the ways in which we are taught to imagine our situation, we must bring the evidence of our own senses.

THE POWER OF THE MERE CONCEPT

Fictions such as "the masses" are created by intellectuals whose imaginations are fertile, and then are reproduced by intellectuals whose imaginations are blank. It is often true that the greater and original intellectual has hold of an idea, sometimes of an insight, occasionally of a truth. But the nature of his imagination is that he must give force to his ideas by erecting them into a huge intellectual construction, in the hope that they will cohere. The creative intellectual is anxious to unify what is stubbornly various, and we have reason to be grateful to him. This act of the imagination, although he would have disliked it being called such, was self-conscious in Hegel, for example; he must impose a form on his knowledge and his ideas by which they could all be comprehended, and that is an original and creative act. But the creation must not be mistaken for reality. Plato did not pursue an existence that was Platonic, Sartre has not lived as an existentialist. They bow in their lives to the actuality of the world, and each of their constructions is merely another model by which to order that reality so that we may try to comprehend it in ways that we did not before. Descartes was visited by his abstract idea in a dream.

The task of the unoriginal intellectual, who is a lowly fellow but with an important task, is to bring against these mighty constructions, their coherence and unity, the presence and variousness of the real world. "But it is not quite like that," should be his voice; "there is something that you have not taken into account." He ought to be the carpenter who tells the architect, "If you lay a beam like that, the wind will blow your palace down." The greatness of any intellectual construction is that it is, indeed, a palace which the wind cannot blow down, because it has within itself its own coherence, and does not require the verification of the outside world. This is why what we call Marxism goes on surviving each successive demonstration that its diagnoses and predictions are invalid; and why Alfred North Whitehead could say that all of Western philosophy has been a series of footnotes to Plato. But one cannot live in these palaces.

The lesser intellectual ought to live in the gatekeeper's lodge, and mediate between the palace and the real world that lies beyond, being careful whom he lets in or out. But in our time he has become careless of his responsibility, aspiring both too high and too low. He allows the traffic to pass one way only. News of the great constructions of the palace is borne to the outside world, but news of the outside world is seldom carried to the palace. From the backstairs of the palace, he hears that a wonderful new idea has been invented: let us say, "alienation." He rushes with the news of it to the outside world: "We are all alienated; I have it from the palace." He does not knock on the door of the palace, as a good steward ought to do, to report: "I went round the estate this morning, and there are only seven alienated people out of five hundred; the rest are healthy, and feel at home in their situation." He imagines that people are alienated in a way in which he would not, just because he had heard of the disease, imagine that a herd of cattle had anthrax.

A characteristic example is to be found in *The Human Condition* of Hannah Arendt, an influential work in which we may find many of the intellectual concepts by which we have been taught to imagine our estate as a "mass society" from which we are inevitably "alienated." Yet she rarely offers any evidence of our societies, past or present, as they in fact have existed or now exist, have worked or work today. Her argument is shorn of facts; in the place of any empirical observation of any actual society, past or present, she concerns herself only with the pure ideas of other thinkers about the working of society, and offers her own pure ideas to set beside them. Yet we begin to think that her picture is real; we are carried away by it.

ITS RELATION TO THE IDEA OF ALIENATION

The trouble with ideas is that they are selective, a detachment from life. "I have chosen the idea of *alienation* as the central point from which I am going to develop the analysis of the contemporary social character," says Erich Fromm.[2] He is entitled to do so; in fact, when someone feels that he must release an idea, give it its own life, he is bound to be selective in this way. He must take a stance, choose the central point from which he will make his analysis, stand at an angle to the world. This ability and daring of the human mind—to select and detach, in short, to abstract—is of incalculable significance to us; but our ideas remain, even the most powerful of them, balloons into which we breathe the air, and we must sometimes let the air out. We cannot treat with them always in the manner in which Engels said that we treat with ideologies, "as with independent entities, developing independently and subject only to their own laws." That is one way of negotiating with them, but in the end we must subject them to the test of our own experience, including our knowledge of the experiences of others.

The three types of human beings which Arendt opposes to each other—*animal laborans* and *homo faber* and *vita activa*—never existed in the past and do not exist now. They are types, perhaps useful to us in thinking about our condition, but not accurate representations of the observable realities of that condition, either in the past or now. The life that was lived in the Greek city-state, for example, was never like the life that is described—typified—in the ancient authors on whom she relies. Indeed, it could be argued that the reverse is true. At least in part, Plato constructed his tremendous scheme in response to the fact that the Greek world was ceasing to fulfill its promise, the life was going out of it. To this extent, therefore, she opposes to the alienation which she suggests is peculiar to our society the writings of a man who was reacting against the alienation that was evident in his own world; and much the same is true of Augustine, on whose work she also leans, who wrote when life was ebbing from the Roman world, and in response to that fact.

One is not denying that the theme of the alienation of man is interesting, only that the fact of his alienation, if that is how we wish to perceive it, is not peculiar to our own society or any other. Even the emergence of the theme in modern literature is not as significant as it at first seems: hints of it, as many of its explorers have demonstrated, may be found in the writings of much earlier thinkers, and its elaboration and prominence in the past one and a half centuries have at least a part of their cause in a number of "accidents."

Ideas feed on ideas, and the sudden prominence of an idea may often be traced to the discovery or the rediscovery, the translation or the retranslation, of an earlier work. The translation into English of the works of Kierkegaard, in the 1930s, for example, and the publication in German in 1932 of the early manuscripts of Marx were "accidents" of this kind, and their impact was in part the result of the further "accident" of a historical situation: it was after the Second World War, as Walter Kaufmann says, "when the world was divided into two camps, that Marxism and existentialism sought common ground in discussions of alienation."[3] In fact, the current emphasis on the theme of alienation in the early writings of Marx is a gross distortion of the general thrust of his work as it eventually developed; it is a false way to read him, to extract merely what one wants.

There have been the "accidents" of individual thinkers who have found the emergence or re-emergence of an idea to be peculiarly timely for them—as did Georg Lukács when he seized on the theme of alienation as one way out of his predicament as an independent Marxist thinker in a Stalinist regime; or who have been deeply influenced by another thinker—as Arendt was by Martin Heidegger and by Karl Jaspers, to the second of whom she was attached, inscribing to him a remarkable eulogy; or whose migration to another country from that of their birth has had the same effect as the discovery or translation of a particular work—as the idea of alienation was "naturalized" in the United States by a number of refugees from Germany and Austria, such as Arendt and Fromm, Herbert Marcuse and Erich Kahler. All of these "accidents" do not make an idea any less significant or less powerful; but they remind us, when we are about to be overwhelmed by the force and pervasiveness of a theme, that it may owe its currency in part to circumstances that are fortuitous.

The danger does not lie in the ideas themselves: to pretend that it does is to make the vulgar mistake of imagining that Herder, because of his ideas, was a forerunner of racism, or Hegel of national socialism; or the equally vulgar mistake of thinking that, if one rejects Communism, one must therefore refuse all the manifold instructions of Marxism. Their danger is that they are taken as comprehensive diagnoses of our actual condition, as accurate representations of our here-and-now lives, and as adequate prescriptions of needed remedies; and it is exactly these confusions which have accompanied the idea of "alienation" during its heady course into contemporary thought, and so into the minds even of those who wish to act.

A sidelight on recent history offers an example. "Where does one begin thinking about manifestos?" exclaimed Tom Hayden as he prepared to draft, for the Students for a Democratic Society, what came to be known as the Port Huron Statement. In his own case, we know at least one of the answers. He "pored over" or "looked into" the works of: C. Wright Mills, Harold Taylor, Albert Camus, Robert Michels, Michael Harrington, Iris Murdoch, Sheldon Wolin, Norman C. Thomas, and William Appleman Williams. This is a mixed bag, but it is also, with perhaps two exceptions, a limited one;

and it is not difficult to understand how, in turn, Tom Hayden and the Port Huron Statement and the SDS drew from it their misleading emphasis on the theme of alienation, both as a diagnosis of the revolutionary situation that was supposed to exist in the United States, and as a prescription for the remedies that were supposed to be needed. At no time—apart from discussions with other students who had no doubt read the same kind of literature—was a serious attempt made to test the idea of alienation against the here-and-now realities of everyday life as it is lived by tens of millions of men and women in the United States and, for that matter, in other societies in a comparable situation.

An idea was floating in the air, like a balloon, the SDS attached itself to its string, and the balloon burst. Marx's exhortation to the proletariat of his day—"You have nothing to lose but your chains"— was close to the truth, at least as a metaphor. It was not just plucked out of the air; it was backed by detailed observation of how entire classes of men and women were condemned to exist, of which Engels' account of the condition of the working classes in England in the 1840s was the most notable, and even so the English working man and woman were not impressed: they had other things to lose, and they knew that they had. How much more, in comparison, does the ordinary man and woman in the United States today have to lose; and, if they are to surrender or even to jeopardize what they have and what they know they have, they will require an explanation of the current impoverishment, real or imagined, of their lives that is considerably more recognizable to them, a great deal closer to the truth about their everyday reality as they experience it, than that which is subsumed in the idea of their "alienation" from a "mass society."

ORTEGA y GASSET AND THE "REVOLT OF THE MASSES"

What is meant by speaking of "the masses"? It is half a century since Ortega y Gasset described "the revolt of the masses" and, although it has often been challenged, the theme has entered deeply into the imagination of our time. It was not, of course, only his theme; but he gave it an expression that was more complicated and penetrating than did anyone else. In challenging the concept of "the masses," we will not rely only on his development of the theme; but so rich was his elaboration of it that it is as instructive a place as any at which to start. He at least was not simplistic.

Ortega insisted that "the masses" are not a social class; in particular, that they are not, "solely or mainly, 'the working class.'"[4] On the contrary, the masses are "a kind of man to be found today in all social classes." In all social classes, there are always "mass and genuine minority," and "the revolt of the masses" is a way of describing the predominance in every class of the first over the second. "The minorities are individuals or groups of individuals which are specially qualified. The mass is the assemblage of persons not specially qualified . . . the mediocre man of our days." He is "the average man": not so much the mere quantity of the multitude, but the "common social quality" of men who are undifferentiated from each other. "The masses" are in any individual who thinks of himself as "just like everybody else," and who values himself on these grounds.

The revolt of "the masses" means the triumph of the commonplace: "The characteristic of the hour is that the commonplace mind, knowing itself to be commonplace, has the assurance to proclaim the rights of the commonplace and to impose them wherever it will." It means the triumph of the vulgar: ". . . not that the vulgar believes itself super-excellent and not vulgar, but that the vulgar proclaims and imposes the rights of vulgarity, or vulgarity as a right." It means the triumph of conformity: "Anybody who is not like everybody, who does not think like everybody, runs the risk of being eliminated." It means the triumph of the unqualified in each of us: "The sovereignty of the unqualified individual . . . has now passed from being a juridical idea or ideal to be a psychological state inherent in every man"; and this last point is at the very heart of his argument.

From this valuing by the individual of what is unqualified in himself, his desire to be judged only generically, as a human being as such, come the two fundamental traits of the "mass man": ". . . the free expression of his vital desires, and therefore of his personality; and his radical ingratitude towards all that has made possible the ease of his existence. These traits together make up the well-known psychology of the spoiled child. . . . To spoil means to put no limit on caprice, to give one the impression that everything is permitted to him and that he has no obligation." In all social classes, this unqualified self is now predominant: the man who "is satisfied with himself exactly as he is," who tends to "consider and affirm as good everything he finds within himself," and who seeks its gratification. Whatever the appetite, it must be satisfied.

Si monumentum requiris . . . Look around, and the prophecy seems indeed to have been fulfilled; the spoiled child to be clamorously everywhere, not least in each of us. Every movement that has been celebrated in recent years—all the happenings in our culture—seem to have rested on this claim of the unqualified self to the uninhibited expression of its vital desires and their immediate satisfaction. It is obvious that the spoiled child is here in our Western societies; and to the particular insights of Ortega—the conservative as prophet, as he so often is—one willingly acknowledges one's debt. But, as has already been suggested in the argument of this book, the arrival of the spoiled child cannot be explained in terms of "the masses."

"The revolt of the masses," if the term is used with any strictness, has been a social event; as Ortega himself said, "There is one fact which, whether for good or evil, is of utmost importance in the public life of Europe at the present moment. This fact is the accession of the masses to complete political power." In contrast, the rebellion of the unqualified self, as he again put it, is a psychological state. Why the two should be connected, he does not explain. He moves freely from the concept of "the masses" as the multitude in society that is now given political power, to that of "the mass" which in every social class is opposed to the qualified minorities, to that of the "mass man" who is in rebellion in each of us; and he does not consider that they may have different causes, and in fact may be different phenomena. In particular, he does not consider that the rebellion of the self may be a cultural event, in the strictest sense, the work of our art and our literature, it's object being a revolt against the "mass society" which they depict.

The rebellion of the self is a denial, not an affirmation, of the "common social quality" of men who are undifferentiated from each other. The malaise in our societies is, not that everybody is claiming to be like everybody else, but that everybody is asking to be judged only by what differentiates him from all others. Far from being proclaimed, the commonplace is allowed no celebration. The truth is, not that the "mass society" exists, but that the spoiled child of our civilization has been taught to think of his estate as the "mass society," and to withdraw from it in his pique.

THE SNOBBERY IN THE THEORY

Let us try, for a moment at least, to keep our feet on the ground. The reason why there are large numbers of people in our "mass societies" is that increasingly, during the past two hundred years, people who have been born have been enabled to live, primarily as a result of the advances in medical knowledge and skill, and of their availability to more than a privileged minority. If we want to be rid of "the masses," all we need to do is have rid of the individuals— while making sure, of course, that this modest proposal does not include ourselves. The thing could be simply done, by the legalization an official encouragement of infanticide. After all, one of the measures by which ancient Greece held down the size of its population was by the exposure of its unwanted infants to the elements, the kind of fact that is neglected by Arendt when she contrasts our "mass society" unfavourably with the Athenian *polis*. The restriction of the *polis*, in numbers as well as territory, was a primary concern; otherwise how could it be governed, asked Aristotle, except by a man with the voice of Stentor?

It is worth remembering, whenever we encounter the idea of the "the masses," that most of us are members of them, that each of us is alive only because each of them is alive. Similarly, when we encounter a large number of people, wherever we go and whatever we do, it is worth recalling that each of us is one of the large number, we are its constituents. To complain of the crowds is for each of us to complain of his own existence. Yet the complaint is familiar, as in this dramatic evocation of Ortega:

Towns are full of people, houses full of people, hotels full of guests, trains full of travellers, cafés full of customers, parks full of promenaders, consulting-rooms of famous doctors full of patients, theatres full of spectators, and beaches full of bathers.

What previously was, in general, no problem, now begins to be an everyday one, namely to find room.

But to find room for whom, if not for oneself? Who is to be kept out, who is to be eliminated? Of those who have not been aborted as foetuses or exposed as infants, who are to be denied a full life?

"On American Airlines they pet you and pamper you, give you scrambled egg among the clouds, and strawberries and cream," wrote Louis MacNeice in 1940.[5] Now that "the masses" travel by air, one is not petted and pampered, there are no strawberries and cream, and in place of the scrambled egg there is food that is uniformly mediocre. But whom is one to keep off the airplane, if not oneself? "My dear, the noise! And the crowds!" the officer of the Brigade of Guards is supposed to have said as he waited to be evacuated from the beaches of Dunkirk; and his cry is now familiar.

It is to be heard in the protest of the art critic Herbert Read at the beginning of the 1960s, a man who interestingly, in this context, believed that art could be an instrument of social revolution:

From July to September, the hordes, bent on pleasure but for the most part achieving frustration, irritation and exhaustion, crowd the same beaches to suffocation, pack the piazzas till there is only standing room, eat in rotation, sleep in rotation, collect the same mass-produced souvenirs, pile impression on impression, and strive desperately to retain an image or two for future remembrance.

. . . The organizers of the recent Picasso exhibition at the Tate Gallery rejoiced in the round number of attendances— nearly half a million visitors passed through the turnstiles in unbroken file, pressed round the paintings, straining their necks, elbowing and tiptoeing, emerging at the end of the labyrinth uninitiated and bewildered but perhaps with a sense of sacrifice.

At the beginning of the century, [Olympia] was visited annually by not more than a hundred scholars, who made the journey from Patras on mules. By 1929 the number of visitors increased to 200, and in 1932 it was not more than 350. Then the tourist organizations began to make their effort—the roads were made possible for motorists and by 1936 the number of visitors rose to 1,000. A tourist hotel was built. . . . This year more than 10,000 visitors paid entrance fees to the museum in the one month of August, and in addition during the same month between 2,000 and 3,000 students were admitted free.[6]

The pain is excruciating. But which of the multitude, which of the students, are to be excluded? A hundred and fifty years ago, say, Read himself would have been unlikely to have seen Olympia, or to have been an art critic.

The lament at our "mass societies" is the same as the lament at our "affluent societies," spreading from the United States to engulf Western civilization. In 1960, an American writer, Marya Mannes, broadcasting from London, told even the British that theirs was an "affluent society. . . . I know because I come from one. . . . I notice all the familiar signs of a hot pursuit of affluence. I see a wealth of things, and a mass of people who can afford them"; and she complained of the evidence in Britain, the traffic in the cities, the indifference of the shop girls to the customers, the presence of "a great many people who have money now" but who "are not educated in its use." At last she sighed: "Easy money, easy vice, a profound cynicism, an encompassing nihilism—all these are the dark companions of affluence; you suffer them also."[7] My dear, indeed, the noise! And the crowds!

In every theory of "the masses" there is always a form of elitism, or simply of snobbery, explicit or concealed. "Looking in any direction," Ortega said again, "our eyes meet with the multitudes. Not only in any direction, but precisely in the best places, the relatively refined creations of human culture, previously reserved to lesser groups, in a word to minorities." Like everyone else fifty years ago, he meant by "minorities" the few who were advantaged; we mean by them today the few who are disadvantaged. Nothing could underline more clearly the change that has occurred. The few used to be those who were allowed in; they are now the few who are kept out. Most of us would not have been fortunate enough to belong to the privileged minorities of the past, and are not unfortunate enough to belong to the unprivileged minorities of today. In both cases, we would have been, as today we are, the majority: members of "the masses."

"Now the average man represents the field over which the history of each period acts," said Ortega, and he concluded, in a phrase with a double edge, "The soldier of today, we might say, has a good deal of the officer." That is most of us. We are the other ranks, but with a commission. If we can imagine ourselves only as "the masses" and our society only as "mass society," we are doomed to diminish our sense of our common humanity and our opportunities as men and women who have "a good deal of the officer" in our privates' uniforms. If any of us is grateful to gaze on a Picasso or travel to Olympia, part of the enrichment of our pleasure ought to lie in our recognition that the other members of the crowd may be grateful also. If the crowds are so large that they become an obstacle to our enjoyment, the fault is not in their numbers, but in our failure to make arrangements for them. The feast of life can be rich for all; and it can be richer for each of us if we share with our fellow human beings, and know that we are sharing, not just a trough of swill and a mattress of straw, but the common experience of the endless inquiry of the human spirit in which we are all and each engaged.

IN DEFENCE OF THE SUPERMARKET

Not one of us is not like every other in his humanness; yet not one is not each his own self. The homogenization of "the masses," as it has been foretold and feared for so long, has not occurred; least of all has it occurred in America, which was described by Ortega as "the paradise of the masses." Instead, there has been the most astonishing individualization of whole classes of people who throughout all previous history have been undifferentiated. Let us consider, for example, "the consumer" in our "consumer societies," which is another of the symbols by which we represent "the masses" in our "mass societies." "The consumer" is commonly taken to be marked by the uniformity of his tastes; but, if we look closely, we will find that his true mark is an increasing individualization of his tastes.

One of the most common symbols of the "consumer society" is, in turn, the replacement of the village (or neighbourhood or corner) shop by the supermarket. One did not know, until one read their writings, that so many of our intellectuals, including some of the most prominent of them, spend so much of their time buying the groceries; or that they suffer such a delicate feeling of estrangement from their fellow men, from society, from nature, from god, or from whatever they feel alienated, when they enter a supermarket. To someone who in fact enjoys trundling his cart round a supermarket, this expression of their feelings is worrying, since it suggests that his own sensibility may be peculiarly dull; and it is even more worrying if he in fact grew up where there were only village (or neighbourhood or corner) shops, and his memory of them, far from being pleasant, is quite the opposite: that they were not pleasant places to go.

Again and again, in the kind of literature we are discussing, we are given a picture of the village woman who used to shop at the village store, where she was served by the village shopkeeper, with whom she discussed the latest gossip, and who is now "at a loss in the metropolitan supermarket where her demands are no longer dictated by her needs, but on the contrary dictated by an abundant supply." At the checkout counter, there is no time for gossip, and she receives only a small slip of paper with the words "Thank you" printed on it, "more for the sake of public than personal relationships. The shopkeeper, focal point in rural face-to-face relationships, has been replaced by machines and anonymous functionaries."[8] The writers seem almost to repeat each other. C. Wright Mills, for example, said that "the small shop serving the neighborhood is replaced by the anonymity of the national corporation: mass advertisement replaces the personal influence of opinion between merchant and customer."[9]

But the village shop, as one knew it personally, and as one can read about it in fiction, was usually an unattractive place, and frequently a malignant one. The gossip which was exchanged was, as often as not, inaccurate and cruel. Although there were exceptions, one's main memory of the village shopkeeper, man and wife, is of faces which were hard and sharp and mean, leaning forward to whisper into ears that were cocked and turned to hear all that they could of the misfortunes or the disgrace of a neighbour. Whisper! Whisper! Whisper! This has always been the chief commodity of the village shop. And not only whispers, because the village shopkeeper, informed or misinformed, could always apply sanctions against those to whom disgrace or misfortune was imputed.

The anonymity of the supermarket is in fact a gain in privacy, even in the equalization of dignity. Anyone can shop at a supermarket without the whole of his life being known and examined; if he is living in sin, or his daughter is mad, or he has dodged the draft, it is of no consequence to the manager or the checkout girl, as long as he can pay the bill.

But let us suppose that the customer is respectable by the standards that prevail: what of the choice, in making a purchase, which is available? There is an impenetrable obscurity in the suggestion that, whereas in the village shop, the customer's demands were dictated by his or her needs, in the supermarket they are dictated by an abundant supply. One really has to do better than that. The demands of most customers at a village shop were dictated, not by their needs, but by their purses; and their purses were very rarely in equation with their needs. The majority of villagers were always poor, and were known to be poor.

It is true that too often at too many supermarkets one may still observe the really poor as they desperately try to balance their purses against their needs, as they rummage for a last penny at the checkout counter. But there is a saving grace in the supermarket even for them. They no longer go into the village shop to be told by the shopkeeper, "Ah! Mrs. Smith, I have saved a few neckbones for you," as if she had no choice, and he was the author of a benefaction. They now enter the supermarket anonymously; no one says to them, "We know what you can afford." They diddle around at the meat counter, as we all do, and even if they in the end have to settle for the neckbones or the chicken feet, they have known, not merely the illusion of choice, as some would say, but something of the experience of choice. The possibility of choice was there, present to them; it was reduced, as they calculated, by the fact of their poverty, but it was not a denial from the beginning, made by others on their behalf, an ordering of the fates, in the person of the village shopkeeper.

What is more, the poor in the supermarket can refuse, with the dignity that anonymity confers, the reduction of their choice. One does not need to imagine, one can remember all too well, Mrs. Smith announcing in a village store that she was tired of cabbage and would try some peas for a change. At once she was reproved by the village shopkeeper—the entertaining fellow— "Ah! Mrs. Smith, you know that the cabbage will go much farther than the peas, with all those mouths to feed," and before she can remonstrate, the cabbage had been popped into her bag. But in a supermarket one can watch the poor decide for themselves that this week they will waste a little money on a frill, and nobody will challenge or reprove them.

This was exactly the point made by George Orwell, when he defended the poor of the 1930s against the accusation that they too often spent their pennies on ice cream and chips instead of on mutton and greens. What they were doing, he said, was asserting their right to regard themselves as human, to be concerned with more than their immediate existence, their mere animal survival. They had a right to a little of what they fancied as much as anyone else.

THE RELEASE FROM CUSTOM

But let us leave aside the really poor, and consider the choice that is available at the supermarket to the large majority of Americans, and increasingly to a large number of men and women in comparable societies. Let us watch them also as they shop. Their demands are not dictated by an abundant supply; their demands on the abundant supply are restricted by their purses. The choice of the poor is reduced to the point at which the nature of the choice is changed; the choice of the majority is restricted, but its nature is not affected, it is a limitation only of degree.

Restriction by the purse becomes more serious if the variety of goods that are available is itself restricted. This has always been one of the faults of the village shop. Not only are its goods more expensive than in a supermarket, because its turnover is not so great, but the variety of goods which it carries is limited. This means that the customer is doubly subject to the necessity, week after week, to purchase the same foods, in order to make the same meals. The choice in the supermarket, if the customer wishes to take advantage of it, is much wider. He can determine to spend more on a foreign cheese—which would probably not be available in the village store in any case—knowing that he can save the extra money that he has spent on the cheese by buying a cheaper vegetable.

These may not seem to be important increases in human freedom, until one considers how astonishingly more varied are the personal tastes of ordinary people than they were even a quarter of a century ago. From this point of view, the recent proliferation of small shops —delicatessens, health-food stores, boutiques—ought to be seen, not as an alternative to the supermarket and the department store, but as an extension of them; they are certainly an extension of the "consumer society," and the true significance of the "consumer society" is this increasing differentiation of tastes. The vegetable counter of almost any supermarket is an invitation to the individual customer to experiment and discriminate with his own taste and, although the significance of this may seem to be slight, it is an expression of individualization, as it is an education in it, far removed from the notion of "the masses."

Not to have to eat the same food that one was brought up to eat, not to have to eat the same food that one ate last week, not to have to eat the same food for all of one's life: this is a release from custom, and from its bondage; and here again one can observe how the critics of "the masses" have a point and then misconstrue it. Even in this simple matter of food, the release from custom does indeed mean the destruction of an old cultural variety. Germans no longer eat only German food, and German food is no longer eaten only by Germans. When the critics of "mass society" talk of the homogenization of tastes, it is usually to the destruction of this cultural variety that they are referring. But this destruction has been accompanied by an individualization of personal tastes that is elaborately various. German food is not lost to the human memory, the arts of German cooking are not forgotten; they have merely become the property, not of a culture, but of individuals, if that is their taste. What is more, the sharing of individual tastes can then become an opportunity for human companionship and interchange, of associations that are voluntary and not just customary.

"Actually we 'eat' a phantasy and have lost contact with the real things we eat," says Erich Fromm. "Our palate, our body, are excluded from an act of consumption which primarily concerns them. We drink labels. With a bottle of Coca-Cola we drink the picture of the pretty boy and girl who drink it in the advertisement."[10] There is a great deal of cant in this kind of imagining. Those whom one knows who drink Coca-Cola drink it because they like it, just as those whom one knows who do not like it do not drink it. There is no evidence that people "drink the label . . . drink the picture . . . drink the slogan . . . drink the great American habit." Above all, there is ample evidence that, as the goods that are available become more numerous, individual tastes are increasingly differentiated.

"The masses" whom one remembers even from one's own child-hood and youth, the working classes and the lower middle classes, ate the same food from day to day, wore the same clothes from year to year, and were uniform in taste and appearance. In contrast, their children or grandchildren are today astonishingly various and colourful in these everyday expressions of their individuality. These gains may seem to be small; but they have their reflections at a more serious level. One does not wish to exaggerate their importance; but it is time that we challenged some of the images in which our society is represented to us, so that we grow to disdain it. The privileged man who was a dandy in the past ought not to be contemptuous or resentful of the construction worker who today is making something of a dandy of himself under his hard hat, which is perched im-probably on his mannered tresses, tolerated even by his employer, and now scarcely noticed by passers-by.

THE ROMANTIC IDEALIZATION OF VILLAGE LIFE

If the village shop has been romanticized in contrast to the super-market, so has the life of the village itself, and the idea of the com-munity which it is supposed to have represented. Villages have usually been, and commonly still are, unattractive and confined, mean in condition and in spirit, unless they are the idealized relics of a rural past which a prosperous and commuting middle class pre-serves for its quasi-pastoral enjoyments, singing the virtues of a vil-lage life that they have urbanized.

Mahmut Makal's bitter description of a village in Anatolia, not in the past but in our own time, can stand for the majority of villages. There is nowhere else to go, not even a thought of anywhere else: "the villager has no desire for any other kind of existence; or—more exactly—he believes that 'the best of all days is today.' . . . So the wheel of fate grinds out our lives, turning as it has done for the last thousand years." Custom is never challenged: "In the eyes of the villagers, women are practically of no value whatever. . . . The man can strike her, curse her, beat her, make her weep, cause her pain, and she may not say a word." Religion is only a thrall of sus-picion: "Our villagers are born to religion. But they show no interest in that aspect of religion which means unity, friendship, love, and respect for others. . . . A charm for the barren woman, a charm for the child who has broken his leg falling off a roof, a charm to make hair grow on the bald head of a baby, a pinch of salt 'breathed' upon an aching tooth—another charm. Charmers and charms; sorcerers and sorcery; such things are a matter of daily occurrence. So it persists. Frustration, ignorance, destitution; hand in hand, saluting each other, they go straight to hell."[11]

If it is said that this is a picture only of a poor village in a poor region of Anatolia, one must answer that most villages in the past have been like it, that in the world today most villages are still like it, and that even in Europe and America at this moment there are plenty of villages in which, although life has been eased a little, it is still bound to the same wheel. To a greater or lesser degree, the mind and life of the villager are, as Marx said of rural India more than a century ago, "bound in the smallest possible compass," from which there is rarely an escape.

But the pastoral myth persists, almost a century and a half after Macaulay hurled one of his magnificent commonsensical tirades at Southey, who was one of its earliest propagators. Southey had described the life of the English rural cottager before the Industrial Revolution in the most fanciful terms: "the hedge of clipt box beneath the windows, the rose-bushes beside the door, the little patch of flower-ground, with its tall hollyhocks in front; the garden beside, the bee-hives, and the orchard with its bank of daffodils and snowdrops"; and so he went on. "Here is wisdom," Macaulay burst forth. "Here are the principles on which nations are to be governed. . . . Mortality and cottages with weather-stains, rather than health and long life with edifices which time cannot mellow. . . . Does Mr. Southey think that the body of the English peasantry ever lived in substantial or ornamented cottages with box-hedges, flower-gardens, and orchards? If not, what is his parallel worth?"

Even thirty years ago, if one may draw on one's own experience, the life of a farm worker on the farm of one's grandfather in one of the most prosperous shires of Scotland was a wretched affair; and as a boy one could react only with discomfort, growing into horror, at the evidence of grown men who were, apart from their strength which was the strength of cart horses—like the blacksmith whom Calvin Coolidge used to watch as a boy, who could throw a horse to the ground if it was stubborn—confined for the length of their days to a boy's life. It was this confinement—the frustration and

ignorance of which Makal speaks, ignorance even of other possibilities—which was even more appalling than the humbling
poverty. The great road which ran at the foot of the fields, eventually
to join the Great North Road south to London and to opportunity,
was not one which they took, unless a war allowed them to escape,
their only escape, into the army.

The question which must be asked of the supermarket is one which
must be asked of every similar imagining by which the theory of
"the masses" is supported: what did the majority of people have to
endure in the past? Arendt speaks, for example, of "the mass
phenomenon of loneliness," and explains it in terms of the "mass
society" which "not only destroys the public realm but the private
as well, deprives men not only of their place in the world but of
their private home"; and one must ask how many people in the
past had a place in the public realm or were able to enjoy a private
home. When she speaks of "the private realm of the household"[12]
—for which she does not, in fact, have much respect—she is talking
of a realm which has been inhabited by only a very few people in
history, until our own age. A private realm—in the mud hovel of
a medieval peasant, in a farm worker's cottage fifty years ago?—it
did not exist. Of what use then is her parallel?

We confront a society, says Robert Nisbet, "composed in ever-
increasing numbers of amorphous and incoherent masses, of people
who have seen spiritual meanings vanish with the forms of traditional society and who struggle vainly to find re-assimilation."[13]
What does he imagine that the spiritual meanings were which the
majority of people found in their lives in the past, except fear and incomprehension and an abject submission to what they understood to
be their fate? To have released men from fear and incomprehension
and superstition, from submission to gods and kings and popes, is
not a loss to them, but the opening of an opportunity, an affirmation
such as their ancestors never knew, that they may remake their own
lives and their own society.

ONE OF THE DEAD FORMS OF EUROPE

In all these hankerings after the village store and the village, it is
the old—and, in particular, the feudal—idea of community that
has travelled like a ghost from Europe, in our time, to haunt the new
society of America. It is community we have lost, cry the Europeans

in their remembrance of times past. It is community we are lacking, echo the Americans in their uncertainty of times future. European or American, in our ill humour with our own times, we imagine that there were golden ages of community in the past. There was community in Athens—but for whom, in a society "whose division of labour was based on the exploitation of man by man"? There was community in feudalism—but for whom in a society which, in the words of Marc Bloch, the great historian of the Middle Ages, "meant the rigorous economic subjugation of a host of humble folk to a few powerful men . . . whereby men exploited men . . . chiefly to the benefit of an oligarchy of warriors"?[14] Are we really to ignore the fact that, in 432 B.C., between 30,000 and 40,000 free citizens in Athens were sustained by an unprivileged class of between 10,000 and 15,000 metics, and by a subjugated class of between 80,000 and 110,000 slaves; or the fact that the humble folk in the Middle Ages were similarly situated, and privilege similarly sustained?

Yet the myth invades even the popular imagination. There have been few more reactionary influences on the modern sensibility than the romantic reimagining of the Middle Ages, which was mindlessly adopted by Charles Reich in *The Greening of America,* in which something that he represents as the medieval peasant is a legendary figure, with none of the squalor and oppression of his actual life. One would imagine from Reich that the peasant lived in the Middle Ages, not unlike the cottager of Southey, in a Garden of Eden, harvesting his fruits in the dawn of time, to eat them in bowers of honeysuckle and columbine as he chanted his roundelays to his lady, amid a gathering of bluebirds and to the song of the lark. Why then did the peasant leaders find so many followers so often in the peasant revolts? We ought not to allow ourselves to be made resentful of the present in which we live by these imaginings of a past that never existed.

In the work of no other American has the myth of community, set against the estrangement in our "mass societies," been so convincingly elaborated as in that of Robert Nisbet. In his major works, there is almost nothing of the experience of the United States. It is thrust aside, and he rests his argument primarily on the written ideas of a handful of Europeans of the early nineteenth century who were in reaction against the French Revolution. "Thirty years ago, while still a student at Berkeley, I came across the writings of the post-Revolutionary conservatives in Europe"; and from that experience and from no evident acquaintance with his own country, he has created one of the most powerful bodies of reactionary ideas in contemporary sociology. His writing is civilized, and it is exactly this that makes the import of what he is saying so influential and so deadly.

He does not bother with Jefferson, he troubles over de Bonald; he does not nourish himself on Madison, he sucks from de Maistre; he does not contend with Adams, he hovers over Tocqueville. There is nothing of the Declaration of Independence, or of the Constitution, or of the Bill of Rights, in his work; only the texts of a reactionary such as Lamennais, whimpering that the French Revolution had "marked the triumph over all social groups in France." (If one believes that, two hundred years later, one will believe anything.) He never asks, in answer to Lamennais, what the first of the revolutions, that of his own country, managed to accomplish, or consider with Crèvecoeur what is the American, the meaning of this new man, or ponders the new forms by which the dead forms of Europe have been replaced.

From the Europeans' lament over their dead forms, he echoes their curse against democracy: "our curse upon posterity is this"—this is Nisbet summarizing their views with approval—"However democratic society becomes, it will never seem democratic enough. . . . Over the whole wondrous achievement of modern technology and culture will hover the ghosts of community, membership, identity and certainty." From them he rescues the ideas which, he argues, ought to be the concern even of American society: "Such ideas as *status, cohesion, adjustment, function, norm, ritual, symbol* . . . , in the important sense that all these words are integral parts of the intellectual history of European conservatism." From all of this, he reaches his conclusion that "the only proper alternative to large-scale, mechanical political society are communities in scale but solid in structure," which will represent the old values of Europe: "hierarchy, community, tradition, authority, and the sacred sense of life."

If he wishes to restore all of these, in the forms which he postulates, one cannot help wondering how much of America would be left. Perhaps the answer is given most plainly in his exaltation of a class society, which would prevent "the rampant invasion of privacy and the erosion of individuality"; would "hold high the banner of intellectualism and cultural standards in our society"; would stand as "one of the most effective barriers against the spread of political demagogism, the lure of the charismatic power-seeker, and the inroads of mindless bureaucracy"; and would make possible a recovery of "the high periods of culture" of the past. This is a man in whom, as Macaulay again said of Southey, "what he calls his opinions are in fact merely his tastes"; and they are the tastes of someone who is inclined to judge the achievements of a society more by its high culture than by the general welfare of its citizens, the convenience and dignity of their lives.

He does not stand alone in his thesis. He says plainly what others put only tentatively. He is right in his statement that, "from an essentially minor position in the nineteenth century, conservatism has come to exert a profound influence upon the contemporary mind"[15]—except that he is speaking of a continental European conservatism, which has always been excessively concerned with the impact of the French Revolution, as if there can be no hope without the restoration of the traditional forms that it destroyed. The imagination of this European conservatism has never reached beyond the possibility of restoration. In the absence of the old communities of Europe, it has been unable to imagine a society that does not suffer from the atomization of the individual, on the one hand, or the homogenization of "the masses," on the other. It can imagine the individual as self-possessed only in the dead societies of its own past.

THE INDIVIDUAL BECOMES SELF-CONSCIOUS

One of the faults of this imagining, of the idea of community as it has travelled from Europe, is that the relationships between people are in danger of being regarded as more real and more significant than the people themselves. This was especially obvious, as Kenneth Minogue has said, in the medieval society, in which "neither the general character of man, nor the particular foibles of individual men, seemed of much political importance beside the political roles which birth determined. Political reality lay in the relationships, not in the individuals related."[16] In fact, we here come to a point that is crucial: in the societies of the past that are held up to our admiration, primitive or classical or medieval, the idea of the individual, to say nothing of his sense of his own identity, did not exist. It was not a matter of concern and it was certainly less a matter of concern than it is in our own societies which are supposed to be composed only of the "mass man," anonymous and unidentifiable.

"However independent or bold in practice," says Herbert J. Muller, "the classical Greeks had no clear theory about the individual, still no precise word for him, for the ego."[17] This was true even of the boasted citizenship of the ancient Greeks. The *polis* knew only citizens; it did not know the individual who was a citizen in only one of his expressions of himself. The citizen and the society and the state: they were all identified as one, whereas to us the state is one, the society is plural, and the citizens are individual. There was only one way in which the identification of them could be achieved: in the *polis,* as one modern interpreter of the Greek city-state has said, "man was a . . . creature bound up with the life of the state. . . . Willing service here, state compulsion there—the boundaries became confused."[18] The freedom that was enjoyed by the citizen of Athens was not the kind of freedom that we expect to enjoy as individuals, and neither was there any individual freedom in this sense, even for the privileged, in the society of the Middle Ages.

The distinction between the individual and his society, and between his society and the state, has been the work of the modern age, and not only is this double distinction most precious to us, there is no way in which we can properly understand either ourselves or our societies if we do not strenuously hold to it. When we talk of "the masses" in our "mass societies," we ought to be talking, first, of the individuals who compose them, each equal in his rights and in his claims on his society and, secondly, of the fact that their relations with their society are personal, not mediated by hierarchy or status, by guild or community, by church or even now by family. The relationships of the individual have ceased to be more important than himself. This is the positive gain of the modern age, of which we are the beneficiaries. If we have lost a sense of community, it is because we have gained a sense of the individual; and this is why the placing of the individual citizen in a direct relationship with his society is today so urgent a task.

The individuality that has seemed to the European to be so

threatened by "the masses" was, in fact, a kind of cultural variety; in particular, it was the individuality of a superior class, as Dewey remarked when he said that the "prized and vaunted individuality of European culture was a very limited affair," in which the peasant and the proletariat did not participate. At no time when the European idea was in the ascendant was there any possibility that this individuality would be conceived and realized as the self-evident and equal possession of all; neither in the French Revolution nor in the Russian Revolution was the individual as such a genuine concern, he was not brought to the fore.

Only in the American idea has there lain this double affirmation of the individuality of each, and of the equality of each with all: the idea of the I released in the En-Masse. The value of thus connecting the idea of the I with the idea of the En-Masse is that it prevents us from being satisfied with the conferment of freedom, in the language of Luther, only on the *homo internus;* it reminds us that the *homo externus* must be freed also, that the individuality of each is to be discovered, not only in his-self, but in his relations with the estate as a social being, and that, since these relationships are now personal, it is to the establishment of each personality in an equal relationship with his society that we must now give our closest attention.

FACE TO FACE WITH EACH OTHER

We can choose, if we will, to be overwhelmed by the size and the shapelessness of the En-Masse, to sigh that it is all too much, that the time has come to draw a line. No one is more anxious to keep out the new arrival than the man who himself has just arrived; and the revolt of the privileged today is his rebellion, "the masses" must be held back while he consolidates his position. But we can also, if we will, choose to concentrate our attention on the evidence of each I in our daily rounds of the estate, on the sureness with which each one is differentiated from any other, the uniqueness of each personality from day to day asserted in even the smallest encounter. It is a matter of habit, of accustoming our eyes and our ears and our imaginations to notice the individuality of each man and woman with whom we come into contact. There is no checkout girl, no mailman, no doctor's secretary, no receptionist, who ever greets us or deals with us in exactly the same way as does any other in the same occupation.

All that we have lost is the ease with which we once could place these individuals in terms of their status, the ranking of each in the hierarchy of his community and his class; now we have only each individual in himself, each of whom we have to place as himself. Fifty years ago we did not, by and large, have to ask why a clerk with whom we had to do business was a clerk, we knew that the explanation lay in the circumstances of his birth and his upbringing; today we are forced to ask why each clerk has remained a clerk, and our answer must be individual to him. Once we contemplate our neighbours in this manner, we find that we have to consider the potentiality that lies in each of them, and then to ask how much of that potentiality has not been realized as a result of the failure of our society to provide for its discovery and its fulfillment. In the En-Masse we are confronted by another I as its-self.

In the end, it is to this that the idea of "the masses" and the "mass society" may be reduced: just as the relations of the individual to his society are no longer mediated by a group, neither are the relations of one individual to any other individual; we are face to face with each other. This is what our art and our literature have understood, as it has in part been their doing; it is what Rilke meant when he said that the most significant revolution of our age was the change in the relations of one individual person to a second individual, that we are only now beginning to look upon these relationships "dispassionately and objectively,"[19] and that "our attempts to live such associations have no model before them" to assure us.

Amazingly, because it has never before been true in history, the individual who is self-conscious as an individual is the unit round which our societies must organize themselves. He is the man who finds his dignity, as it was put by George Herbert Mead, in the fact that, when he calls upon himself, he finds himself at home. If we are bound to imagine the individual in this manner, we are no less bound to reimagine our societies in such a way that he will be enabled to participate fully as an individual in the common life, so that each may know and feel that he is a citizen.

Our societies need the assurance that, when they call upon the individual, they also will find him at home. The uneasiness that we feel in our societies is that the individual does not know how to call upon them, and they do not know how to call upon the individual. There seems, so to speak, to be no appropriate etiquette by which the one can address the other, so that we go on vainly trying to restore the communities and hierarchies and classes of the past, or some simulacrum of them, in the hope that they will mediate, as once they did, between our societies and ourselves, and ourselves and others.

THE MODEL IN AMERICA

One is not denying the immensity of the challenge—to imagine and then to create a society in which the individual day by day negotiates with it as himself, and it day by day addresses him as an individual—but at least we have a model before us. Whatever its faults, the vast commonalty of the middle class of the United States is a society of individuals, in the sense that we are trying to imagine; it is here that most obviously the I has been released in the En-Masse, with no mediator between the two. The result is not yet rewarding to the individual, or satisfactory to society; but there can be no doubt that here is where the challenge may be met, that it is in "the paradise of the masses" that the I must be established, not only as an individual in his own right, but as fully a citizen.

It ought to be a boast, not a lament, that the example of the En-Masse is being spread by America to the rest of the world, with its power and its commerce. "We do indeed share a common culture," says Edgar Z. Friedenberg of the United States. "And the commonness goes further. American mass gratifications, from soft drinks to comic books and movies, have turned out to be the common coin of mass culture the world over. This is not conquest, but genuine cultural diffusion. All over the world, man in the mass has turned out to be exactly our type of fellow."[20] His point is correct, but the voice is familiar in its disaffection. As always, the emphasis is put only on the material manifestations—and these the grossest—of the culture that is being spread.

But it was again Dewey, whose voice is so sorely needed at this time, who invited us to look deeper and farther ahead:

. . . a peasantry and proletariat which have been released from intellectual bondage will for a time have its revenge. Because there is no magic in democracy to confer immediately the power of critical discrimination upon the masses . . . it does not follow that the ineptitude of the many is the creation of democracy.[21]

It is not only the wholesomeness of this voice, the lack of pettiness in its vision, to which we need to listen, but its truth. The idea of the revenge of "the masses" has been prominent in the literature, not least in the work of Ortega; but more than fifty years after Dewey wrote his careful words, the evidence is that the desire for revenge has been neither deep nor long-lasting.

The questioning of traditional standards has not proved to be the negation of all standards; the desire to replace has not proved to be an ambition to destroy; the claim of equality has not proved to be a denial of liberty. We have only to look around us in the public estate of America to see that the I released in the En-Masse is neither impatient nor placid, that even in so short a time, year by year, generation after generation, the search is being made for new forms to replace the dead forms of the past. Perhaps it requires an outsider to affirm that the commonalty of the middle class in America is experimental and invigorating and rich in promise, and that it needs only a further exercise of our imaginations to recover for it a sense of direction and a common understanding of its purpose.

There are "situations in social life—exceptional situations, to be sure—when it might be said that history is 'free,'" Francis D. Wormuth has said; "the resolution of a small group of leaders who can capture the revolutionary movement can turn it into a channel which it could not follow without their action."[22] This is a prescription for the kind of revolutionary action of a Lenin or a Mao or a Castro; and the answer of the United States must be, as it can be, that history is "free" in its society, not exceptionally, but habitually. It is free in this sense because it is the I who has been released as the main actor, never for long to be subdued even in the En-Masse; and it is to the condition of the individual in this En-Masse, as it is open to our inspection in the commonalty of the middle class of America, that we must now turn to find the causes of our disaffection.

PART VI

The Revolt of the Privileged

The doctrine that all men are equal is gradually being dropped, from its inherent absurdity, and we may at any time find it expedient to drop the jingle about a government of the people, by the people, and for the people.

—WILLIAM GRAHAM SUMNER, in *Folkways*[1]

CHAPTER 13

The Boundaries of Affluence

The idea of the "affluent society" has entered deeply into our imaginations, and not only in America; as we have seen, an American writer could even imagine that Britain was an affluent society in 1960—an image which seems more than a little inappropriate even a decade and a half later—and reacted to it with a puritanism that is not evident in the rest of her writing. To the outsider as he at first travels in America, the evidence of what appears to be affluence is even more striking; and it is a common theme. "This is not the first time in history that luxury appears as a phenomenon in society," wrote Marías in the late 1950s. "The difference is that this time luxury is majoritarian," which is an echo, of course, of his master's thesis that "the masses" have now arrived where only "the minorities" were once able to go. Marías even claimed to have uncovered what he called "the American beggar, the indigent American: he is not the man who has nothing, but rather the man who has everything, the one who lacks incentive. . . . But for these American needy, the spirit of charity has invented 'the newest model.' "[2]

But "the man who has everything" is a figure in the advertisements in magazines like *The New Yorker,* and his "luxury"—a word which illustrates how far the idea of the "affluent society" may be carried—is not that of the majority; no one has yet been able to demonstrate that the patrons of Tiffany's are majoritarian. Marías was probably reacting to another phenomenon. It is only in the last century or so that luxury has meant the ability to "have everything": the technology to make this possible was simply not there. The very rich man, until about a hundred years ago, lacked many conveniences; and the main advantage of the very rich man over those who were less wealthy was that he could hire an abundance of cheap labour to overcome the inconvenience. He can still hire labour when others cannot—this ability is one of the main attributes of wealth—even though what he now needs are likely to be special skills and not menial work.

THE LACK OF AFFLUENCE OF THE GREAT MAJORITY

The impression of affluence in the society as a whole is equally a result of technological invention, rather than of the spread of economic wealth. The services that are today available to the ordinary American householder would in ancient Rome have required the labour, it has been estimated, of several thousand slaves. To turn on a switch is to have the equivalent of slave labour at one's finger tips. A disposal unit is an alternative for the many to the slave labour that would once have carried out the garbage for the few. Only in this sense—the conveniences that have been made available by technology—is it legitimate to talk of the United States, or of the countries of Western Europe, as affluent societies. Technology has been the real equalizer.

Beyond that, it is a falsehood to say that the majority of the American people are affluent. At the beginning of the 1970s, the U. S. Bureau of Labor Statistics estimated that it required almost $11,000 to enable a family of four to live in an urban area for a year at what it called a "moderate living standard." At that time, the average income of an unskilled worker was only $6,866 a year; of a semi-skilled worker, only $7,915 a year; and of a highly skilled worker, only $9,627 a year. A majority of American families earned less than $9,000; and the median annual income of all families, *based on the income of all wage earners in a family,* was $8,632.

Let us use these figures as our base. If we accept $11,000 as providing a moderate standard of living, the very lowest figure at which we can begin to talk of affluence for a family of four in an urban area is that its total earnings should amount to at least $15,000 a year. (One deliberately chooses so low a figure to strengthen one's argument; in standard of living and way of life, such a family on such an income would not in fact be affluent.) Even on this basis, then, at the beginning of the 1970s, only about thirty million Americans—that is, about one seventh of the population—lived in families that annually earned $15,000 or more, and could therefore be called "affluent." What is more, most of these families were able to enjoy even this level of affluence only as a result of the multiple incomes of its various members; and the second paycheck was, in most cases, brought home by the wife. The image of the "affluent society" is already looking a little pale.

Let us put it another way. According to the same government study, a city worker, aged thirty-eight, with a wife and two children, had to work forty hours a week, for fifty-two weeks a year, at a wage rate of $4.50 an hour, if he was to earn the more than $10,000 which was needed in 1968 for a "modest but adequate standard of living"; to enjoy the same standard today, the wage rate would have to be substantially more than $5.00 an hour. But the gross average hourly earning in July 1973 in the manufacturing industries was only $4.07 and, if overtime was excluded, only $3.89. One is not suggesting, of course, that the American worker is not well-off when compared with his counterpart in the rest of the world; one is merely pointing out that even the highly paid worker in the automobile industry cannot be regarded as a member of the "affluent society"; and it is somewhat impudent to suggest that he does.

It is the seventh of the population, then, who live in families that earn more than $15,000 a year or more who can, by any stretch of the imagination, be regarded as affluent. Why, in that case, did the wholly misleading phrase "the affluent society" become immediately popular when John Kenneth Galbraith used it in 1958? At least part of the answer is that it was what the privileged, who are reasonably educated and buy books, wanted to hear. After all, when one says that such a phrase is popular, one means that it is popular only within a comparatively small group of people who read, and a larger group of people who pick up the gist of what other people are reading. In particular, the professional middle class had by 1958 been among the more obvious beneficiaries of the general prosperity of the country, rising in the ranks of the affluent, to enjoy a standard of comfort, and even of privilege, that has not obviously benefited their souls.

There was only one reference to poverty in *The Affluent Society;*

and the subject has not preoccupied Galbraith in the succeeding volumes of his scripture which he has published in the intervening years, revising and reinterpreting his views so regularly and with such conscientiousness that it is no longer possible to know which we should include in his canon and which we ought to count as his apocrypha. In the last of his testaments, *Economics and the Public Interest,* published in 1973, poverty is again not his concern, although he announces himself at the end of the book as a kind of socialist, with the kind of aplomb that one would have expected from Beau Brummell, if he had suddenly declared that henceforth he would adopt the attire of a sansculotte.

But it is not with poverty as such that we are concerned here, and especially not with the poverty of the disadvantaged groups. Our interest is in the commonalty of the middle class in America, and in the fact that the majority of this commonalty does not enjoy affluence. It may be well-off by the standards of the rest of the world; it is not affluent by any standards, and in particular by what American society has set up, and from day to day advertises, as decent standards of convenience and comfort and dignity, and above all of expectation.

One does not need to turn to statistics to make the point, but only to roam the country, and to live in it; to ride a bus, to shop at a Woolco or a Sears, a Safeway or a Montgomery Ward, at any ordinary department store or any plain drugstore; and one can observe this commonalty, not very well dressed, not obviously used to comfort or even convenience, anxious at the cost of each purchase, even of necessities. They certainly do not have everything: they are needy in a plainer sense, forced to scrimp with each dollar, as the poor are still forced to scrimp with every penny. Amidst the advertised affluence of their society, they are harassed by their own lack of affluence; and the sly justification of the revolt of the privileged is the pretence that this majority is equally the beneficiary of the nation's prosperity with themselves. The truth is more complicated and more disturbing.

THE ABSENCE OF A CLASS SYSTEM IN AMERICA

We must first address ourselves to a mystery: do classes or a class system exist in the United States and, if so, what is their character?

We can begin with a certainty. There is no class *system* in America; and what there is not in the United States is perhaps most easily explained by describing what there is in England. The class system is a preoccupation in England because it is a reality. The country is permeated by it, and it does not go away. J. D. B. Miller, a level-headed Australian political scientist, wrote in 1962; "The survival of a habit of deference to the wealthy and the well-educated, in spite of the advance of 'democracy,' is evident to most foreigners who visit England for the first time."[3]

It is not primarily—and this is sometimes hard to explain to Americans, who imagine no other measure—a matter of money. The upper class has maintained its position in England even when its pockets have been empty, which has been at least as often as when they have been full. Its estates have been plundered by monarchs, taxed by governments, improvidently neglected by prodigal sons, ruined by adventurers, but still as a class it remains; still the individual families manage to survive, to take precedence in society's ranking, and to enjoy the deference of the many. Not much of the substance is ever lost; the opportunity to recoup is granted by the deference of the society, and it is taken.

But important though these relics are, they are not in themselves what matters most. They are merely the most visible symbol of a society that knows no other way of arranging itself but by rank. The gardens of England are renowned, but what is less well known is that, such are the refinements of the class system, even flowers and shrubs, fruits and vegetables, are ranked by social class. To be a member of the Council of the Royal Horticultural Society is to have a badge of one's rank, but even that is not the top. "There is the gardening equivalent of the Royal Yacht Squadron," an inquiring sociologist has written, "an exclusive—and elusive—organization, known as the Gardens Club, which is almost unknown." Its members are the owners of the few large gardens that still exist; but the purchase of a well-known house with a famous garden "out of money made in quick property deals" would not be acceptable. The resistance of old wealth to new money, especially if that money has been made in "trade," is of course a part of its *noblesse oblige,* and has done much, it must be admitted, to temper the influence of capitalism.

But even among the various annual shows of fruits and flowers there is a social scale that cannot be upset. At first reading, the ranking of the superior and the inferior may be baffling, but in no madness is there more method than in the refinements of the class system in England:

1. The Royal Horticultural Society's Fruit and Vegetable Competition
2. The Rhododendron Show
3. The Camellia Show
4. The Daffodil Show
5. The Flowering Tree and Shrub Competition
6. The Alpine Garden Society's Show
7. The Orchid Show
8. The Rose Show
9. The Geranium Show
10. The Delphinium Show
11. The Dahlia Show
12. The Early Chrysanthemum Show
13. The Carnation Society's Shows (Pinks, Borders, and Perpetuals)
14. The Sweet Pea Show
15. The Late Chrysanthemum Show
16. The Cactus and Succulent Society's Show

"As a rough general rule," says John Street, "it can be stated that the social value of any flower is in inverse ratio to the amount of work in its successful cultivation," which is an almost perfect demonstration of one of the basic principles which was enunciated by Thorstein Veblen in his *Theory of the Leisure Class*.

But why, then, are fruits and vegetables, which need a lot of labour and which can be grown anywhere in England, at the top of the list? The answer is one of infinite subtlety: ". . . the shows held by the Royal Horticultural Society exclusively for fruit and vegetables are the last stronghold of the old regime, a world ruled by head gardeners. . . . The owners of the gardens seldom appear at the fruit and vegetable shows and . . . entries are always credited to the head gardener concerned." It has taken centuries to work out this intricate scaling. The cactus is easy to grow, for example, but it is at the bottom of the list because it does not need a garden, only a windowsill, and thus it is fixed in its station.[4]

This habit of ranking is the habit of a society as a whole. A few years ago, another sociologist made a study of the crews of British and American merchant ships, and he found, which can hardly have been a surprise, that the British crews were much more rigidly and intricately divided than the American crews. For example, on the British ships, the bosun and the carpenter ate with the engine-room supervisory men, or petty officers; but on the American ships the bosun and the carpenter and the petty officers ate with the able-bodied seamen and ordinary seamen, although usually at separate tables. The quality of food for seamen on the British ships was inferior to that enjoyed by officers; but the unions on American ships had already won the right to equal food for all, which is an extension of the Declaration of Independence that Jefferson cannot have foreseen. The British able-bodied seamen and ordinary seamen collected their meals from the cook, and after eating they did their own cleaning up; American able-bodied seamen and ordinary seamen were provided with a steward, who took the orders from the men, acted as waiter, and afterwards cleaned up the utensils and mess room. On the British ships only the officers had tablecloths; on the American ships tablecloths were provided for all hands. It need hardly be added, since it is in part the purpose of the whole system, that obedience on the British ships was more automatic.[5]

All of this amounts to a system—a class system such as does not exist in the United States—and this is why the commonness of a greeting like "Hi!" insignificant though it is in many respects, is nevertheless striking to an outsider. The cleaning woman or the shop girl in England may address one as "luv" or "dearie" or "ducks," but these are the badge of her class; not only does one not use them in reply, one does not use them at all. The familiarity on her part is a familiarity of deference.

The intricacy of the class system in England, and its rigidity, are maintained by many factors, but in particular by an educational system whose primary purpose is still to instruct only a limited number of those who are already, and those who have been recruited to be, members of the governing and educated classes; and by the cultivation in these classes of what used to be called the "Oxford accent" and later the "BBC accent," a manner of speech that is easy to distinguish from the speech of the majority of the population. It sets a few apart, as is its intention. The many in England are in effect ruled by a few who speak an alien tongue; they are literally—in their letters—in the position of barbarians, speaking a different language from that of the ruling minority who decide what language should correctly be spoken.

American speech is in contrast a democratic speech. It is in speech that the significance of regional and ethnic differences, compared with class differences, may be observed in the United States. Raymond Williams, the English social critic, observed in 1962 that "the most easily available alternative standard," to the class standards of the traditional culture in England, "is American or pseudo-American." This was especially true in the popular culture, where the American or pseudo-American accent of pop singers, for example, was "more acceptable, in many contexts, to a majority British audience than the traditional accent which once monopolized the BBC."[6] He could have added that this "American" accent is also more acceptable to the representatives and guardians of the minority traditional culture than would be an English accent of the traditional lower classes; and it has again been noticeable that in the decade that has followed even the most famous English rock groups have not sung in the speech of their class or even of their provinces, but have transmuted it into a kind of mid-Atlantic accent that is acceptable as classless.

One means something of this, putting it at its simplest, when one says that, with the jeans and the colas, the records and the dances, travels also an idea. The Americanness or pseudo-Americanness is in part a promise of release from the fixed station in life to which the majority are confined in a country such as England. The commonalty of the middle class in America is the only promise of a different future that is available: the only land to which they can "emigrate" even as they remain in their own country. Class in America, to whatever extent we find that in some form it exists, is not systematic. It is not an adequate, certainly not a complete, and therefore a misleading, explanation of the stratification of its society. The patterns of its society are not those of a system, but those of a kaleidoscope. Stand at any angle to English society, and the patterns of the class system are still dominant; change the angle at which one stands to American society, and the patterns of class are at once disturbed and rearranged into quite different patterns.

A UNIVERSAL AWARENESS OF DIFFERING NEEDS

But still the most important element is missing. "French and English working men," said Ferdinand Lassalle, the German socialist in the nineteenth century, "have to be shown how their miserable condition may be improved; but *you*"—he was addressing the workers of Germany—"have first to be shown that you are in a miserable condition. So long as you have a bad sausage and a glass of beer, you do not notice that you want anything"; and in a telling phrase he referred to "the accursed absence of needs."[7] Perhaps the most obvious characteristic of the American middle class is its common noticing of what it wants, what some would call the accursed presence of its needs. Needs are defined in a class society in terms of class; in America they are taken to be needs that are common to all individuals. That is how they are understood, even if they are not uniformly satisfied.

These needs are usually described as only materialistic. But the material improvement of human life, if it is genuinely an improvement, directed to the increase of comfort and convenience for the individual, is not something to be despised, especially by those who already enjoy these advantages and who, themselves well dressed, would hang the sackcloth on other shoulders. An increase in comfort and convenience is an increase in dignity and opportunity of choice; and these should not be disdained, especially when so few people in the world as yet enjoy them. They may not be the end of life, but they can be the beginning of a transformation of life. Who is it that we wish to keep in, or return to, the washhouse and scrub brush, pail and washing board, for all of their days?

It is a part of the revolt of the privileged to describe the "consumer society" in terms merely of the material benefits that are most visible and most easily measurable. This is particularly true in the denunciation of the "consumer society" that is given by Arendt. One of the faults of *The Human Condition*—which might be subtitled *A Guidebook to Attitudes Appropriate in an Elite*—is that she consistently presents what are social phenomena as if they had the same character as biological phenomena. Thus at one point she describes men's earning and spending as "only modifications of the twofold metabolism of the human body." Things "appear and disappear" daily; one consumes and evacuates. In this way, we are presented with a picture of people—the masses of the people—who want only to guzzle. But the parallel from biology is as crude as it is misleading.

It was in the societies of the past that rested on scarcity that consumption was merely biological for the majority of people, as it still is for the majority of people in many parts of the world. They did very little but stuff their bellies with roughage to "keep body and soul together" until the next day. They lived "from hand to mouth," and the effort to sustain merely biological life was intense. Increasingly in the "consumer society" it is the enjoyment, and not merely the consumption, of food that is becoming a vital concern. Eating is becoming for more and more people a matter of taste, of discrimination by the palate, to which the biological necessity is no longer the solitary concern. Even with food, the most combustible, as it is also the most biological, of the materials that we consume, consumption is ceasing to be the only determining consideration of the consumer.

In fact, one of the marks of the "consumer society" of "the masses" is the discovery by innumerable individuals of needs that are not primarily a function of the necessity to sustain their mere existence. The "durable consumer goods" on which the commonalty of the middle class in America is most anxious to spend its money are not really consumer goods at all. They are not *devoured,* as Arendt would put it, to sustain the life process for a day or an hour; they are *used* for years, to make possible a different kind of life. For all the talk of built-in obsolescence and new models, the vast majority of the middle class is not constantly replacing its refrigerators or its television sets or even its automobiles; and the enamelled refrigerator today is no more a consumer goods than the oak wardrobe was yesterday, or the car than the carriage.

What we find in America now is a universal awareness of differing needs, in contrast with the accursed absence of needs that still keeps too many people fixed in their stations, inert in their class, in other parts of the world. At the beginning of 1974, a coal miner in Wales, who had started working underground when he was fourteen years of age, and was still working underground at the age of fifty-one, was earning the equivalent of fifty dollars a week. The acceptance for so long of this level of wage may be traced directly to the absence of needs, to the lack of expectation that life can be different and more varied and better. In a class society, needs and expectations are not regarded as individual; when the coal miner in Wales tries to improve his condition, it is solely by trying to improve the condition of his group; he rises with it, staying within its well-defined boundaries, and by his place in it his needs and expectations and tastes are determined.

A society may be regarded as having no class system when any individual may imagine his needs and expectations and tastes as personal; and this is, even if in promise more than in performance, the distinguishing characteristic of the commonalty of the middle class in America. (After all, when we are talking of needs and expectations, we are talking of promise.) The contrast may again be pointed by returning to England, where there has been a long controversy about the supposed *embourgeoisment* of the "affluent worker," revealing that his condition is very different from that of his American counterpart.

John Goldthorpe and his collaborators were, in the fullest and most satisfying of the studies, able to demonstrate that, in spite of the increase in his earnings, the affluent worker in England is still "a worker," that he still regards himself as such; in short, that there are still "two nations," as Disraeli named them, in the one country. In particular, they were able to show that the high-paid (by the standards of England) industrial worker is still significantly separated in his attitudes and his manner of living and his relationships from the low-paid white-collar worker, who in merely economic terms is his equal, yet both in and out of work follows a different way of life. To the industrial worker, for example, his kin is still relatively prominent in his social life, and the place of the kin, if these are absent, "is taken, not by friends chosen from among the community at large, but rather by neighbours, roughly defined as persons within ten minutes' walk." In contrast, the white-collar worker has far more friends and acquaintances who are neither kin nor workmates nor nieghbours; socially, he is much more mobile.[8]

The picture of the affluent worker which we are given here is of a class which, as a class, has been able to improve its class conditions, but remains tightly bound as a class. There is a bond in the sense that changes in the way of life, and action to effect the changes, are both collective. As an individual, the worker does not move, socially or geographically, because he does not expect to move, and therefore does not feel the need. The distance of the "ten minutes' walk" is a social as well as a geographical symbol. Class is still the measure of men, the frame in which they congregate, from birth to death. This is the bond, powerful and constraining: that one is bound to one's workmates, bound to one's union, bound to one's neighbours, bound to one's kin, and above all, perhaps, bound to one's job; in short, bound within the ten minutes' walk.

This picture cannot be translated, without significant alteration, into American terms, even though there is enough in it that is recognizable in Pittsburgh or Detroit, say, to warn how easily, as it pursues the image as well as the reality of "the great, always self-renewing middle class as the matrix of society," America could ignore the growth of an increasingly rigid stratification within its own commonalty. Nevertheless, the awareness of individual needs, the existence of individual expectations, is sufficiently a characteristic of American society, and the satisfaction and fulfillment of them is achieved by a sufficiently large number of individuals, to make the model of a class system a singularly inappropriate way of trying to interpret its nature. The land of promise is, for the individual, sufficiently often a land of performance for us to distinguish it as unique, and as the example of the future.

MOBILITY IN AMERICA: GEOGRAPHICAL AND SOCIAL

Nowhere is the awareness of needs, the expectation of improvement, seen more clearly than in the mobility, geographical and social, that is so often noticed in American life. The geographical mobility is frequently misinterpreted. It is true that, when one travels to a strange city in the United States, checks into one's hotel room, and goes to the bar for a drink, one is as likely as not to sit next to an American who is about to move his family a thousand miles for the gain of a slightly higher income or a marginally better opportunity; he is there like a scout, while his family awaits his return—as they might have done for Daniel Boone—when he will beguile them with the assurance that the pasture is more lush beyond the horizon, and life can be fairer. But one does not meet this mobile American more than one would expect in a country that is the size of a continent.

Moreover, the talk of a "nation of strangers" is usually based on as misleading a figure as that, for every hundred people in the country, there are nineteen changes of residence in each year. Such a figure is impressive. But, in fact, of this nineteen per cent, two thirds move to a new house in the same county, and therefore are not making a dramatic alteration in their lives by settling among strangers; and one half are people who had already moved in the preceding year. For the most part, therefore, they do not move far, and they are often the same people who move. One was only mildly surprised to be introduced once to an American couple who moved twenty-five times in twenty-three years.

Nevertheless, the geographical mobility is a reality, especially in the sense that it is always a present possibility in a country in which movement is not regarded as extraordinary or even eccentric. Once again, however, the motive is usually described in terms only of material wants, and the material wants are not allowed to have anything but a material significance. But the desire to have a better job, or to live in a better neighbourhood, or to give one's children a better education, is not necessarily only a materialistic or a snobbish aspiration; and we will usually find that it is the privileged, already living in surroundings of their deliberate choice, where the schools are already good, and who have jobs that satisfy and reward them, who sniff at "the masses" when they search for the same advantages.

The geographical and social mobility of the commonalty of the middle class in America represents the expectation of ordinary people that they and their children may improve their lives by moving from the place and the station into which they were born; it is the very opposite of the image of "the ten minutes' walk." This has not been a common expectation of most people in the history of the world, not even in the industrialized countries of Western Europe, and insofar as it is growing in them it owes a great deal to the example of the United States. One is not denying that there are many stratifications within the American commonalty, but merely saying that the individual person may have a reasonable expectation that either he or his children will move about within it, each rising or falling as individuals, that the more mere existence of this expectation is an agitating force, and that it is fulfilled enough to be more than a popular delusion.

All of this is real in America. It is the boasted equality of opportunity of American society, which is held to be a sufficient answer to the demands for an equality of results. Its significance is no more to be underestimated than its achievements. It means of course that, since the social mobility is a matter of individual movement, the upward social mobility of some is accompanied by the downward social mobility of others. The larks may rise, there is little doubt of that; but the sparrows stay on the ground, or fall to it.

The effect of this two-way movement is astonishing. Initially at least, the outsider is surprised by the frequency with which members of a single family will be engaged in occupations that are socially as well as economically on a different level. It is common to encounter a family in which three brothers are employed in occupations, one of which is manual, the second is clerical, and the third is professional. He cannot deny the claims of such a society: although the inequalities in it are endemic, it is classless; although there is stratification, there is also individual movement on a scale that alters the character of the social stratification.

But, as he grows used to the society, and looks more thoroughly at the meaning of its achievement, he begins to wonder whether another dimension is not now needed. There can be no doubt that the commonalty of the middle class in America is a presentiment of the future for other societies. The movement of individuals within the commonalty, rather than the periodic adjustment of classes within a social order, is what the future will be like; and it will be a gain. Yet one thinks of the sparrow who falls to the ground, and of the lark who does not know that he is a lark and has not tried to rise. Moreover, what is lacking in it all is a social purpose; the achievement is personal; the commonalty has no sense of its own being, and certainly no sense of its direction. All the I's that have been released in the En-Masse, to rise or fall, seem to have no common recognition of each other, and to be joined in no common endeavour; and so they grow feckless.

THE GROWTH AND VINDICATION OF PRIVILEGE

The boundaries of the "affluent society" are not only as confined as we have noticed, there is evidence that they are being more tightly drawn than before, that it is in danger of becoming a society that excludes, rather than includes. The promise of affluence ought to be that it is shared: that, with the abolition of scarcity, the enjoyment of abundance is majoritarian, as Marías put it. But this is not what appears to be happening in America at the moment: the affluence that is so much remarked is creating a habit of privilege for the few, even within the commonalty.

It is not the affluence of the very rich, who are unostentatious in the use of their wealth. They do not employ, as did the aristocrats of Europe, craftsmen to gild their furniture and their carriages. Their private planes are like commercial planes; the fuselage is not inlaid with gold, the fabrics are not embroidered, nothing in them is carved or lacquered, embossed or tapestried. Even if their homes are hung with paintings, it is not art as "conspicuous waste" that they are displaying, but an investment which advertises their thrift; the Cézannes and Matisses hang on their walls like certificates of stocks and bonds. For the most part, the very rich in the United States use their fortunes only in order to maintain and increase their fortunes. Luxuriousness is not a habit in them, and they may even be said to have forfeited one of the few justifications of great wealth, that it is able and willing to waste money. The very rich in America are little more than their own safety deposit boxes. They are dull.

The affluence that is interesting is that of the thirty million people —the one seventh of the population, to put it at its very highest— who earn more than $15,000 a year: of those who have risen, or are rising, to the top within the commonalty of the middle class, not of those who have stepped beyond it. To the outsider at least, it is clear that there is growing, at this level, a rationalization and vindication of privilege, and a sullen tolerance of it by those who do not share it, that is wholly alien to the character and intent of American society. It is not the privilege of some new class; a theory of class is no more, perhaps even less, relevant than ever it was. It is the privilege of the aggregate of individuals who, with however many or few advantages they began, have moved upwards, separating themselves as they have risen from those they have left behind. Between the flight of the lark and the fluttering of the sparrow, the song of the one and the chirp of the other, the coincidence is year by year growing fainter.

This is a matter of one's own observation, of the conviction that has grown, as one has watched and listened, that the seventh of the population who may be described as affluent are increasingly, not only reaping the rewards of their success from society, but exacting from it privileges that amount to an expectation of deference to their needs of comfort and convenience, leisure and decoration. It is they who ride on the surfboards; and they ride on the great deep of "the masses." The revolt of the privileged is in part their rebellion against any claim or threat of "the masses" to follow where they have arrived. There are themselves and there are the rest; "gentlemen" and "players."

If the first inclination is to resist this interpretation, one has only to ask why it has been with such astonishment that the "blue collars" and the "hard hats" and "Middle America" have been discovered by the privileged in recent years, as if no one knew that they were still there? Not only have these been absent from as representative a liberal canon as the work of Galbraith; they are even absent from as allegedly radical a thesis as *The Coming Crisis of Western Sociology* by Alvin Gouldner. They have been written off by Herbert Marcuse, as they were slighted by the New Left; and the everyday concerns of the women among them have only a small corner in the imagination of Women's Liberation. The most convincing explanation is that the professional leadership of the middle class, which at one point felt itself firmly in alliance with the "average man," has now been separated from the commonalty by its privileged enjoyment of a different manner of life.

One of the reasons for the decline of public services in America, such as public transport, or the failure to develop them, such as a health service, or the increasing neglect of them, such as the public schools, is that the professional leadership of the middle class—the people who read and write and teach, who know how to act and how to use "the system"—are no longer dependent on them. For their way of life, they rely increasingly on private services; and the expanding demand for these services is met by what economists would call a low-wage force. But what is being ignored is the size of this force, which supplies the services, in comparison with the relatively small numbers of the professional and managerial elite, which consumes them. In effect, a large proportion of the employed population in the United States are servants to a new class of masters.

THE MANY WHO MUST LABOUR SO THAT THE FEW WILL NOT BE BORED

In sketches such as that given by Daniel Bell in *The Coming of Post-Industrial Society,* we read abstractly of the United States as "the first service economy . . . the only nation in the world in which the service sector accounts for more than half the total employment and more than half the Gross National Product." Already about 60 per cent of the population is employed in the provision of services; he predicts that by 1980 the figure will have risen to 70 per cent.[9] If we are not satisfied with abstractions, the most immediate question that suggests itself is: to whom will the 70 per cent of the population be supplying these services? To some extent, they will be supplying them to themselves, they will be exchanging services, whether these are gas stations, or banks, or schools, or hospitals, or just the services of the bureaucracy, federal and state and local. But we all know that these common services are only a part of the story; that the services are not equally distributed.

We have only to look around us in the United States to observe, year by year, the steady growth in the number of men and women who are engaged in the service of privileges to the one seventh of the population who are affluent enough to afford them. More and more, to take an example that is significant, even the unemployed graduate may be observed drifting into occupations that exist solely to provide for the comfort and amusement of the thirty million Americans whose affluence has made the anxious pursuit of their leisure a daily problem to them. Increasingly one has the impression of a country in which six sevenths of the population must labour so that one seventh will not be bored. The exaggeration is pardonable if it helps to emphasize that what is growing in the commonalty of the middle class in America is an acceptance of privilege, to be enjoyed, not only by the few who are very rich, but by a new managerial and professional elite.

Increasingly today the professional leadership of the middle class is itself privileged, separated from the commonalty for whose welfare it is responsible; and this is one reason why American society, which largely is the commonalty of its middle class, seems today to be without a bond, without any intent. It is the existence of this privilege inside the commonalty that Norah Sayre was describing in 1970, when she visited California: "Bombing down those great silky highways, in a souped-up Mustang, with electronic rock ribboning out of the radio, made three adults feel about twelve years old. . . . When you feel so extravagantly healthy, your own body seems more important than any world events. . . . Hence the surfers on the beaches seemed justified in their isolation, their ignorance of everything but the next wave. . . . The car makes it easy to see life as a movie: watching your own footage." We are back to the surfer as an image; and it is at this point that we are able to make an exact connection between the rebellion of the self, preoccupied with its body and the revolt of the privileged.

THE OCCUPATIONS OF THE UNPRIVILEGED

The inequality that is causing this separation is not only economic. It is now widely understood that the stratification of a society has at least as much to do with the kind of occupations in which its individual members are employed as with the size of their earnings from these occupations. There is evidence that, in the commonalty of the middle class in America, this stratification by occupation is becoming more rigid at a time when the general prosperity of the society should be making it more flexible. The privilege that is growing is not that which has always been enjoyed by great wealth, and against which there is no protection but punitive taxation against the accumulation of large fortunes; it is the privilege of an aggregate of individuals in certain occupations for which exceptional favours are now claimed, on no other basis than the nature of those occupations.

It is the condition of the unprivileged in the commonalty—that is, of its majority—that their work is to them little more than labour; that many of them are ready to surrender the remote possibility of work that they might find satisfying for the immediate reward of a job that offers a larger paycheck; that to many of them shift-working and systematic overtime are part of the pattern of their work, therefore dictating the pattern of their lives outside work; and that the large majority of them do not look forward to any advancement, they do not think in terms of a career.

The importance of this description is that it thrusts our attention away from the earning and spending of the worker—the "affluence" that he is supposed to enjoy—to the other constraints on his life, on his expectations of it, for himself and for his family. Affluence cannot be counted in terms only of dollars or pounds, of earning power and spending power; it is related to the manner of life by which the salary or wages are earned and in which they are spent, and to the opportunity to enjoy the kind of life that society as a whole can offer and which its members are nourished to expect. "To be able to work at and for what one most wants to do well should be gospel in our democracy," said Frank Lloyd Wright.[11] It is a gospel whose fulfillment is open to only a small minority of the commonalty.

It is worth putting side by side two quotations, separated by approximately sixty years. The first was issued by the International Harvester Corporation to its workers as a brochure, about 1912:

> I hear the whistle. I must hurry.
> I hear the five minute whistle.
> It is time to go into the shop.
> I take my check from the gate board
> 　and hang it on the department board.
> I change my clothes and get ready to work.
> The starting whistle blows.
> I eat my lunch.
> It is forbidden to eat until then.
> The whistle blows at five minutes of starting time.
> I get ready to go to work.
> I work until the whistle blows to quit.
> I leave my place nice and clean
> I put all my clothes in the locker.
> I must go home.

In 1971, the management of General Motors in La Grange, Illinois, issued the following instructions to the supervisory staff of the engine division:

> BELL TO BELL POLICY: It is the policy of the [electromotive] division that all employe[e]s be given work assignments such that all will be working effectively and efficiently during their scheduled working hours, except for the time required for

allowable personal considerations. EACH EMPLOYE WILL BE INSTRUCTED ON THE FOLLOWING POINTS: 1. Be at their work assignment at the start of the shift. 2. Be at their work assignment at the conclusion of their lunch period. 3. All employe[e]s will be effectively and efficiently at work until the bell of their scheduled lunch period and at the end of their scheduled shifts. 4. Employe[e]s are to work uninterrupted to the end of the scheduled shift. In the most instances, machines and area clean-up can be accomplished during periods of interrupted production prior to the last full hour of the shift.

As we know from the strike of workers at the General Motors plant at Lordstown, Ohio, not only do they resent such conditions, but they have developed their own ways of "bucking the system"; it is a preoccupation to them.

These are "affluent workers," even by American standards, and must be counted as part of the commonalty of the middle class; as much as any they regard themselves as installed in its way of life, to which they adhere. But the question may be approached also by contemplating the condition of the white-collar worker. Already by 1970 he outnumbered the blue-collar worker by five to four. The most notable fact about the white-collar worker is that he is "a worker," even a "wage worker," as Marx said, prophesying his advent. No one is more clearly a member of the commonalty of the middle class in America, yet economically he falls below— usually far below—the lowest level of affluence as we have defined it; the nature of his work, although it is not manual, is mechanical, and often it is menial; and his chances of getting ahead, making a career, although they are greater than those of the industrial worker, are still severely limited, especially for women.

Perhaps the only significant differences between him and the industrial worker lie in his out-of-work activity and companionships, and in his expectations for his children. It is here, in contrast with a society such as that of England, that the classlessness of America, the existence of its commonalty and the mobility of individuals, up or down, within it, may be most clearly observed. The refinements of upper-working and lower-middle and middle-middle in England are constraints on the life and the opportunities of the white-collar worker that do not exist in the United States to nearly the same extent.

Again our attention is being turned from considerations only of earning and spending to the terms of the employment and the nature of the occupation. As much as earning and spending, these must be taken into account before we talk of affluence. There must, if we are to regard a person as affluent, be at least some of the characteristics of self-employment, the opportunity in some way to choose the manner and the hours in which one works, and to some degree at least the chance of self-satisfaction in one's work, even within the demands of a large organization. Before we speak of an "affluent society," we must ensure that these conditions are satisfied for the majority of the population. For six sevenths of the population of the United States, the work that they do, or that they may expect to do when they leave high school or the university, is demeaning to them, in respect both of the terms of their employment and of the satisfactions it offers; they are not affluent.

THE THREAT OF "TWO NATIONS" IN AMERICA

A redistribution of wealth and income is of course a necessity; but that is not really where the thrust must be made, it is merely the ground from which the thrust must be prepared. In the commonalty of America at the moment, two different ways of work and life are being allowed to solidify, and one can foresee the day, if the effort is not made to restore the fluidity of the society, when the individuals who enjoy the one will not be able to communicate with those who endure the other.

Increasingly the few who are privileged seem, not only to have abdicated the responsibility for, but to be surrendering the hope of, educating the many to the enjoyment of their own advantages; and it could happen that, fifty years from now, six sevenths of the population will barely be able to read or write, beyond the minimum that will be necessary to survive in a modern society, to read a label, to address an envelope, to perform the mechanical tasks of their occupations, to complete their tax returns, and then to watch television, which the privileged one seventh has considerately provided for them. It is not inevitable; it could happen.

In this way, there could be created the reality of "the masses" to confirm the theory, the majority of the population being encouraged to consume, as long as they are willing to be governed; a gross national appetite fed by the gross national product, thus confirming also the theory of the "consumer society" by bringing it into existence. As has already been argued, neither of these theories is an accurate description of our modern societies as they now exist, or an adequate imagining of the kind of societies that they could be if they were hopefully and intelligently remade. But it would be equally a folly to deny that the possibility that they will be realized is present: that the great majority of the human race, having been released from the slavery of centuries, will now be enabled to exist only as a race of helots, and as helots to reproduce in whatever numbers the privileged determine is socially useful and environmentally practicable.

It is only to the United States that we can look for the recovery of its own idea: that each individual can be made equally a citizen of his society, to participate to the full in its life and culture, and to the full to accept his responsibility for its welfare and good governance. There is no other ambition that is worthy, or that today is even tolerable. Its realization can alone restore the commonalty that is the only alternative to the realization of "the masses"; it alone can overcome the divisions in the commonalty that are now hardening; and meet the bidding, as Mark Van Doren once put it, that "the necessity is not to produce a handful of masters; it is to produce as many masters as possible, even though this be millions."12

CHAPTER 14

Created Equal but Everywhere Unequal

Call it equality, call it justice, call it fairness: the issue is clear. Galbraith in *The Affluent Society* may have sniffed that "few things are more evident in modern social history than the decline in interest in inequality as an economic issue"; and he may even have been correct in saying this of economists or of Harvard. But almost from the day that he published these words, the inequalities in American society, political and social and economic, have been a dominant concern, and Zbigniew Brzezinski was perhaps nearer the truth when he said that "We have reached the stage in mankind's history where the passion for equality is a universal, self-conscious force."[1] Even this, however, is pejorative, carrying the implication that as a passion the aspiration is irrational.

It is more appropriate to say that the idea and the ideal of equality have become the dominant concern of democratic politics and political philosophy, because there is no longer any other political value that can be affirmed except within the framework of an egalitarian principle. In fact, we are here at the crux of the matter, at the meaning of the release of the I in the En-Masse in our times. We have to attempt nothing less than a restatement, suitable to our times, of the proposition in the American idea that "all men are created equal." Until this is done, the bond of American society will be weak, and the world will not hear from it.

The inequalities in men's attributes and their circumstances are clearly one of the facts of existence that we have to take into account in our daily rounds as well as our philosophies. But it is equally clear that we do not allow our perception of these inequalities to be the sole arbiter of our attitudes and our behaviour towards other men; these are governed at least as much by the fact that we perceive them also to be equal in one overriding aspect, that each human life has its own intrinsic value; and this perception is a "fact of existence," too, because without it our discourse and conduct as moral beings would cease. Indeed, the perception of each individual of his own intrinsic value depends on his perception of it in all other human beings.

We either all have an equal value, or none of us has any intelligible value. This is one reason why, as Isaiah Berlin has said, "Belief in equality . . . is a deep-rooted principle in human thought," and why he went on to attribute to it an absolute value: "Like all human ends, it cannot itself be defended or justified, for it is itself that which justifies other acts—means towards its realization."[2] Apprehension of this value has been the work of centuries; and its sheer persistence, as it has gathered its own justifications in our thought, and our increasing commitment to it in our practice, must tell us that we are dealing with an idea and an ideal without which men have found it difficult to imagine their common humanity, and each his own intrinsic value as a moral being.

A MODERN RESTATEMENT OF THE AMERICAN DECLARATION

If we are to restate the proposition of Jefferson, we must take our stand in our own age, on the evidence of our science. We must gaze and reflect on our genes. If we can no longer say with the Christian that we are all the children of god, and that in his fatherhood we are all equal, our science tells us something that is at least as interesting: that in each individual there is a unique genetic code, which never existed before in any other individual and which will never exist in any other individual again. Although it is not in that code that the whole of the self is to be found, it is there that we find the justification of the claim that each self is entitled to an equal respect. There is no way of contemplating the existence of that code, singular and unrepeatable in every Jack and every Jill, without according to each human being an equal intrinsic value; for, although the genotype is the source of the self in each of us, it is only an array of potentialities, and the development of these potentialities will depend to a great extent on the kind of environment which they encounter and with which they must negotiate.

By basing the claim to equality on the unique genetic code of each individual, we deal at one stroke with the difficulty that human beings are not equally endowed in their genesis. The uniqueness of the endowment of each man and woman means also the inequality of the endowment and its potentialities. It follows, therefore, that since it is to what is unique in each of them that we have to give equality of consideration, it must also be to what is unequal in them. Men's claim to equality is based on their uniqueness and therefore on their inequality; and in this apparent paradox is the key to the whole problem.

Let us begin our restatement: *all men are created equal because it is to what is unique and, therefore, unequal in each self that the equal consideration of all to each and each to all must be given.* But the full sweep of this statement will be recognized only if its implications are well understood: the equality of consideration that must be given to what is unique and unequal in every individual is thus given to the potentiality of every individual. At this, the proposition that all men are created equal comes alive for our times: each individuality, we are saying, has an equal right to realize the potentiality of its own genes; and once again we can see how closely the ideas of equality and of individuality are related, the meaning of the I in the En-Masse.

Once we speak of the potentiality of each individual, we know that we are in our own times. During the past century and a half, we have been vouchsafed by our art as well as our science—by all that we call our culture—revelation after revelation of the different compositions of every individuality, and of the different ways in which each may need to express itself, if it is to be fulfilled and to find contentment. This is the truth, as was acknowledged at the beginning, in the modern idea of the self, and it remains a truth in spite of all the exaggeration, all the wrongheadedness, all the foolishness, that has accompanied it. In understanding what has happened to us as a result of this new knowledge, we are only at the beginning of what Rilke called our "timid novitiate." But, as a result of the novitiate of these past decades, of which the experience of the past few years has only marked a new stage, we can today notice in people what we once did not see; we can see as people those to whose humanity we once were blind; and we give consideration to natures by which we were once affronted. These are gains, for humanity as a whole, and for each of us as individuals; for what we can now see in others, we may notice also in ourselves.

We may now add a rider to our restatement: *all men, being created equal, have an equal right to the realization of their own potentialities, to the extent that in the pursuit of this right they do not interfere with the similar and equal right of others.* When we have said that, the twin problems of what we mean by equality of opportunity (which is clearly not enough) and what we could ever mean by equality of results (which is clearly not attainable) are at once—not easy, by any means—but less intractable. To some extent, we can now do without both these phrases, which is the form in which the problem is usually posed, and substitute for them the enlivening thought of equality of realization.

What this means is that our societies must strive, so far as it is within their power, to ensure that each individual starts from an equal level of expectation: that they must then, as each individual sinks to the level of his own incompetence, strive to ensure that his incompetence is not the result of any extraneous factor which it is within their power to remove; and that they must finally, when each individual has found the level of his own incompetence, strive to ensure, so far as it is within their power, that he will there find the realization of his own potentiality as rewarding as does any other individual at his own level.

There is, for our times, no other concept that will suffice. That men are born equal, but are everywhere unequal, has become an affront to our sensibilities and our intelligences. The idea of the self, in spite of its distortions, is nevertheless an idea of which we cannot be rid. But it is an idea that desperately needs to have conferred on it some moral vindication, otherwise the selfhood that has been discovered will degenerate into self-centredness and self-indulgence, and so attenuated it will wither. In our-selves we are not of much interest, and we need a renewal of our moral sense that will turn us outward again. Morality is concern for others; and in the end the satisfaction of ourselves as moral beings can be found only in our concern for the strangers in our estate.

We urgently need a public philosophy that will persuade us again that all men are equal: not only in their situation, that they are all domiciled for their lives in an estate that they share; but each in his right to the full development of his personality, the realization of his potentiality in the self that he may become. There is no way in which the individual claim to this realization can be made without making it for all individuals. This is the profound meaning of the I released in the En-Masse; this must be the working out of the American idea in our time, in the third century in which it is carried restlessly to the world, still agitating us in our complacency, still loosing the bonds of men, still freeing us from all narrow walls. The truth that was so daringly proposed in the Declaration of Independence is a truth for which the evidence is now irrefutable. The self that has been described to us by our science, and reimagined for us in our literature and our art, is not something we can shed; but it needs to be given a sense of its society, of its companionship with all the selves that are other than it, all of them unequally endowed but each endowed with the demonstrable right to equal consideration.

THE REDRESS OF INEQUALITY

"Natural inequalities are not beyond all remedy," John Rees has said in his essay on equality; and he points out that some people who are born with defects "can be provided with artificial aids which enable them to overcome, largely or partially, their natural disadvantages."[3] Increasingly other artificial methods, such as surgery, can be used to alter what hitherto we have had to assume were our natural properties. We can now give life, and not merely an existence of frustration and harassment and futility, to the deaf and the dumb; we know now how to find the intelligence in the child whom we once set apart from his fellows as the village idiot, and to release it; we are now able to acknowledge the worth in the woman whom once we burned as a witch, and to allow it its fulfillment. No longer do we automatically accept what appears to be the natural condition of any individual, for we know that his natural condition is only the preface to the development of his whole and cultured personality. This is the work of our estate, and of the individual in his negotiations with it; and, just as we can remake our societies to any purpose we intend, so we can determine, if we will, that we will remake them in such a way that each individual is nourished and stimulated to find within them the fullest expression of his-self.

The life of every individual in the estate must be imagined as a continual process of education. The ideal is the growth of each person, and this ideal of growth, in the words of Dewey, results in "the conception that education is a constant reorganizing or reconstructing of experience." This transformation of the quality of experience is not confined to any single period of life:

Infancy, youth, adult life—all stand on the same educative level in the sense that what is really *learned* at any and every stage of experience constitutes the value of that experience, and in the sense that it is the chief business of life at every point to make living thus contribute to an enrichment of its own perceptible meaning.

The purpose is, not merely to add to the meaning of any immediate experience, but to increase the "ability to direct the course of subsequent experience."[4]

In its widest sense, then, the purpose of this lifelong process of education, and not merely of schools or universities, must be what Alfred North Whitehead called "creating the future": the creation by the individual of his own future within his society, and all assisting in the re-creation of the future of the society. If this is the purpose of education, the messages that it carries must be revolutionary, for what they will open to each individual, and to the whole of society, as Edmund D. Pellegrino put it, is "the secret of what knowledge and reason can do to make life more human"[5]: a statement that was made at a Benedictine College in 1971, and reprinted in the *American Benedictine Review* in 1972, a reminder of how deeply into Roman Catholic thought in recent years has gone the awareness of the new humanism that men and women are "the artisans and authors" of their cultures and their communities.

We must act in the belief, which year by year is confirmed by our science, that there is no man and no woman who cannot be educated to the reconstruction and reorganization of his experience, so that he may create his own future and assist in the re-creation of the future of his society, in order to make life more human for himself and for his companions. He is not subjected, from the day of his birth, only to natural stimuli. "The savage deals largely with crude stimuli," as Dewey again said; "we have *weighted* stimuli."[6] In knowing that, we know also that we can alter the weighting. At the present moment, the vast majority of the people of the world are subjected only to crude stimuli. The power to change this is in our hands, and the inspiration to change it has been in the American idea from the beginning.

Its bidding to us is that we should, wherever it is possible, seek to redress the disadvantages with which an individual is born, and those of the environment into which he is born. We are aware, for example, that the influence of the home and the parents is significant in the development of the child. To underline the point a few years ago, two enterprising sociologists in England examined the differences in the kind of toys that were available to the child in middle-class and working-class homes, and in the purposes for which they were intended. Their conclusions were hardly surprising, but they were a reminder, which sometimes is necessary, of the disadvantages in their early environment to which many children are subject. For the working-class child, even before it goes to infant school, "a whole order of potential learning may not be available"; and the middle-class child also enjoys the benefit of a continuity between his learning at home and his learning at school.[7] This is not a matter of the willingness or unwillingness of the individual parent to care for the child; it is a matter of an entire social environment in which the parent has been, and the child is also to be, raised.

If the difference in upbringing were individual, caused by the particular aspirations that one parent has for his child in contrast to those of a second parent, then perhaps we ought not to take exceptional measures to compensate for them, even if we could. But a great part of the inequality of opportunity from which many children suffer in their upbringing is not individual, it is social, and "it is the office of the school environment," as Dewey said, "to balance the various elements in the social environment, and to see to it that each individual gets an opportunity to escape from the limitations of the social group in which he was born, and to come in living contact with a broader environment."[8] This is the "principle of redress" which has been so forcefully described by John Rawls in *A Theory of Justice:* "the principle that undeserved inequalities call for redress; and since inequalities of birth and natural endowment are undeserved, these inequalities are to be somehow compensated for. Thus the principle holds that, in order to treat all persons equally, to provide genuine equality of opportunity, society must give more attention to those with fewer native assets and to those born into the less favorable social positions."[9] No prescription for the working out of the American idea in our times is more commanding.

THE UNTRIED EXPERIMENT

The tremendous American experiment in universal public education is today under a severe intellectual attack; and we may be satisfied to begin with the response, made some years ago of Robert M. Hutchins, one of the greatest as he was also one of the most American of educators in this century. He admitted that universal education might be accompanied by "superficiality and mediocrity," producing "an educational system largely devoid of content, emphasizing time spent, amounts memorized, credits acquired, and certificates, diplomas, and degrees received." But he went on: "It is impossible to tell whether the attempt to educate everybody can succeed. It has never been tried. In the United States, the attempt has been made, not to educate everybody, but to get everybody into school and keep him there as long as possible."[10]

It has not been tried. There can be no real success in the experiment in public education, proclaimed Dewey again, "until the democratic criterion of the intrinsic significance of every growing experience is recognized." This has to be the insistent voice of the American as he confronts the meaning of the I released in the En-Masse. A democracy must make the effort to educate all its citizens, because it has substituted for external authority the "voluntary disposition" of its members; because it is not only a form of government, but "primarily a mode of associated living," in which the area of shared concerns and communicated experiences must constantly be enriched by "the liberation of a greater diversity of [the] personal capacities" of each individual.[11] In the search for the equality of all, our attention is bent once again to the particularity of each: this is again the American rope that is always in tension.

Peter Viereck, one of the few of the breed of American conservatives whose mind is civilized, once observed that, if democracy was to be acceptable at all, it could only be by making of each of its citizens an aristocrat.[12] Mark Van Doren, an American liberal who was writing about the same time, said that a liberal education in the modern world "must aim at the generosity of nature, must work to make the aristocrat, the man of grace, as numerous as fate allows."[13] But it is the generosity of these natures, conservative and liberal, that is absent from so much of the discourse in the United States at the moment, as it ponders, not the I in the En-Masse, but only "the masses."

Nowhere did this generosity of imagination, of concern for the quality of each individual, receive a truer expression than in the famous Harvard Committee Report of 1945 on *General Education in a Free Society,* a perfect example of the kind of spirit by which the professional middle class was inspired at that time. "There are two aspects of American education," said its authors, which reflect "two characteristic facets of democracy: the one, its creativity, sprung from the self-trust of its members, the other, its exposure to discord and even to fundamental divergences of standards precisely because of this creativity." The second of these two facets means that education is "conceived as education for an informed responsible life in our society": that, while seeking to "help young persons to fulfill the unique, particular functions in life which it is in them to fulfill"—*there is the I*—it must also seek to "fit them in so far as it can for those common spheres which . . . they will share with others"—*there is the En-Masse.* The purpose of a general education is "the preparation for life in the broadest sense of completeness as a human being rather than in the narrower sense of competence in a particular lot."[14]

The banality to which this idea of educating everybody may be reduced was demonstrated, at that time, in the enthusiasm, not least of Mark Van Doren himself, for what was then called "liberal education" in general, and in particular for the programme of "Great Books," to which serried monuments may still be found, gathering dust, on the shelves of many middle-class homes in the United States. The great minds of our civilization were to be commanded to yield their secrets and their pride in a rapid perusal and desultory discussion of less than a hundred and fifty of their more obvious works. It was an adventure at which Don Quixote might have faltered: the mind of the "common man" was to be made to blossom with seed packets of knowledge, summarized in a "Synopticon."

Beside the hundred and fifty works in the list of St. John's College, there were the hundred works proposed by Robert Hutchins. In the Middle West in particular, the enthusiasm spread. By 1946, the Hutchins list was being read and discussed in fortnightly seminars by more than two thousand people in Indianapolis alone, and by an almost equal number of people in other towns of Indiana. "It certainly looked like some kind of dawn," commented an observer at the time. But by the beginning of 1948 at least five of the Indianapolis groups had dissolved; and six of the seminars in the rest of the state had evaporated. The same was happening in the remainder of the country; the idea was dead.

The idea can be mocked, and it ought to be criticized. There was something that was madcap about the lists. As he scanned them at the time, Alexander Meiklejohn asked of the works that were proposed two unanswerable questions: "Why so many? Why so few?"[15] Yet there is a moment at which our mockery and our criticism must give way to other reflections. The inspiration was genuine, and even today it is a reminder of the confidence in its own values which, as was said at the beginning, the professional middle class in the United States has lost since 1945. The separation of the "intelligent man" from the "common man" in the vast commonalty of the United States was not contemplated. In spite of the sentimentality of the liberalism of Van Doren and his collaborators, one must in the end incline to their hope, without prejudice and without jaundice: "to secure that human beings shall be precisely and permanently human. . . . The main thing is that there are powers within the person which liberal education, and only liberal education, can free him to use . . . not merely to know or do, and there can be no compromise with the proposition"[16]; and so the faith is recited.

American or otherwise, we feel arch today if we repeat such a creed, yet we need at least something of it if we are to restore our care for other men in our estate; we need to discover again our shared concerns even at the deepest level of our culture, believing that there are none to whom its messages cannot be communicated. "Democracy cannot flourish," as Dewey affirmed, "where the chief influences in selecting subject matter of instruction are utilitarian ends narrowly conceived for the masses, and, for the higher education of the few, the traditions of a specialized cultivated class."[17] We cannot release the I in the En-Masse, and then rob most of the I's of the very opportunities to know their heritage and their culture that their release was meant to offer, confining the enjoyment of these to only a few who are privileged in talent and in circumstance, and are bent to keep their privilege.

Yet it is exactly this kind of separation that is taking place year by year in American education, and year by year growing more rigid. The true education that must be given to all cannot be done with a hundred and fifty Great Books; except in a few individual cases, it will not be done in a generation. But it must be the social ideal of a democracy that it can in time, by the higher education of everybody, so widen the area of shared concerns and communicated experiences that the I released in the *equality* of the En-Masse can recognize his or her own *quality* and acknowledge that of others. The conflict between equality and quality will be a genuine one only so long as the education, in the widest and truest of its meanings, of the commonalty of the people is not attempted. For it has not yet been tried; and neither has equality been tried, never in the history of man.

CREATING AN ELITE

The attack on the principle of universal public education in the United States began to gather its strength only when it was extended, beyond the grade school and beyond the high school, to the universities; and it is an attack, of course, by a privileged elite who think that the universities should exist for them and their pursuits. "Nor will any trace of virtue—honor—of an original idea be found in the avoirdupois of our stupendous mass-education," said Frank Lloyd Wright in a comparatively early protest in 1949. "By its capacious ministry, insignificance becomes dear to the common herd and true significance disturbing to authority." But it is worth listening in more detail to his complaint, in which he talks of "standardized mimicry" and "overgrown knowledge factories," and concludes that "wholesale barter of freedom for intellectual slavery is what we are calling "higher education.' "[18] He is at least right in his last point: what we are *calling* higher education. Much of it in the United States, and in other countries to which the idea is spreading, does not deserve the name. But this is not the fault of the aspiration; it is the fault of the lack of imagination and effort in its execution. More than any other form of educating everybody, it is the higher education of all that has not been tried.

This confusion of the aspiration with its execution needs to be removed, because it is at this point that a legitimate criticism of the *kind* of higher education that is being given is transformed into an illegitimate claim that higher education *as such* should be the privilege of only a few. One of the foremost educators in England once spoke wryly of the American experiment: "Anyone who has completed a high school course may claim admission to some university or other. The degree course is an obstacle race to all competitors who care to enter it. . . . There are prizes in the form of degrees for over half the competitors." But the wryness vanishes when he drives home the contrast: "In Britain we follow an entirely different policy. . . . By the age of twelve the door to full-time higher education is all but closed to eighty out of a hundred schoolchildren. The remaining twenty per cent are selected for specialized privileged schooling which brings them to the gates of colleges and universities, but only about eight of the twenty get in." The contrast is familiar, but he points it well; and what he is discussing is "investment in man."[19]

The attack on universal higher education which is developing in the United States today has as its immediate, even if covert, purpose the reproduction of the English system in America. When the report of the Harvard Committee was issued in 1945, F. O. Matthiessen observed that "Harvard wants to join America"; thirty years later, the elitism of many of the voices that may now be heard from Harvard gives the impression that it is ready—perhaps on the Bicentennial?—to leave America, to make the recrossing to Europe, to turn the prows of the three caravels back to the high castles. It has been called a retreat from education; properly it is a retreat from the idea of equality in education, the idea that education can, and ought to be, used as an equalizer.

For the moment it is enough to say that all of the prescriptions for abandoning the idea can have but one outcome: the creation of what Daniel Bell openly admits—advertises, boasts—would be a meritocracy. His definitions have the coldness of a shackle that is at last to be fastened on the spirit of America:

> A meritocracy is made up of those who have earned their authority. An unjust meritocracy is one which makes these distinctions invidious and demeans those below. . . . The meritocracy, in the best meaning of that word, is made up of those worthy of praise. They are the men who are best in their field, as judged by their peers. A society that does not have its best men at the head of its leading institutions is a sociological and moral absurdity. . . . a well-tempered meritocracy can be a society, not of equals but of the just.[20]

A meritocracy of the "best men" as judged by "their peers" is to rule "those below" in a society that is composed "not of equals": these are hardly the ideas by which it was hoped that the chains of the world might be loosed.

What we are never told by these new elitists is how the "best men" are to be discovered, so that they may be chosen. (Would they think of looking in the bullrushes, or in a manger?) Soon after the Second World War, the classes at Harvard University itself were almost equally composed of students from private schools and those from public schools; yet of sixty students in the classes of 1957 and 1958 who graduated *summa cum laude* forty-seven were from public schools, and of the three hundred and forty-four students who graduated either *summa cum laude* or *magna cum laude* two hundred and forty-four had also come from public schools. It is worth considering these figures—from a time, not so long ago, before the admissions policies of universities had become politicized and controversial—for only a few years earlier many of these students who did so well at Harvard would not have been admitted, and one may therefore put more precisely the question: How do we know who is capable or incapable of benefiting from a university education of high quality?

It is true that the public schools in the United States are today labouring under peculiar difficulties, that they are ill equipped to prepare many of their students for the university, and that many of the students who arrive at the universities are poorly nourished to take advantage of a higher education. But no one who has spent any considerable length of time with these students, at a state university of high standing, can doubt that the fault is not in them. Their minds are lively, their curiosity is eager, their intelligence is marked, their independence has a flair; but they have difficulty in learning because they have simply not been properly taught before they have come there. He must be a man of hardening prejudices and a jaundiced estimate of the potentiality of each individual who cannot see the promise in them, and aver that the promise has been betrayed.

A NATION OF HELOTS OR CITIZENS

By placing the education that we receive at school and university in the framework of the wider education that we receive in the course of our lives, Dewey helps us to understand why the principle of equality in schooling has become a ruling one in our age. What we learn in our total education—in the process of socialization in which our circumstances and our family and our environment each plays so large a part—is bound to be unequal and, although some of the inequalities, such as poverty, could and should be removed, it will remain so. What we learn in our schooling, on the other hand, can and should be used to redress at least some of the inequalities in our total education, just as it can and should be used to redress at least some of the inequalities in our genetic endowment and our initial social circumstances. This is why, if there is a retreat from education—and Christopher Jencks's talk of the school as a marginal institution would seem to be part of one—it is also a retreat from the idea and ideal of equality.

The most obvious difficulty in the principle of redress—and it is both a logical and a practical one—is the danger of defying one's own principle by giving unequal treatment to those who are favourably endowed or circumstanced. Much is made of this by both Bell and Jencks, as when Jencks—and his influence on public policy is important—pursues it to its logical conclusion:

If, for example, some students have more trouble learning to read, this strategy implies that the teacher should ignore the fast readers and give the slow learners extra help. Taken to its logical conclusion, this strategy would imply that anyone who was reading above the norm for his age should be sent home, and the entire resources of the school devoted to laggards.[21]

To argue thus, by a *reductio ad absurdum,* is of course no argument at all. There is no reason why our wealthy societies—America in particular—should not provide simultaneously the teaching that is appropriate to all and each.

But the difficulty that is presented by the principle of redress can be met in another way. Let us return to the proposition that men's claim to equality is based on their inequalities, that each individuality has an equal right to the realization of the unique and unequal potentialities of its own nature. Inequalities must be redressed, in other words, by making the effort, not only to correct them, but to cater to them: we should try to remove the effects of some, but to give equal consideration, including encouragement, to others. This has been the justification of all the experimental movements in education which have been so fertile in the past century, and which, in the United States at least, owe so much of their inspiration to a reading but also a misreading of the works of Dewey. Many of them have been dotty; one has a deep suspicion, for example, of unstructured curricula and teaching; in some forms they imply such a catering to inequalities of endowment that they in fact confirm them, by assuming too easily that there are some people who are not capable of certain activities, especially of intellectual activity; play and therapy too often take the place of teaching and learning. Nevertheless, the experimental movements have reflected our new awareness of the differing potentialities of every individual, and the traditional schools are still absorbing what has been of value in them to their obvious benefit.

To "help young persons fulfill the unique, particular functions in life which it is in them to fulfill" is at the heart of the idea and the ideal of equality, and schooling must be one of the ways in which we seek deliberately to do this. If it is impossible to claim that schooling is of equal value to everyone, there is no way of determining in what way it is of unequal value that can be made the basis of an educational policy. We must stick to the fact, which once was unquestioned except by the most candid defenders of privilege, that schooling is one of the few social institutions, and is the most important, by which we can try to redress the undeserved inequalities in people's circumstances.

If we turn to the second task of fitting people "for those common spheres which they will share with others," the case for equality, and for maintaining the creation of equality as one of the objects of schooling, is just as strong; for there is no way of making sense of this second task without saying that the purpose is to fit people *equally* for the sharing of their common spheres. They must be enabled, so far as it is possible, to address each other in those spheres —in the commonalty—with an equality of consideration; there must be a continual and equal exchange of deference between one human being and a second individual; and no such equality is possible unless each individual perceives himself to be equal with all other individuals, and all other individuals perceive him as equal with them. This is the social bond that is required by our democratic societies, and especially by the commonalty of America.

The traditional faith in public education in the United States is being lost; if lost, there is no institution of equivalent value by which it could be replaced. In the past, the public school was shared and trusted by the commonalty of Americans; and no consequence of the revolt of the privileged has so far been more harmful than this willingness to let the public school system of the country, from the grade school to the university, slide more and more steadily into purposelessness, inefficiency, weariness, and disrepute. "If a nation expects to be ignorant and free," wrote Jefferson in a famous letter in 1816, "in a state of civilization, it expects what never was and never will be." His bidding is even more urgent today, when the I has already been released in the En-Masse. He can be left ignorant and careless of his society, educated neither to cope with it nor to love it, no more than a helot; or he can be brought, each and all, fully into the estate, fully a citizen, and the United States again will find its common pride in its stubborn citizen heart.

CHAPTER 15

Fixing People in Their Station

We must take our stand on the unique genetic code of each individual, because there is no other way of stating, in terms appropriate to our age, that each individual has a soul. But, having done so, it ceases to be interesting. As Howard Higman has said, what is important about heredity is, not that it does not exist, but that it is dull. The basketball player may owe a lot to his exceptional height, which he has inherited, but it is not his height that we go to watch; we are entertained by the exceptional skill with which he uses his height, and that is acquired. The unusual height of John Kenneth Galbraith has not made him a basketball player; he has acquired other forms of agility by which we are entertained, to which his inherited physical height is irrelevant, and which the rest of his heredity only in part explains. He might well have been raised in an environment in which he did become a basketball player, but he was not. When at last a man's life is done, we do not inscribe on a gravestone our memories of his inherited characteristics, which are uninteresting, but our remembrance of his acquired qualities, for it was by them that we singled him out as an individual.

Our realization that what we acquire is more interesting than what we are born with owes much to the idea of culture as it has developed in this century; and "the idea of culture, simply put, is that there is a design or pattern which one learns after he emerges from the womb. That is the main point, he learns it after he is born." The important question therefore becomes: "Who gets to learn what?" This is why we have in the past hundred and fifty years attached a large importance to education, and why the questioning of the significance of education is today at the heart of the reaction against "the masses." We are being invited to lean more heavily on the inequality of the genes at the beginning than on their adaptation by education and socialization after birth. This is also the danger of the recurring emphasis on "what we are in ourselves"; it can too easily be made to mean only "what we are born with," and in this way the question "Who gets to learn what?" is neglected.

THE SYSTEMATIC RETARDATION OF MINORITY GROUPS

The systematic retardation to which many of the children of minority groups are subjected, as a result of being poorly taught or learning the wrong things, has been vividly described by Higman as a result of the work with which he has been associated on the Pine Ridge reservation of the Oglala Sioux. "At the ages of three, four, five," the Indian children and the white children on the reservation "are all interchangeable and exciting and wonderful"; then the Indian children enter the first grade of the white school, and "find themselves missing from their books"; the abstractions which they must learn to handle they have customarily heard expressed "in the chatter of their Lakota-speaking parents, but we will not allow them to speak Lakota in school"; they enter the third grade, and learn "that Columbus discovered them in 1492"; by the fifth grade, they are coming home from school and saying, "When I grow up, I'm going to be a cowboy"; in the ninth grade "they start to drink heavily"; in the twelfth grade, "we find the highest suicide rate of which we have a record."[1] It was not in their genes that this must happen; it was the result of what they had learned.

More than seventy years ago there was an unforgettable little story recorded in the *American Journal of Sociology*. "The attention of a friend of mine was once called," wrote the author, "to a singularly bright and attractive little coloured boy. He sighed and said: 'Yes, the boy will continue to be clever until he finds out that he is black.'" He was born black, but the disadvantage that he suffered was not genetic, it was environmental. In the same way, Virginia

Woolf, in the long footnotes at the end of *Three Guineas,* set out quotation after quotation from the memoirs of Victorian women which are no more than screams of pain at their discovery at a certain age that they were not, as women, allowed to be clever. The answer to the question "Who gets to learn what?" was for them negative.

We have all, in fact, something to learn from Women's Liberation, the sense in the movement and not the nonsense. As has been pointed out earlier in this book, the fundamental point that is made by Women's Liberation is that what is most interesting and most significant in women as in men is, not their biological equipment, not their inherited traits, but their learned behaviour; and this is the genuine truth that lies in the "liberation" movements of our time. Women's Liberation is opposing a genetic view of our personalities; it is the relics of a "genetic society" that they are challenging. That is why some of their rhetoric, which at first seems to be exaggerated, proves on examination to be justified. The relegation of women to an inferior position in our societies can justifiably be described as a form of what we call "racism," because what we understand by racism is no more than a genetic view of the human personality.

"Social roles are learned phenomena," said Wilma Scott Heide in 1970 before the Senate Judiciary Committee. "Home-making and child-care are learned social roles without biological imperatives as to who performs them." In the terms of the understanding of our human nature that we have by now acquired, her statement is irrefutable. We cannot ignore our genesis, as some of the more radical wings of Women's Liberation seem inclined to do. But equally we cannot take what is irrelevant in our genesis and artificially make it significant. In the words of Leo Kanowitz:

As long as organized legal systems . . . continue to differentiate sharply, in treatment or in words, between men and women on the basis of irrelevant and artificially created distinctions, the likelihood of men and women coming to regard one another primarily as fellow human beings and only secondarily as representatives of another sex will continue to be remote. When men and women are prevented from recognizing one another's essential humanity by sexual prejudices, nourished by legal as well as social institutions, society as a whole remains less than it could otherwise become.[2]

The real significance of Women's Liberation—illuminatingly preceded by Black Liberation, making the same point—is its assertion that the differences in our genes as individuals, which are natural and relevant, cannot be a justification for creating distinctions in our estate that are irrelevant and artificial. That is all, a plain statement of our commonplace view of our human natures, yet it must even now struggle to be accepted.

THE ARTFUL SUPPORT OF PRIVILEGE BY A COMPUTERIZED SOCIOLOGY

What is at risk in the genetic view of human personality is our historic sense of ourselves in our societies; and it is only in this sense of our historical existences that we can, in the words of Saul Bellow, "defend the possibilities of the present," choosing to make our lives in our estate more tolerable, with an assurance of "happiness not extinct, hope not unjustified." The genetic view is precisely a denial of our historical existence; we are to be allowed no narrative, nothing of any fundamental importance happens to us after we are born. The renewed emphasis that is being given to the genetic contribution to our intelligences is, or can be made, a direct refusal of "the possibilities of the present"; we are what we are born with, and with that we are fixed, stationary and passive, in the situation to which it has pleased god to call us in this life. This may not be the intended consequence, but it is the logical conclusion, of the present exploration of the genetic element in our intelligence quotients; and it needs to be fought, with no bending to the artfulness of its seductions, before it seizes our imaginations, and becomes yet another way of dividing men from men, separating them into the few and "the masses."

The artfulness is in the method: the statistical method of a computerized sociology. Daniel Bell, in an article, "Meritocracy and Equality," in which he comes down firmly on the side of meritocracy, has one sentence that is memorable: "The logic of the argument has been pushed further by Arthur Jensen of Berkeley—that 80 per cent of a person's I.Q. is inherited, while environmental factors account for only 20 per cent—and Hernstein proceeds to extend the implication."[3] In this way, the data that has been assembled by Jensen, which is only a collection of statistics, passes to Hernstein, and from him to Bell; and the absurdity of it all is not altered by the fact that, in this case, Bell questions the conclusions of Hernstein. For what matters is that this body of data, circulating in the hanging garden of computers at Harvard University, is fictional. The figures of Jensen are not facts, they are his conclusions; they are what he has made by arranging the figures; he has made them up. They may be turn out to be "true," but they have not been proved to be "true" as yet. Even if they did turn out to be "true"—and that seems unlikely—they would be "true" only in the world of mathematical symbol, and not in the actual world. Only in the world of mathematical symbol can one say that 80 per cent of a person's—that is, any person's—I.Q. is inherited; there is no such 80 per cent in an actual person in the actual world.

In the works of men such as Arthur Jensen and James Coleman and Christopher Jencks, we are, as two social scientists have said, in the field of "statistical augury." Jencks does not explain how he reaches the figures in a statement like this: "Whereas Arthur Jensen and others have argued that 80 per cent of the variance in I.Q. scores is explained by genetic factors, our analyses suggest that the correct figure is probably more like 45 per cent . . . environment explains 35 per cent, and . . . the tendency of environmentally advantaged families to have genetically advantaged children explains the remaining 20 per cent."[4] Even a layman, when he is confronted by the roundness of these figures, and by the striking differences in the estimates which are made by different experimenters who are using the same method and the same data, must wonder whether they are more than guesses, inspired by a hypothesis, which the computers are then programmed and manipulated to prove.

The figures in fact seem to lose all meaning. Thus, at one moment, the possibility that the supposed fifteen-point advantage that the average white child has in intelligence tests over the average black child might be reduced by social policy to five points is dismissed by Jencks as trivial compared with "the differences within ethnic groups." The individual student who might gain from the ten-point—that is, two-thirds—reduction of the disadvantage is lost in the mathematical abstraction. Similarly, the figures in which he states the correlation between, say, a white child's educational attainment and his father's occupational status (0.50), or between a father's occupational status and the status achieved by his son (0.50), may seem to the layman to be trifling, when they are stated in that manner, and Jencks himself regards them as comparatively small. But to other sociologists, equipped in the field, correlations of such an order are significant; and those of us who are statistically unsophisticated ought not to be intimidated by this kind of computerized legerdemain.

It is important to understand that it is not just a single work—such as *Inequality* by Christopher Jencks—that one is criticizing, although its influence can already be seen. (David Brinkley in one of his television journals said that the points that Jencks argues had been proved; he was taking the statistics as proof.) A vast amount of money was poured into Jencks's enterprise: by the Carnegie Corporation, by the Office of the Secretary of Health, Education and Welfare, by the Office of Economic Opportunity, by the Urban Institute, by the Department of Education of Massachusetts, by the Guggenheim Foundation. We are talking, in other words, of a sociological method that has become a part of the conventional wisdom of our times; and part of the purpose of this book is to show how many of the different ways in which we are being taught to look at ourselves and our societies in fact are leading us, willy-nilly, in the same direction, without our questioning.

We cannot resist the argument unless we resist the method; and the method ought to be distrusted on the simple ground that, in the course of the method, something is put into the "facts" in order to make them prove the argument. A hypothesis is fed into the digital information as it is fed into the computer; and when the scientific sequence—hypothesis, experiment, test of hypothesis—is used in the examination of social questions, the hypothesis that is put into the facts becomes a much more controlling factor than in the natural sciences. The facts with which the physical scientist must deal have a stubbornness of their own—are less available to control by the experimenter—in a way that is not true of the facts with which the social scientist chooses to deal; in fact, the social scientist can choose the facts with which he will deal with a freedom that is not, ultimately, open to the physical scientist.

The method ought also to be distrusted, as has already been hinted, because the data that are used too often turn out to be only the data of other social scientists. In spite of the lavish endowment of Jencks's enterprise, which enabled him and his seven colleagues to labour for three years, there is little evidence in the book of any original research, and certainly none of any field research. When they talk of the Head Start programme, for example, they depend entirely on three previous studies, of varying length and of questionable authority. They did not make their own study; and of course they did not, on the evidence that they offer, visit one Head Start project, interview one Head Start teacher, talk to one Head Start pupil. In this way, the entire programme is dismissed in two brief paragraphs, which even they seem to regard as of so little worth that they did not even bother to list them in the index. This is not scientific observation at all.

Yet the evidence in the earlier studies, fed once more into the computers to prove a hypothesis, is used to repudiate the idea that preschooling can help to "narrow the gap between rich and poor or between blacks and whites," and this argument is at last allowed to rest on the statement that "no study has yet suggested" that this is possible. If they had conducted their own study—and conducted it among teachers and pupils in Head Start—they might have discriminated between its successes and its failures; they might have considered the pressures that distorted its promise; and above all they might have understood that it is still too early to judge the influence which it had on the future life of a single child, which is what matters.

But what we need to notice is Jencks's own announcement of his method and his intention, of the hypothesis that he will work to prove:

The reader should also be warned that we are primarily concerned with inequality between individuals, not inequality between groups. This accounts for much of the discrepancy between our conclusions and those of others who have examined the data. There is always far more inequality between individuals than between groups. It follows that when we compare the degree of inequality between groups to the degree of inequality between individuals, inequality between groups often seems relatively unimportant. It seems quite shocking, for example, that white workers earn 50 per cent more than black workers. But we are even more disturbed by the fact that the best-paid fifth of all white workers earn 600 per cent more than the worst-paid fifth.[5]

This is atomic sociology with a vengeance; indeed, it could, if its logic is extended, be an argument for having no sociology at all, but only psychology, especially that form of psychology that has its grounding in the mechanistic view of man, in "the properties of man's being that can neither be increased nor diminished," which physical science, as we saw at the beginning, has shown to be insupportable.

THE ISOLATION OF THE INDIVIDUAL IN ORDER TO ELIMINATE THE MANY

The reactionary consequences of this isolation of the individual may easily be demonstrated in the case that we have been considering. It is as a class that women are as individuals seeking to raise their incomes; and it is as a class also that they are seeking as individuals to replace some of their existing desires, hitherto prescribed by their social roles, by others which promise a greater satisfaction of their whole natures. If this is true of women, it is also true of blacks and chicanos, and of various groups of unprivileged whites. Of course the differences between the individuals within these groups will remain when the differences between the groups have been removed. But it is impossible to perceive the meaning of these individual differences, and to do something about them, until the "hidden injuries" of belonging to a disadvantaged class are brought into the open.

Twice in *The Scarlet Letter* we listen as Hawthorne muses on Hester Prynne's feelings about the status of women:

Indeed, the same dark question often rose into her mind with reference to the whole race of womanhood. Was existence worth accepting, even to the happiest among them? A tendency to speculate, though it may keep woman quiet, as it does man, yet makes her sad. She discerns, it may be, such a hopeless task before her. As a first step, the whole system of society is to be torn down, and built up anew. Then, the very nature of the opposite sex, or its long hereditary habit, which has become like nature, is to be essentially modified before woman can be allowed to assume what seems a fair and suitable position. Finally, all other difficulties being obviated, woman cannot take advantage of these preliminary reforms, until she herself shall have undergone a still mightier change, in which, perhaps, the ethereal essence wherein she has her truest life will be found to have evaporated.

At the close of the book, he says of Hester in her old age that she held the firm belief that "at some brighter period, when the world should have grown ripe for it, in Heaven's own time, a new truth would be revealed, in order to establish the whole relation between man and woman on a surer ground of mutual happiness."

It is the historical situation in which women find themselves in our actual society that Hawthorne puts first, even though a still "mightier change" may be needed in the consciousness of women themselves, before they accomplish what in time they must. Hester Prynne is aware of the learned behaviour that has prescribed her social roles and dictates how her personality will express itself.

The individual as he is presented to us by Jencks, and by those of whom he is representative, is not a historical figure. He is not regarded as the creature of his learned behaviour, which can be changed, but as the creature primarily of his genetic endowment, which cannot be changed. He is to all intents and purposes fixed in his station at his birth. But we know of the Indian on the Pine Ridge reservation that he was made into that kind of an Indian, that kind of a failure, by what he was taught; and we know of women that they have been made into the kind of women that they have been, the kind of failures that they have been, by what they have been taught. There is something that is not benign in so belittling—and thus inviting people to neglect—the injuries of class (and of other sources of inequality) that it is in our capacity to remedy.

The only failure that is tolerable to any human being who is permitted fully to be one is that boasted by Antigone in her flaming retort when she is told by Ismene that she will fail: "When I have *tried* and failed, I *shall* have failed." Much the same idea was once voiced by Bergil Killstraight, one of the younger leaders of the Oglala Sioux, when he said: "What we are denied is the right to fail." It is a remark of crucial significance. Almost everyone is able to cope with the fact that, in the course of his life, he will sink to the level of his own incompetence; and those who cannot cope with it we regard as disturbed, and we care for them in suitable ways as individuals. But the right to sink to the level of one's own incompetence is important because it implies the right of everyone to begin with an equal expectation of what she or he may achieve. Our societies are bound to try, as far as is possible, and as far as is consistent with other values to which they give recognition, to remove the inequalities of expectation with which individuals begin their lives: the inequalities of expectation, that is, which are the result of the differences in both their genetic endowment and their initial social situation which it is within the power of a society to remove.

THE TRUE PROPHECY OF WOMEN'S LIBERATION

We can learn much from Women's Liberation at its present stage of development: there can be no doubt that it is one of the most significant movements of the modern age. When it is true to itself, Women's Liberation is the attempt to change our cultured or learned behaviour; when it is untrue, it comes near to denying the significance of any cultured behaviour, and returns the individual, male or female, to his or her genetic endowment, to what they were born with, and so to the pinpoint of the self as something that is just there inside, and to which she or he has only to give free and spontaneous expression. This conflict has existed within the movement itself, and it is at this point that we begin to see how many of the themes that have been approached in this book begin to draw together, and to become concentrated in one of its central concerns: the confusion that today exists in the relationship between the self and our societies. The true prophecy of Women's Liberation is that the individual, male or female, is a social being, taught by the society how to respond, not only to it, but to his or her own self in the station in which he or she is fixed. The false prophecy is that the self is just there in its-self, magically there inside, waiting only to be released in some act of self-expression.

Consciousness raising is an illuminating illustration of many of our contemporary notions. It became a procedure of the New York Radical Women when they began to find that, in their meetings, they were recalling their experiences as individuals, and that these were leading them, "slowly and hesitantly," to the conclusion that what seemed to be "a woman's idiosyncratic pattern of behaviour was in fact a prescribed social role." (This is in many ways quite as significant a "discovery" as Freud's revelation that hysteria was not an idiosyncratic pattern of behaviour of his female patients.) From this there developed an "educational process used throughout the country," and "the small group has become the most widespread organizational unit of the movement." The point of the process was to relate "the personal to the political," and in that intention the method is of interest.

In a paper which Kathie Sarahchild read to the first national conference of Women's Liberation in 1968, consciousness raising was firmly given a social and political context: "We always stay in touch with our feelings. . . . We assume that our feelings . . . mean something worth analyzing . . . that our feelings are saying something *political*."[6] But the danger of the process is that it will, as in many of the "encounter groups" of our day, merely be a form of the indulgence of the self in its-self, of stroking and massage. Consciousness raising, Marlene Dixon has said, became to some women a messianic prophecy that "calls up women to recognize at the deepest emotional level their own contained resentment flowing from frustrated aspirations, their loneliness as the givers of understanding who are themselves not understood."[7] This is useful if the personal experience is taken to be a metaphor which then needs to be rigorously analyzed in a generalized social or political context. But too often consciousness raising is arrested at the first stage. The metaphor—and at the deepest emotional level we express ourselves metaphorically—is taken to be a sufficient expression of reality: the release of the I in its own immediate expression of itself, unrelated to its historical situation, is regarded as its "liberation."

The warning in the Redstockings Manifesto of 1969, that the purpose of consciousness raising is not therapy, which implies the existence of solutions for the individual and falsely assumes that the "male-female relationship is purely personal," could have been taken farther. Even the personal relationship is itself a society, between two people, and it needs to be imagined in the context of a whole society; the two ought to reflect each other. The request of John Wilson that we rediscover some sense of style in our sexual relationships is in fact a request that we seek the assistance of our society in the conduct of our personal relationships. It is clear that for a long time our societies have been failing in this respect; their morals and manners are in a state of anarchy, and one of the reasons, as Women's Liberation makes abundantly clear, is that they have been lagging disastrously behind our changed awareness of ourselves in the sensibility of the modern age. But that is all the more reason why we must look to them for a restoration of that style. We need from them a framework of manners and morals that can be accepted and reliable measure, both of our attitudes to ourselves and of our conduct to others, even in our personal relationships.

If this is the bidding of Women's Liberation to itself, it will be an instrument of the radical transformation of our estate that is long overdue. The prophecy of Rilke, seventy years ago, was that there were in "girls and women," even then, signs of the "timid novitiate" in which we were exploring a revolution in the relation between one human being and a second individual; and this is the true prophecy of Women's Liberation. Its task is that of our humanity, not of a sex; to assist in the establishment of new manners and new morals in our estate, fences against the disordered personal experiences of our lives: a reshaping of our conventional awareness of each other in our learned behaviour.

It is only as a social being that the individual can be truly liberated. The forms of personal liberation that are today so seductive can be seen, especially at moments of crisis, to leave the individual fixed in the same station in life as before. Whatever else he may imagine that he has altered, he has not altered his relationship with his society, and he finds, usually with some rancour, how far his personal role is still socially determined, by his place in a society that he has disdained to understand or to reform. He is still trapped by the learned behaviour that he has sought to modify only in his-self or in his personal relationships, and not where it can be truly modified, in the co-operative life of the human estate, in association with others. It is not only in our sexual relationships that we need to recover a sense of style; it is our societies that need a style, so that we enjoy with less perturbation our relations one with another.

THE REBELLION OF THE SELF AGAINST THE HIDDEN INJURIES OF CLASS

We may now attempt a definition of "liberation," which, as was said at the beginning, is one of the coded words of our time, and which has emerged directly from the political tradition and experience of the United States, in which the I is released in the En-Masse. Liberation is a rebellion of the self—not of a class, but of the self—against a lack of opportunity for self-realization which is perceived as being in great part the result of the learned attitudes and behaviour of the individual.

Each and all, we have been taught how to think and feel as blacks, taught how to think and feel as chicanos, taught how to think and feel as women, and so on: this is the cry common to them all, and the demand for liberation is then understood by others who begin to realize that they have been taught to think and feel as whites, taught how to think and feel as men, and one does not know how far the ripples will in the end travel. What we are witnessing is the individual self in rebellion against his learned attitudes, where he recognizes that those learned attitudes have injured him or her; and as long as the liberation movements keep in mind that it is learned attitudes and behaviour which they are trying to change—that it is learned behaviour that helps to keep them fixed in their station—they are true to themselves and are effective. This was the point driven home by Betty Friedan in 1969, when she said, "the gut issues of this revolution involve employment and education and new social institutions, and not sexual fantasy." She was talking of changes in what individuals are taught in their society.

Again, as we approach the close of the argument, the themes of this book may be seen to converge. None of the liberation movements—Black or Women's or Gay, or any other, serious or trivial—would have taken place without the radical redefinition of the self that has occupied our culture for the past hundred and fifty years. The "timid novitiate" of Rilke is now ceasing to be a novitiate, and it has ceased to be timid. It is this emphasis on the self inside its-self—on the "hidden injuries" of class that are done to the individual psyche—that distinguishes Black Liberation from the more traditional black movements, and Women's Liberation from the more traditional women's movements, and which has often been disturbing to the more conventional groups. It is not militancy as such that has been shocking, but the sight and the sound of so much internalized injury being suddenly given vent in public, spat out and screamed out. The individual psyche, its sense of individual wrong and its need for self-realization, has been made a weapon of social protest, and this is one of the coded meanings in "liberation."

Given the times in which we live, and the manner in which we have reimagined the self, all of this is legitimate; but the danger of it is obvious. To put the emphasis on one's blackness or on one's womanhood is to run the danger of resting one's case solely on the genes, solely on what one was born, solely on one's inventory at birth; and not on the array of one's potentialities as they have developed. That this plays straight into the hands of those who hold a genetic view of the human personality has not prevented some of the sects of the liberation movements from taking up such a position. My humanity is the blackness with which I was born, my humanity is the femaleness with which I was born, and to this cry their opponents respond: As you say! Blackness and femaleness are genes; and if it is by them that one's humanity is to be defined, there is no reason why one should not reply that red hair or freckles ought equally to be definitions of it.

The liberation movements are the products of a historical situation. They have emerged in a particular society at a particular stage of its development. They are the creatures of the very tradition and experience against which they protest. The ideas of liberty and equality, of the individual and the self, have been given to the "oppressed" by the "oppressor." The proper stance of the black or the woman is to say to the white or the male: I am the victim of the attitudes and the behaviour that I have learned from you, but I am also their beneficiary; against the mischiefs of what you have taught me, I bring the truth of what you have taught me; it is not from what I was born with that I make my claim, for that cannot be changed, but from what I have learned, and that can be changed; it is as an individual *of* my society and *of* my culture that I claim the self-realization that I have so far been denied by them.

It is only if they couch their protest in these terms that the liberation movements can escape the narrowness that has too often afflicted them, that the "oppressed," can avoid separating themselves, as once they were separated by their "oppressors," from the society and culture in which each is installed and to which each is bound to adhere. This is the warning in the words of Dag Hammarskjöld that were earlier used as an epigraph, that "To separate himself from the society of which he was born a member will lead the revolutionary, not to life but to death," because he is a creature of that society. It is in the human estate of which he is a member that our shared humanity has been won and secured; it is there that it can be redefined.

As we have seen, much of "The Movement," especially the hippies and the yippies, was almost bound to separate itself from the society in order to make its gesture of protest, partly because it is a separation that is normal in adolescence and even in delayed adolescence, but also partly because the learned attitudes and behaviour of the adolescent are still very slight. He has no resource in society with which to combat it; he has only the fragile weapon of his-self. But an adult movement, such as that of women or blacks, has a much stronger claim to make, and a much stronger argument to use: I am what I have learned in my society, and I wish now to use what I have learned in order to change what I will learn in the future. Only in this way can the individual hope to unfix himself from his station.

This is what was meant earlier when it was said that the individual can be fully liberated only as a social being. "As long as woman's socialization does not nurture her uniqueness, but treats her only as a member of a group of some assumed average characteristic, she will not be prepared to realize her own potential in the way that the values of individuality and self-fulfilment imply she should." This statement was made in the hearings on discrimination against women before a subcommittee of the House of Representatives in 1970, and it is worth a careful perusal. In it is every right idea, but in it also is every potential source of confusion.

There is the statement that it is a "woman's socialization" that is the true issue; in other words, what she learns. The task of this socialization is to "nurture her uniqueness"; this is true enough, but it is not adequately precise, since it could mean the nurturing only of a fixed inventory of what she was born with—"to be a woman"— and not of the array of potentialities that even her present socialization has made available to her to realize. "To realize her own potential" is open to the same ambiguity of interpretation; as also is the talk of "values of individuality and self-fulfilment," with no indication that even the woman's awareness of these "values" is the construction of the society on which she is making her claims. In spite of its initial premise, the passage could be read as no more than a claim for a woman "to be a woman," much as the antifeminists say that she should be a woman. The passage is interesting because, as in so much of the literature, the problem is correctly approached, but then carelessly mislaid.

HUMAN SEXUALITY AS CULTURED BEHAVIOUR

An illustration that is relevant in this context is the current emphasis on our sexuality. As with our idea of the self, our idea of sex appears to be that it is something that is just inside ourselves, and not something that has been put there: that it is merely an instinct or drive. But this is not true and, if it were true, it would be, not a sexual instinct, but a reproductive instinct, as in animals, a drive to mate. At some stage in man's history, however, his sexual activity was not confined to a mating season. It has been calculated that it takes about a thousand acts of intercourse by a human being to produce one baby—the kind of statistic that has no meaning except as a metaphor—and the rather obvious conclusion is that human sexuality has acquired other uses and interests than mere reproduction. These other purposes and interests of our sexuality are not natural, we are not born with them; they have been placed in us by the history of our race, and are still placed in us by our culture.

We have been and are educated to our sexuality; it is more in our heads than in our loins. Our sex is mannered behaviour that we learn or, as William Simon and John Gagnon have put it, "scripted behavior, and not the naked expression of a primordial drive." As they point out, it is obvious that we do not become sexual all at once, in infancy or in childhood or in adolescence. There is a development, a continuity from one stage to another, even when the development has been interrupted by periods of latency; and during this development, the arrangement by the individual of his sexual desires is associated with his arrangement of his other desires, the one often being an expression of the other, each in association with all, and all with each, in the whole personality that is constructed by him in negotiation with his society. It is only insofar as sexual activity is the expression of this whole personality that it is rewarding to the individual and to his partner, and of any possible interest to the rest of us. To isolate the sexual impulse as an instinctual drive of the untutored self, to be gratified in isolation from all other desires, is to deny its rich potentiality and its infinite expressiveness of the human valuing of another's life.

We are not in the Garden of Eden, there has been no Garden of Eden in history, we have no Garden of Eden to which to go; there have been and there are no "primitive peoples" who stand naked before each other without artifice or affectation. But, if we cannot enjoy our sex in paradise, neither is it simple, something that we have only to get into perspective, as natural as urinating: when the gland has filled, then empty it, with as little ado as possible. This is not who we are, nor who we have become. "We are a complex race of people with an imprint of a history on our spirits," and even if we wished, we cannot refuse that history. If one thing has been made clear, it is that in all human societies, as Robin Fox has said, "there is a regular assignment of mates—regulated sexual access. Random mating is rare or non-existent."[8] When the whole of human history speaks so unanimously, we should have at least the humility to realize that it is not speaking idly about our needs and desires, and that it speaks to us.

The false side of Women's Liberation made an ado about the "discovery" of women's sexuality, for as such it was presented; but it was presented as something that was just there inside women as part of what they are born with. It is no more just inside them than it is just inside men. It has been taught and learned: perhaps it should be taught differently, but it is of a cultured and not of a natural desire that we are speaking. Given this fact, it ought to be the ambition of Women's Liberation, and of men, to assist in the creation of a new style for our sexual relationships, in which the whole personality of the partners may find a satisfying expression, in which the attitude that everything is worth trying is replaced by the rewards of something that is worth enduring. Otherwise, the self reduced to its-self has no resource but to behave like a spoiled child, dodging from experience to experience, seeking to contrive an authenticity that has no art, no convention; with no narrative, no plot, to his life, but merely a conspiracy for each occasion.

THE HELPLESSNESS OF THE UNPRIVILEGED

If we are not to fix people in the station into which they are born, we cannot be satisfied with an equality of results. It is on such a proposal that Christopher Jencks leans in what, on the surface, appears to be the most radical suggestion that anyone could make. Although it is impossible to educate people out of their inequalities, he says, the effects of those inequalities could be overcome by giving them equal incomes, for whatever work they do. He admits, of course, that there is no obvious strategy by which the American people might be persuaded in the future to resort to such a measure; it would merely require a long campaign of political education—but why should education work in that?

The more serious objection to his proposal is that he will make people equal in one respect—their earnings—but leave them unequal in every other respect; in brief, he will fix them in their station still, and pay them to stay there. The society is to be left divided into the educated and the uneducated; and, if we consider only the ability to cope, we can at once see the fallacy of the position. By the equalization of incomes, it might be ensured that everyone can pay for a lawyer; it would not ensure that everyone knows how to use a lawyer, or knows that he should use a lawyer, or knows that he could use a lawyer. This is only one aspect of the ability to cope, but it runs through every day-to-day activity in the common spheres that we share with each other.

The poor and the unprivileged in our societies are often helpless; and they are helpless, not only or even primarily because they are poor, but because they are uneducated. This helplessness is one of the most widespread and intolerable forms of inequality that persists in our societies, and it would persist even if incomes were equalized, for the ignorance that is its true cause would not be eradicated. Moreover, devastating as this helplessness is in diminishing an individual's perception of himself as equal, and in diminishing our perception of him as equal precisely because he appears to be so helpless, this is not the only form which the lack of ability to cope can take.

Even if it is true that the best people should be at the head of our institutions—one hesitates only because it is not clear what is meant by the best people—the governed must be able to cope with their governors. To do this adequately, they require information and an educated perception of their own interests and the interests of their society. People who are ignorant do not know how to criticize the elite, how to articulate their discontents; they may not even know what their discontents are, or even that they have discontents. In short, even the exercise of his political liberty by an individual depends, not merely on his equality, which was established in the Declaration of Independence in the beginning, but to a large extent on this primary equality: that of the education that he receives.

But what is lacking above all in Jencks's proposal, and in many others that are related to it, is that it would fix people in their stations in every respect but that of mere cash. Even the spending power would not be equal, since it requires knowledge to spend well. As David Caplovitz pointed out, "the poor pay more," and although his study was subtitled *Consumer Practices of Low-Income Families,* the lesson is not really about income, but about ignorance. But, beyond that, people would be fixed in their station in their capacity to read, to listen to music, to enjoy what is unfamiliar, to discover what they never expected, to hold discourse at different levels, to enrich themselves with the knowledge of their cultural heritage, and in turn to enrich it. This is a terrible demeaning of the human spirit to come from a socialist and from Harvard; it is also a terrible diminution of the American idea and the self-evident truths it proclaimed.

What is lacking in Jencks's proposals and in so many others today is any real understanding of the variety of ways in which people now expect to be, because they know that they can be, unfixed from their stations; in the fullest sense, to be liberated. There is no more unconsciously agitating force in our societies than television. It gives to millions of people a nightly glimpse of worlds—and possibilities —other than their own. One has only to recall how slight was the awareness of other worlds in a small town only thirty years ago to realize what has happened: life than *was* confined to the "ten minutes' walk." But give a person a television set, and one gives him boots with which he can stride the earth in his imagination, asking why he cannot be other than he is. Even the soap operas encourage him to recognize, and therefore to express, emotions that he might otherwise have suppressed and kept hidden; even on this level, we live in societies in which we are face to face with each other, our relationships not mediated by any group.

We cannot just ignore the I released in the En-Masse. He is the prophetic figure of our age; and he is all about us. During the miners' strike in late 1974, it was possible to gaze on the television screen on miners of two generations: the older who might still have been in Appalachia in the 1930s, the younger who were in dress and manner all but indistinguishable from the students who cross Harvard Yard. There is no way of fixing these younger men in their station; they are already liberated from an ancestral past even if they have not yet been fully liberated to the realization of their own potential futures. We can either educate them to the enjoyment of the individuality of which they are already aware; or we can condemn them to the anomie of "the masses" and, in doing so, condemn our societies to a state of perpetual siege by the majority of its citizens.

CHAPTER 16

The Revolt Against the Democratic Idea in America

Democracy is the idea that what is common to all men and women is more important in the making of our estate, and in the determination of its policies, than what is different in one from the other. It takes the idea of the individuality of each, and the right of that individuality to liberty and its own self-realization, and attaches it to the idea of the commonness of all. It fixes the tail of liberty to the kite of equality; and the kite must be kept in the air if the tail is to dance with the *hilaritas libertatis* of which the English medieval philosopher spoke: the laughing and dancing joy of liberty.

Unless liberty is attached to the idea of equality, it is privilege, conferred by status; and the status is conferred by someone else, god or pope or monarch, and so is not liberty at all. It has been the genius of democracy that, once there were no cosmologies or priesthoods or monarchies, it understood that the fragile claim to individual liberty must be given an egalitarian foundation. Why should "I" be free? There is no answer that can convince except that all men need the same liberty as do "I" for the full expression of their own I's; and that they therefore have the same right to it as do "I." The liberty that is required is not a grant from another, and it is positive: the right to the conditions, shared with others, in which each individuality may be fully realized and fully express itself.

The democratic idea is part of the public philosophy of America, and it is under attack. It is impossible in these pages, as it is unnecessary, to show the breadth of the attack, or the length of time in which it has been building. But one can give some idea of its depth, for it is this that matters. It is not just the capacity of democracy that is being questioned, in this or that respect; every political and intellectual and moral justification of it is being challenged; and what is more, the challenge is not being met. There is no better way to begin than by showing how the attack is developed by one influential writer, Irving Kristol, a man who was once talked of as the favourite intellectual of Richard Nixon. His views are those of an elite, self-appointed, fashionable, and powerful.

THE DEPTH OF THE ATTACK ON DEMOCRACY

His object is profound. It is to attack the idea of democracy *as it has developed* in the United States, and to attack it by presenting it as alien to the idea of democracy *as it was initially put forward* by the founding fathers. He believes that "the way in which a democratic political philosophy was gradually and inexorably transformed into a democratic faith seems . . . to be perhaps the most important problem in American intellectual—and ultimately political—history."[1] The "democratic political philosophy" was that of the founding fathers; and of that he approves. The "democratic faith" had emerged by the time of Andrew Jackson; and of that he disapproves. He would return America to 1787.

But there is not a shred of evidence, in spite of the American idea in the Declaration of Independence, where it lay embedded until it slowly worked its way into the imagination of the country, that the founding fathers in general had a democratic philosophy, that they either established a democratic government or believed that they were doing so. Their characteristic institutions—the Electoral College, the Senate, the limited suffrage—were rigidly exclusive; their characteristic philosophy was that of John Randolph of Roanoke: "I love liberty, I hate equality." The founding fathers did not speak of democracy—except in the very limited sense, as in *The Federalist Papers,* No. X, of the "pure democracy" of the ancient world, which they could easily reject—because they did not believe in it; they did not understand the seed they had sown, because it was not a democracy which they thought they were establishing.

The idea that Jefferson had planted had yet to grow, and democracy in the event grew very fast, in spite of the checks and balances and interests which were intended and which sought to resist it. "You and I did not imagine, when the first war with Britain was over," wrote Harrison Gray Otis to a friend at the time of the War of 1812, "that the revolution was just begun." Men such as Kristol would like to eradicate the whole of that further revolution, to purge the American people, not only of their "democratic faith," but of the democratic experience of which it was born, and return them, cleansed and purged of their history and their heresy, to the "democratic political philosophy" which was available to them in the beginning. This interpretation has the nature of sorcery: the story of the American people is to be made to evaporate; they never grew; they have had no narrative.

From this curious reading of history, from which all history after 1787 is eliminated, it can be shown that we are already visited by the calamities that an unbridled democracy must bring. "Self-government, the basic principle of this republic, is inexorably being eroded in favor of self-seeking, self-indulgence, and just plain aggressive selfishness . . . One wonders: how can a bourgeois society survive in a cultural ambience that derides every traditional bourgeois virtue and celebrates promiscuity, homosexuality, drugs, political terrorism —anything, in short, that is in bourgeois eyes perverse?"[2]

The connection must now be made between these cultural changes and the "religious faith" in democracy which has overtaken the American people. We are asked to believe that there was, before this faith had triumphed, "an older idea of democracy . . . for which the conception of the quality of public life is absolutely critical." Since democracy is a form of self-government, "you have to care about what kind of people govern it," be "solicitous of the individual self," and educate that self in "what used to be called 'republican virtue.'" In short, "in this version of democracy, the people took some care not to let themselves be governed by the more infantile and irrational part of themselves."[3]

The growth of democracy was accompanied by the growth of large cities, which are places of "moral experiments" in contrast with the "conventional morality" of the provinces; and with that we are ready to move to the most daring proposition of all. The population in the city is, in its political essence, a mob, whose potential "does not go much beyond riotous destructiveness." That is an old hat to wear, fashionable in the nineteenth century in England, but one does not expect the next leap: "For something very odd has, in the past decade, been happening to the bourgeois masses who inhabit our new urban civilization. Though bourgeois in condition and life-style, they have become less bourgeois in ethic and strikingly mob-like in action."

But it is not enough to identify only this "bourgeois urban mob." It is the whole American people who are to be condemned: "I am not asserting that the American people, at this moment, are a corrupt people—though it worries me that they are so blatantly free from self-doubt about this possibility. What I am saying is that they are more and more behaving in a way that would have alarmed the founding fathers, even as it would have astonished them. To put it bluntly, they are more and more behaving like a collection of mobs."[4] In this manner the people of the United States are set beyond the pale of political virtue, no longer responsible citizens. The idea of "republican virtue" has been used, as it was intended to be used, to undermine the justifications of democracy.

THE UNTENABLE STANCE OF THE AMERICAN CONSERVATIVE

The attack on democracy has been building for a long time and, although it does not always or even often take the form in the United States of an avowed conservatism, the attempt to construct a native American conservatism has received more attention in the last thirty years than at any earlier time. It therefore needs to be said that it seems to the outsider, even though he may himself be regarded as a conservative in Britain, that it is impossible to be a conservative in America without occupying a position that is in the end intellectually untenable and even morally disreputable.

At its best, European conservatism—and at its best it is, in very large measure, English conservatism—is an imaginative recollection of a utopian past, with which to challenge the defects and inadequacies of contemporary society. The radical imagines a utopia in the future, the utopia of the conservative is imagined in the past; and they both use these unreal worlds as criticisms of the actual world of the present. They are both critics of the status quo. The imaginative act of the conservative was described by Roy Cambell, when he described himself as a pre-Victorian "who never was put through any mill except that of the pre-industrial European culture of an equestrian, slightly feudal type, a sort of inhabitant of the moon, a foreign being who cannot imagine what such words as 'rights,' 'progress,' 'freedom,' and 'liberty' mean." There is no shilly-shallying in this statement. He is defending an idealization, that is why he is like "an inhabitant of the moon," wishing for an "equestrian" ideal in the age of the automobile.

In standing on his ruins in the dead past, the European conservative is saving his position from the mere facility of reaction. He is not proposing that the past should be restored. He is saying something much more profound: that history is a matter, not only of what succeeded and therefore is present to us, but equally of what was vanquished; that the destroyed alternatives need to be taken into account as well as the victorious survivors; that history is to be understood *ex memoria passionis,* as the memory of suffering, of the possibility that was overwhelmed as well as the one that prevailed.

But this has not been, and is unlikely ever to be, the attitude of the American to his past. There are no ruins on which the American can take his stand; between the past and the present there is no separation; the destroyed alternatives can hardly be a part of a history that is considered as the unfolding of a destiny that was initially ordained. From the start, therefore, the conservative in America is on ground that must shift, if he is on any ground at all. Whenever he makes an appeal to or from the past, it is always more than a little preposterous. At one moment he may seem to want to restore the United States as an agrarian community, governed locally by a benevolent magistracy, and nationally by a parliament; at the next to restore even a monarchy, and not the demure constitutional monarchy of England at that, but a continental monarchy of Catholic and absolutist pretensions, so that he appears to be almost a Carlist.

The reach of American conservatives to dead Europe for their inspiration is indiscriminate, as in this list of their mentors, taken from the writings of two of them: Thomas Aquinas, de Maistre, Maurras, de Bonald, Croce, Ortega y Gasset, Madariaga, Savigny, Scheler, Bosanquet, Bradley, Voegelin, Husserl, Heidegger, Burke, Coleridge, Roepke, von Mises, Gilson, Christopher Dawson, J. C. Murray, Bryce, A. V. Dicey, and so on. Almost the only American mentors who are acknowledged are John Adams, Calhoun, and

William Faulkner. One has to ask, on the basis of their writings, whether conservatives can be native in America: do they not have to go abroad because they cannot find what they wish at home?

The aristocratic tradition to which the conservative appeals in England does not represent to him any actual aristocracy or aristocratic system that he believes in fact existed. It is a model—a rather playful one—from which he challenges the presumptions of the capitalist system, of what he refers to curtly as "trade." Not only is there no such aristocratic tradition to which to appeal in the United States, but the American conservative is usually a defender of capitalism, of "free enterprise," of competition: in short, of an unrestrained individualism that has always been opposed by traditional conservatism. To almost all that the English conservative has always loathed in Adam Smith—especially his view of man as individualist and hedonistic, competitive and acquisitive—the American conservative gives his support.

The reformer in America, said Emerson, was always trying to bring down the great capitalist in order to make a small capitalist of every man. This is the mythology of the expectant capitalist: that since some can be capitalists, others may be capitalists. "That some should be rich," as Lincoln put it in 1863, "shows that others may become rich." To none has this mythology appealed more than to the American conservative. He has therefore placed himself in the position of defending a society of isolated atoms. If the American people were the "collection of mobs" that Kristol finds in the "bourgeois urban society" of today, the cause would not be their democratic faith but their extreme individualism: the I released in the En-Masse with far too little sense of himself as a social being in a public.

The belief in capitalism—even in circumstances in which it is possible to say that capitalism no longer exists—is today the main obstacle to the rediscovery of the public in America; and again the conservative in America has no resource to which to reach in order to take a confident stand. The conservative in England has always believed in a strong central government: this is part of the true Tory's attachment to the monarchy, his looking to the "Crown" for the effective and sure governance of the people. That is why the Tory Democrat is in England a possible creature. But there is no such tradition in the United States to which the conservative can appeal. All too easily, therefore, he is reduced to defending the private at the cost of the public, the individual at the cost of the social, self-interest at the cost of communal interest: in short, his concerns are the very opposite of what they should be.

His defence of capitalism forces him to excuse the excessive individualism that is a part of American life; and when he confronts the competitiveness and covetousness that are its effects, and which threaten the harmony of the society, he reaches to prescriptions of authority and hierarchy and tradition that are usually taken from European conservatives such as Tocqueville and Burke, Oakeshott and Acton, to whom Daniel Patrick Moynihan appeals in his own description of his personal movement from liberalism to conservatism. If he had his way, the American conservative would impose on his society the very forms that the United States was created to reject; and the one idea that never seems to occur to him is that, given the release of the I in our times, it is not the obedience or submission or acquiescence of that I that is required, but his participation and co-operation with others in the public. Instead of being a critic of democracy, a position that is today as necessary as it is tenable and reputable, the American conservative is an opponent of it, and so sets himself outside his own times and in isolation from the political tradition and experience of his own country.

AMERICAN LIBERALISM AS A DISTRIBUTOR OF RANDOM CONCESSIONS

If democracy is under attack by the conservatives, it cannot at the moment look for a very strenuous defence from the liberals. At the heart of the difficulty, once again, is the deference to capitalism. By the end of the Second World War, it seemed to have become the mission of the liberals to show that the capitalist system could be managed in such a way that it would realize the promise of endless growth in the economy, and endless abundance for the consumer. In this way, the Gross National Appetite fed by the Gross National Product, the expectant capitalist was to be turned into an expectant consumer. Liberalism seemed to be satisfied to make "random concessions to groups within the community," August Heckscher said of the Fair Deal at the time, until its actions seemed to demonstrate no more than "a kind of habitual deference to claims, pressures, and interests."[5] In 1948, a group of liberal economists published a manifesto, *Saving American Capitalism,* and the ambition has not changed.

This is the true criticism that is to be made of the "consumer society": that the people have, to the degree that was described, been made prosperous, but there has been no transference of power to them. The concentration of economic power in the corporations— what Franklin Roosevelt called "private socialism"—ought to be a primary concern of the liberal. In the late 1960s the outside board members of the Morgan Guaranty Trust Company, New York, consisted of representatives from: American Machine & Foundry; American Telephone & Telegraph; Bethlehem Steel; Campbell Soup; Coca-Cola; Columbia Gas System; Continental Oil; E. I. du Pont de Nemours; Gillette; International Nickel; New York Life Insurance; Pennsylvania Railroad; Procter & Gamble; Singer; Standard Oil; J. P. Stevens; and State Street Investment. When these men sit round the table, they together have a decisive voice in determining much of what the ordinary American will buy during any week, and the price at which he will buy it. They in fact exercise a coercive power over the day-to-day lives of the ordinary citizen, and the liberal ought to find this intolerable. The corporate system is one of organized coercion, and yet the liberal in this century has almost ceased to be concerned to restrain its exercise.

The tragedy of liberalism is that it has again and again allowed its support of "free enterprise" to undermine its own doctrines. It was by "free enterprise" that the great corporations were first formed, and then combined, enabling them to impose restraints on trade that are the very opposite of "free enterprise." Moreover, as the corporate system from year to year showed that it was incapable of sustaining either its own stability or that of the economy, the state had to come to the rescue with a massive intervention of its power which is used to uphold the corporations in their restraints on trade. Liberalism has, in other words, been too ready to associate itself with the promise in the Constitution of the right to property, instead of with the promise in the Declaration of Independence of the right to the pursuit of happiness. The balance between these is today upset, and it needs to be restored by an imaginative display of political energy.

But the liberal will be incapable of this energy as long as he remains in "the vital center" which Arthur Schlesinger, Jr., discovered and announced in the 1950s, as long as "the broad liberal objective is a balanced 'mixed economy,' thus seeking to occupy that middle ground between capitalism and socialism whose viability has so long been denied by both capitalists and socialists." Its imagination will not be released in an atmosphere of consensus. It needs to invite opposition even from the most dangerous quarters, to recover some of Theodore Roosevelt's disdain for businessmen, "very powerful in certain lines and gifted with the 'money touch,' but with ideals which in their essence are those of so many glorified pawnbrokers." It was the imagination of Veblen that struck deep into the minds of a whole generation who came to Washington in the 1930s to give direction and vigour to the New Deal. The economist who today has a comparable influence is Galbraith, and it is precisely the imaginative force to electrify a generation that his work lacks.

The liberal in the United States has become too much interested in being pragmatic, too ready to identify himself with the avowed "realism" of Hamilton instead of with the avowed "idealism" of Jefferson, too willing to be satisfied with "gradual and piecemeal reforms" without placing these in the context of a reimagined vision of what society might be. It is the essence of liberalism that it believes that man can master his society as well as nature. Detached from this idea—this deeply American idea—liberalism may as well concede its ground to conservatism, as in many respects it in fact has done. The voice of liberalism that has been transmuted into conservatism is heard most clearly in Moynihan: "The great questions of government have to do not with what *will* work, but what does work."[6] It is also the voice of the politician who has been transmuted into a manager.

The faith of the liberal is that man can order his own progress, and he has surrendered in this century to the denial of the idea of progress. "It is possible," wrote the English socialist R. H. S. Crossman in 1948, "that we are approaching the end of the liberal epoch," during which man believed that he could make his own society as he wished.[7] But the epoch that was coming to an end was European, as has been argued repeatedly in this book, and as was so well put by Nicola Chiaramonte in 1953, when Europe had for the second time ravaged itself:

For some time now a major segment—perhaps all—of the world has been living in a state of bad faith. The beginning of the time can be given a definite date. That date is August 2nd 1914, the outbreak of the First World War. On this date there began the destruction of the only belief in modern times that had taken the place of religious faith—the belief in the progress of humanity. From that day in August 1914, not only the intellectuals, but the whole of European society, found itself in a state of nihilism.[8]

But one must ask again, as one has already asked so often, why the American, and the American liberal in particular, should be overcome by the darkness of this foreboding, and surrender his own enlightenment.

LOCKING THE PEOPLE OUT OF POWER

Among conservatives and liberals alike, the most obvious form that the revolt against the democratic idea in America takes is in the persuasion that "We, the people" cannot be trusted to govern themselves, but must be governed by elites. Once more the idea has travelled from Europe, not only in the classic works of Pareto and Mosca and Michels, but in the hardly less influential works of the intellectual refugees from Central Europe during the 1930s and 1940s who were so impressed by the rise of totalitarianism there that they found the explanation in the "authoritarian personality" of "the masses," and in the incapacity of democratic institutions to restrain that personality. For twenty years the idea travelled into the public mind of America, there to infect it, until "We, the people" appeared to vanish from all discourse.

The steadiness of the American people under an endless series of provocations during this century, and the resilience of their democratic institutions, was not taken into account. They were blamed for Joe McCarthy—who was taken to be *the* "authoritarian personality" of "the masses"—but not praised for getting rid of him. Throughout the 1960s, it was forecast that a "backlash" would develop among them, but when it did not occur they were given no credit. If ever a people has shown that it is capable of self-government it is the Americans of this century: the immigrants, and children and grandchildren of the immigrants, who have shown a remarkable steadiness as they have waited for the land of promise to prove itself a land of performance.

Now that they have become the vast commonalty of the middle class in America, they are to be locked out of power. Daniel Bell tells them that in the new post-industrial society they must be ruled by a meritocracy. Irving Kristol tells them that they are only mobs, and cannot be trusted to exhibit the republican virtue that would alone fit them for self-government. Christopher Jencks tells them that only a few of them need be fully educated, and so be able to occupy positions of power or influence. Patrick Moynihan sniffs that "few persons think, and fewer still take notice of those who do." These are only among the leaders of a chorus that is swelling.

What is proclaimed by all of these voices—and many others on whom they draw and yet others who follow like a pack behind them —is that the purpose of a democracy is merely to govern. "He committed the mistake of supposing that the *business* of human affairs was the whole of them," said John Stuart Mill of Jeremy Bentham, and his words apply with equal force to those whom we are considering. Mill regarded one of the functions of government to be the education of the citizen. It is "a great influence acting on the human mind," and therefore participation in it can help promote the right kind of individual character. It was for this reason that he rejected a benevolent despotism, even though it might perform the business side of government efficiently; and he asked, as we must ask of the "benevolent despotism" of an elite or a meritocracy, "What sort of human beings can be formed under such a regime? What development can either their thinking or their active faculties attain under it? . . . Their moral capacities are equally stunted. Wherever the sphere of action of human beings is artificially circumscribed, their sentiments are narrowed and dwarfed." There is a connection, therefore, between the development of the individual and the activity of the citizen, the very connection that it has been part of the purpose of these pages to establish.

In the absence of participation, "the man never thinks of any collective interest, of any object to be pursued jointly with others, but only in competition with them, and in some measure at their expense," Mill went on, and engaged in these selfish pursuits, he "fastens his attention and interest exclusively upon himself, and upon his family as an appendage of himself;—making him indifferent to the public . . . and in his inordinate regard for his personal comforts, selfish and cowardly."[9] This is exactly, as has been argued, what has happened to the individual self in our times. Here is the intersection between the rebellion of the self and the revolt of the privileged. The many may withdraw into their private pursuits so that the few may govern.

The commonalty of the middle class of America as it was described at the beginning, will not fulfill its promise, as the portent of the future, if the individuals in it are not educated and nourished, and provided with the opportunity, to participate fully in the public life of their society. The cause of their present discontents is that they are not fully citizens. The impact of the modern state on the individual is today so great that the nature of the relationship between him and the government can have profound consequences. If the relationship is narrow, the individual will lose his citizenship, and what that means is that he will lose his right "to share to the full in the social heritage and to live the life of a civilized being according to the standards prevailing in society."

The participation of the individual as a citizen needs to be nourished wherever he is in contact with and affected by one of the institutions of society. The first of these is his place of work; and there is now a sufficient body of evidence about workers' participation in the regulation of their own conditions and the management of the industries in which they are employed to make it clear that in such solutions there is considerable promise if they are pursued with enough conviction. If the worker, blue-collar or white-collar, is given the opportunity to exercise his own suffrage, so to speak, at his place of work, not only does his life have more meaning and more dignity, but his exercise of a wider suffrage in the wider society will also change in quality.

But these are not the only reasons for nourishing the participation of each individual as a citizen in the government of his estate. "We do not educate the people only to teach them," said the Greek poet George Seferis, "we educate them also to learn from them."[10] This humility of the true intellectual is at a discount in America today. Yet there is no country in which the voices of "We, the people," of the I released in the En-Masse, need to be heard more clearly, if they are not to disintegrate into atoms, coalescing only as the mobs that Kristol fears. The danger to the commonalty, as has been said, is that a seventh of it will soon be unable to speak to the other six sevenths. This is why it seems to lack cohesion, and to have no sense of a common endeavour or purpose. Those who are undermining the justifications of democracy in America, whether by denying the ability of the people to govern themselves or by refusing their right to be educated, are undermining also the only possibility of that harmony in society which they seek to uphold and restore.

PART VII

Rethinking the Purpose of America

The United States must invent some program for its collective life. . . . it is now incumbent upon the United States to search out and find a plot for its future history.

—JULIÁN MARÍAS, in *America in the Fifties and Sixties*[1]

CHAPTER 17

The Restoration of Politics

The American is not, unless he chooses to throw up his hands, out of control of his society; his estate is still available to him to make of it what he pleases. It is not too large, or too impersonal, or too mechanical, unless that is how he chooses to imagine it. In order to improve it there are things that he can do; he need not have recourse to hopes of a revolution that will not occur, or retreat into an intimacy that has no reward. He is in charge of what he has made, more than any other in the world.

It is an old idea that we have been alienated from our societies by our technology. "A mechanic becomes a sort of machine," said William Godwin in 1805, "his limbs and articulations are converted, as it were, into woods and wires. Tamed, lowered, torpified into this character, he may be said perhaps to be content."[2] In all the literature that has followed in the almost two centuries that have intervened, nothing much has been added, and it is usually said less well. The idea has dominated our century, even in America, which has used the machine with more intelligence and to better purpose than any other country. Man will become, according to Lewis Mumford, "a passive, purposeless, machine-conditioned animal whose proper functions, as technicians now interpret man's role, will either be fed into the machine or strictly limited and controlled for the benefit of depersonalized, collective organizations"[3]; which is the kind of mesmerizing prophecy which once caused a critic to say that his works were "a lot of typical after-dinner conversation in intellectual suburbia."

Frank Lloyd Wright was also for many years a name with which to keep the conversation going. "Spirit only can control" the machine, he exclaimed. "Spirit is a science mobocracy does not know."[4] Once again, "the masses" make their appearance, brought forward to be contemned, the creature of the machine and out of control of it; "liberated from the fetters of labor," as Arendt puts it, but with no knowledge of "those other higher and more meaningful activities for the sake of which this freedom would deserve to be won." Within this society of equals, she laments, "there is no class left, no aristocracy of either a spiritual or political nature, from which a restoration of the other capacities of man could start anew."[5] It is again the voice of the snob.

THE MACHINES THAT WE HAVE MADE

One of the puzzles in the propaganda against our technology is that we made the machine, just as we made god, and we made nature, and we made the self; it is another part of our creation, and it cannot be out of our control unless we are not properly imagining what we ourselves have made. There is nothing that a machine can do without us; there is no way in which our machines can take over.

Perhaps a part of the difficulty is that our machines have become invisible. If one goes to an old mill, for example, the water from the millrace runs onto a great wooden wheel, splashing as the wheel turns; inside the mill, this visible force, which seems so slight, turns a majestic and visible system of other wheels and cogs and gears. One may walk from floor to floor, watching the wooden teeth as they couple with wooden teeth, driving the wooden wheels which turn the wooden axles, which themselves run through holes in the floor. It is a geometry in wood, and it is gratifying; and at the end of the process, one can hold one's hand in the newly ground flour as it pours into the open sacks.

Of course we miss it. Our machines have all but disappeared; they are all in casings, the transistor as well as the computer. Even if we open them, we find only wires and spools, mere castings; there are no pistons, no levers; they have no body and bulk. There is nothing that moves, nothing to watch, nothing to touch, nothing to fondle. In a modern brewery, the operation is encased in metal and glass, removed from the touch of human hands and the taint of human breath, and there is no smell of the beer. How dull is a spaceship, in spite of its complication, when compared with the *Mayflower* or with the *Spirit of St. Louis*. It is sad, no doubt, but what in the end does it signify?

Does it mean any more than that, if we wish to have things to look at and to touch, we must now make them, not for our use, but for our enjoyment, for our play? If our work has become boring, is not the other side of the coin that we now have the opportunity to make our leisure more delighting? To be "alienated" from our work may mean no more than that, the character of our work having changed, we need to reimagine both it and its place in our lives. After all, when we go to the Smithsonian Institution and revel in the visibility and vigour of the machines, we need to remember the labour—the animal labour, indeed, as Arendt says—which was needed to drive them. They were, when they were used, dirty and heavy and dangerous; and there was nothing very admirable, although it may have been picturesque to those who did not have to do the work, in the mere brawn and muscle, straining for long periods, that was needed to move them.

We are told that the worker has been alienated by the machine from a reality that was "sensual" and "immediate." But what was this reality? It was a kind of hell, its furnaces as singeing; it was the sweatshop; it was endless toil and painful endurance and meagre reward; it was working in dirt and carrying home the dirt, to be dirty for six days of the week, to wash on a Saturday evening, and then for one day only to wear one's Sunday best. The reality was as "sensual" and "immediate" as filth. Physical labour that is voluntary is easy to admire when there is no danger that one will be involuntarily subjected to it. It is simple to agree that the miner at the coal face with his pick was not alienated from his work, until one remembers the coal in his lungs and his veins and his eyes; the gas and the explosions; the cracking pit props and the falling roofs; the water in the seams that might become a deluge; and the living tomb.

Our machines are the uses to which we put them, and the uses to which we put them is a great part of our civilization. It was this that John Dewey proclaimed in the accent which the American needs to recover: "These appliances of art supply a protection, perhaps our chief protection, against a recrudescence of those superstitious beliefs, those fanciful myths and infertile imaginings about nature, in which so much of the best intellectual power of the past has been spent."[6] If we have misused our technology in the past, it is still the resource by which we may contrive to do better in the future. "The world," said Dewey elsewhere, "has not suffered from an absence of ideals and spiritual aims anywhere nearly so much as it has suffered from the absence of means for realizing the ends which it has prized in a literary and sentimental way."[7] Is it one's own imagining that one hears in this the accent of Jefferson, the voice of the American in his estate?

The machine does not exist apart from our use of it, it is not a machine without our participation, as Daniel Yankelovich and William Barrett have well said:

> Children playing around an abandoned cyclotron are not using it as a technical apparatus. It does not even become a technical instrument in the hands of a single scientist: a whole team of scientists is needed to operate this machine, and only then does it become, properly speaking, a piece of technology. It is of the essence of technology that it requires, in addition to machines, the calculated organization of men.[8]

One may go further. The invention and the gadget and the machine are profound liberations of the human spirit, not merely because each is a triumph of man over his environment, but because they are essentially a form of the reimagining of his estate in which man is continually engaged.

THE HIEROPHANTS OF THE NEW TECHNOLOGY

But the habit today is to think of our machines, not as gadgets and appliances which we can control, but as systems which can control us. We think less of a telephone that is convenient to handle than of a telephone system that is out of our hands; not merely of a telephone system but of a communications system. In this manner, we form the idea that the system in fact exists, that it is an objective reality, whereas no system exists except in our minds and imaginations; that is the point of systems, that we make connections. The systems of communications by which we are surrounded today, and of which the telephone and the airplane, say, the computer and the transistor, are parts, are the ways in which we imagine how these may be used.

We can change these ways and change the systems; they are only in our heads. Yet one would not know this from most of the literature about technology, whether it is approving or disapproving. Even our knowledge is presented as something that has an existence that is independent of us, even it is regarded as a system that is in some fanciful way thought to be beyond our control. The accounts are breathless. We are told by Brzezinski that "the volume of digital communication will shortly exceed human conversation across the Atlantic; it has already done so in the United States. Moreover, within the next decade, the value of information export from the United States to Europe will exceed the value of material export."[9] This is stuff and nonsense, because the digits of course have no existence in themselves, no meaning and no value and no use, apart from the conversation by which we determine what meaning and what use they may have; the conversation is still what matters.

"A national information grid that will integrate existing electronic data banks is already being developed to pool the nation's accumulated knowledge," and we are asked to contemplate with wonder "the ultra-microfiche technique, pioneered by NASA, by which a thousand-page book can be reduced to a transparency smaller than the average book page."[10] This kind of excited description is misleading, for even the thousand-page book, in whichever of its forms, does not exist until a meaning and a use are bestowed on it by a reader. There is nothing in a library until *someone* opens a book.

This new "intellectual technology," as Daniel Bell calls it, is almost deified by him, which is perhaps not surprising, since he is self-appointed as one of its high priests. He writes of it with stark obscurity:

An *intellectual* technology is the substitution of algorithms (problem-solving rules) for intuitive judgments. These algorithms may be embodied in an automatic machine or a computer program or a set of instructions based on some statistical or mathematical formula; the statistical and logical techniques that are used in dealing with "organized complexity" are efforts to formalize a set of decision rules. . . . without the computer, the new mathematical tools would have been primarily of intellectual interest, or used, in Anatol Rappoport's phrase, with "very low resolving power." The chain of multiple calculations that can be readily made, the multivariable analyses that keep track of the detailed interactions of many variables, the simultaneous solution of several hundred equations—these feats which are at the foundation of comprehensive numeracy—are possible only with a tool of intellectual *technology,* the computer.[11]

But the computer is just a toy, and that is how we need to imagine it, before its priesthood fixes it like a yoke on our necks. It is something with which we can play; and beside it our intuitive judgments are still our seriousness.

The elevation of this "intellectual technology"—a phrase without any fathomable meaning—is one of the most reactionary of the currents in our societies today. We are being told that the "average reader"—the "layman," the "citizen"—can no longer have the knowledge that is required for purposeful action in his society. So a new priesthood must be created—those whom Bell in fact calls the "hierophants of the new society"[12]—to interpret to us the sacred mysteries of the new knowledge. He celebrates their arrival, which is his own arrival; but Arendt, fifteen years ago, was more accurate in her dismissal of them:

It may be well to remember . . . that throughout ancient history the "intellectual" services of the scribes, whether they served the needs of the public or the private realm, were performed by slaves and rated accordingly. Only the bureaucratization of the Roman Empire and the concomitant social and political rise of the Emperors brought a re-evaluation of "intellectual" services. In so far as the intellectual is indeed not a "worker" . . . he resembles perhaps nobody so much as Adam Smith's "menial servant," although his function is less to keep the life process intact and provide for its regeneration than to care for the upkeep of the various gigantic bureaucratic machines.[13]

Bell says that the new hierophants have "either to compete with politicians or become their allies." This is too exalted a view of their position. In their priesthood, they are servants of, ironically enough, "the system."

What is dangerous in these "intellectual technologists" is that they in fact accept their menial condition, their own subservience to the machine, and therefore ask us to accept our subservience as well. "The post-industrial society is becoming a 'technetronic' society: a society that is shaped, culturally, psychologically, socially, and economically, by the impact of technology and electronics—particularly in the area of computers and communication," says Brzezinski, and he concludes that "it is an open question whether technology and science will in fact increase the options open to the individual."[14] But we can answer that question in our favour if we hold on to the fact that our technology and our electronics are of our creation, and that what we have created is accessible to us and at the disposal of our decisions. "It is no longer resources that limit decisions," said U Thant. "It is decision that makes the resources. This is the fundamental revolutionary change—perhaps the most revolutionary man has ever known." How we respond to this situation is a matter of our own determination.

"We define technology as the organization of knowledge for the achievement of practical purposes," said Emmanuel G. Mesthene in the report of the Harvard Program on Technology and Society.[15] If we organize that knowledge to the wrong purposes, it is not the knowledge or the nature of its organization that are to blame, but the interests which we ask them to serve. The truth is, as Dewey wrote more than forty years ago, that the uses to which we put our technology are largely determined by considerations of private profit, but that is exactly the kind of observation that is resisted by the intellectual technologists, who dismiss it as ideological. But their own passivity before the machine is itself ideological, an acquiescence in the status quo. A remedy of the secondary evils which flow from the dominance of private interests is available to our decision; we are not bound to be the creatures of the machines that we have created.

MAKING THE BUREAUCRACY ACCESSIBLE TO ALL

In this imagining of our estate, there are not only machines to which we are subject, there is the machine or system that controls our lives: the bureaucracy. "Bureaucracy" is only a word and, used descriptively, it refers only to a system of rational co-ordination of complex organizations. That is all, but it becomes in *Webster's*

New International Dictionary: "A system of carrying on the business of government by means of departments or bureaus, each controlled by a chief who is apt to place special emphasis upon routine and conservative action. . . . Hence, in general, such a system which has become narrow, rigid, and formal, depends on precedent, and lacks initiative and resourcefulness." Above all, we are told, this machine or system is impersonal. "They, the people to be administered," says Erich Fromm, "are objects whom the bureaucrats consider neither with love nor hate, but completely impersonally,"[16] a statement for which, of course, no concrete evidence is offered.

It is in fact hard to find any evidence of this rigid and impersonal machine in the United States, or in any other country that is similarly placed. None of the bureaucracies that one encounters are like "the Castle" of Kafka; they are a great deal more like "the Custom House" of Hawthorne, which he describes at the beginning of *The Scarlet Letter.* Since the idea of "bureaucracy," as we have received it, is generally credited to Max Weber, it is worth remembering that he built his theory, at least in part, on his acquaintance with the Prussian bureaucracy which, since the days of Frederick the Great, had exhibited many of the features of a medieval retinue in the service of an almost absolute monarchy. Many of the ideas by which we imagine our reality have origins that are local and historical.

In fact what we know of our bureaucracies, public or private, is the opposite of the Weberian picture that haunts us. Within any bureaucracy there is a continual and intense struggle for power between different personalities—one has only to think of the administration of a large university—and round these contending figures there coalesce different interests and ideas; the bureaucrat is, above all, an in-fighter, and the meaning of this day-to-day contention within the bureaucracy is that it is a great deal more open to external influence than is generally realized. A bureaucracy is known best, not for its impersonal efficiency, for the rationality of its organization, but for its personal fumbling, for the irrationality of its errors. We recognize a bureaucracy when we read that it has fed into a computer an out-of-date list of employees for next week's paychecks, or when it prints millions of coupons for gas rationing with the same picture of George Washington on them as appears on a dollar bill, so that the coupons could have been used in dollar-bill change machines; the impersonal machine is reassuringly given to human error.

When it is organized to a single purpose, such as the development of the atomic bomb, a bureaucracy can act with single-minded efficiency, and we often have reason to be grateful for this. But ordinarily a bureaucracy is cumbersome and unwieldy, changing direction only with as much displacement of water as does an ocean liner; and this resistance also is often valuable to us, since it means that our day-to-day lives are less subject than they might otherwise be to arbitrary decision and change. If we look closely, a bureaucracy is a refuge of idiosyncrasy just as often as of the "organization man" in our imaginations; the bureaucrat is frequently as eccentric as a lepidopterist, hovering over his precedents as the other does over his specimens, and it is through him that the organization is often humanized. The truest characterization of the bureaucrat is that given in many of his stories by Gogol, and we would be better off if we contemplated his quirkiness with something of Gogol's wry sense of the constant intrusion of human beings in even the best-laid schemes.

A bureaucracy is not only a formal structure, it is also an infinite number of informal arrangements. It cannot be otherwise. The kind of large and complex organization that we think of as "bureaucratic" cannot be managed only by rational procedures: it would break down every day, if that were the case; break when it ought to give. In actual life, it gives. It pursues its course as much by improvisation as by precedent, the improvisations often in time becoming the new precedents. There is always something in the In tray that is untidy, and that is still untidy when it is put in the Out tray, that no rule can quite cover. The bureaucrat becomes an artful dodger, capable of creating a "channel of circumvention," as Charles H. Page has called it; and without the artful dodger most bureaucracies would not function effectively.

We are capable of terrifying ourselves by our own imaginings; and we need to overcome our fear of the large-scale organization by realizing that it is only very rarely that it functions as a large-scale organization. For the most part it is an aggregate of smaller organizations that have grown side by side—out of one another, and on one another—and which interlock as a result more often of personal contacts and improvisations than of hierarchical procedures and rules.

It grows like a coral reef, an accretion of live organisms round dead organisms, and it is the live that matter.

It is the live ones that are accessible to us, that we can master. We as well as the bureaucrat can circumvent the organization by using our wits; at least, we can do it if we know how to do it, and this is the point. Those who have enjoyed a certain degree and quality of education are usually skillful in coping with a large organization, in getting round it. We know to whom to go. We know the point in the system where our request or complaint is most likely to be given consideration. We do not go too high or too low. We do not enter the fortess of a bank or a department or a corporation, awed by its size and anonymity. We know how to find someone in it with a name, who at once ceases to be faceless to us.

But this is exactly the point, because those who are ignorant as a result of their social disadvantages do not have these skills and the confidence that they engender, as they do not have the confidence that engenders the skills. The fault does not lie in the size or the impersonality of the organization, it lies in our own failure to educate them to cope with modern life, and this we can remedy. This is the point that was made earlier, when one said that, by not educating a large number of people, Jencks would leave them incapable of coping with their lives from day to day, even if they all enjoyed an equality of income with other people. It is foolish of us, a diversion that we cannot afford, to go on trying to reimagine our societies as if they can be based on small social units, when what is required—at bottom, all that is required—is to educate everyone into the skills and confidence by which our large social units can be mastered.

The effort at reimagining our society in terms of smallness is, again, a part of the revolt against the masses. Our organizations are large because they are trying to give services—usually of comfort and convenience, promising an increase in choice and dignity—to large numbers of people. Social security is given to more and more people, as is medical care, as is higher education, and so we have, not only the *massif* of Health, Education and Welfare, but the complex administration of the large university; cars are made for more and more people, milk provided for them, telephones made available to them, and so we have the great corporations, and the brindled cow organized into something that is called the dairy industry. All of these are gains. The large organization, private as well as public, is the distributor of goods to the commonalty, and it is as mischievous to nourish people to fear it as it is to disdain it. We need it, and we need to reimagine it with a sense of our own measure, so that we can master it. Its largeness needs only to be brought under our control.

THE FAILURE OF THE SOCIOLOGICAL IMAGINATION

In fact, there is something that is false in the whole of our present imagining of our societies, that pits us against them, instead of encouraging us to care for, and to cope with, them as things of our own creation. Few things have been more sad in the past century than what may be called the failure of the sociological imagination. There can be little doubt that sociology has been the most promising, as it has also been one of the most characteristic, of our ways of imagining ourselves and our societies in the past century and a half. It was in part a response—as its "father," Auguste Comte, made clear—to the failure of the French Revolution. No reliance could, after that, be placed in ideology or revolution, so society would be remade, first by scientifically studying it and, secondly, by applying the discoveries of that science in social engineering. But here was the misconception. Sociology was set off on the wrong foot.

Psychology turned in the wrong direction when it broke from philosophy—there was an actual break of psychology from the schools of philosophy in the older universities—in order to claim to be a science; and sociology was set in the wrong direction from the beginning by regarding itself as a science, and setting itself firmly against the kind of reimagining of values that an alliance with philosophy would have demanded of it. It is not just a question of method, but of what the subject of man in his societies is thought to be. Thus, Durkheim could write:

> The social realm is a natural realm which differs from others only by greater complexity. Now it is impossible that nature should differ radically from itself in one case and the other in regard to that which is most essential. The fundamental relations that exist between things cannot be essentially dissimilar in the different realms.[17]

This is in effect a denial that our society—the human estate—is something that we have created apart from nature; and to say that the social realm is a natural realm is to preclude the possibility of sociology itself.

In the first number of the *American Journal of Sociology* in 1895, the great American sociologist Lester F. Ward recited the liturgy: "We all know what an improvement physics has been upon natural philosophy, and biology upon natural history. Sociology stands in about the same relation to the old philosophy of history . . . the last and highest of the sciences . . . we may regard sociology as one of the natural orders of cosmical phenomena . . . the cap-sheaf and crown of any true system of classification of the sciences."[18] Fifty years later, another American sociologist, W. Lloyd Warner, was still making the same claims: "Social facts are capable of scientific treatment. . . . It seems likely that once we place the study of civilization in the framework of an inductive, systematic, comparative sociology, we can increase our knowledge of our own social behavior with the same rapidity that biologists did when they placed the knowledge of our physical structure in the framework of comparative biological science."[19]

What inevitably was the consequence of this approach? The answer may be found in Durkheim, when he said, "We study various aspects of man's social behavior to show an essential and permanent aspect of humanity." Here is exactly the fault that we noticed at the very beginning, and which must occur if the Newtonian synthesis is used in the human sciences: that "we have to find out, by observation, experience, and even experiment, the fundamental and permanent faculties, the properties of man's being that can neither be increased or diminished." This is not only a terrible diminishing of the nature of man, it is also a terrible diminishing of the subject matter of sociology, and of the possibilities of using its insights to reimagine ourselves and our societies.

What happens when we think that we can study ourselves and our societies by the same methods and to the same purposes as those of the natural sciences? For one thing, we are tempted to the approach of one American anthropologist, that "the most realistic and scientifically adequate interpretation of culture is one that proceeds *as if* human beings did not exist."[20] Or again, we get the "philistine obtuseness," as Brand Blanshard has called it,[21] of behaviourism, which grew out of the persuasion of its pioneer, John Watson, that he must "either give up psychology or else make it a natural science," and who denied the existence of mind and consciousness because they could not be found in the test-tube of his science. Of course, the behaviourist is in fact not being scientific. The statement that he presents as scientific—such as that mind does not in fact exist—is usually found to be unverifiable and unfalsifiable, and as such is unscientific; and although this is most obviously true of the behaviourist, it is also true of many of the allegedly scientific propositions and assertions of psychology and sociology. Moreover, the science that they claim as a support has already corrected many of the methods that they still follow.

This is one of the explanations of the essential conformism, and even conservatism, of sociology and, indeed, of all the studies that are significantly known as the "behavioural sciences." Man is reduced to his behaviour, and his behaviour is reduced to his conditioning. In this way, it is easy to return man to nature, human nature to animal nature, as Konrad Lorenz does. He describes the behaviour of animals in terms that have rich and complex associations in human life, and then he proceeds to say that in their behaviour men are doing what animals do, and that it is therefore possible to deduce—implying that the method is scientific—the principles of men's behaviour from the ways in which animals can be seen to behave. From this, the conformism follows. What men have hitherto, as a result of their values and beliefs, thought to be evils, can be shown by Lorenz to be inevitable in our animal natures, and we cannot correct them. As Auden put it in a posthumously published article, "our kinship with the higher mammals" is used as "an excuse for bad behaviour."[22]

Lorenz is not a sociologist, but he is characteristic of the failure of the sociological and psychological imagination in our times, in which man is reduced to little more than a bundle of the properties and attributes of his being that can be neither increased nor diminished; and that therefore there is no way in which he can be reimagined, either in himself or in his societies. Sociology is thus reduced to no more than describing; it does not judge; it claims to be free of values, as does most of psychology. But even this claim is as false as the claim to be scientific. For the denial that judgments of value are being made in fact only conceals the values that are being employed. They are determinist; and it is this determinist standpoint that too often makes sociology today a conservative force, making in effect an inventory of the fixed attributes of man and his societies, instead of contemplating the array of his and its potentialities.

The evidence of this determinism, leading to passivity and conformism, was noticed by Veblen in economics, when it claims to be a science: "Such a quasi-science necessarily takes the current situation for granted as a permanent state of things; to be corrected and brought back into its normal routine in case of aberration. . . . It is a 'science' of complaisant interpretations."[23] It is for the same reason that as influential a political scientist as Ralf Dahrendorf can boast that the concern of his studies, like that of other social sciences, is to identify the "more stable social groupings" behind the changes and contentions of the day, thus ensuring that the purpose of his studies is conservative. The statistics on which these social sciences to a large extent rely are themselves an expression of the belief that men can be relied on to behave consistently in large numbers according to fixed and permanent patterns.

A sociology that fixes its attention on numbers, in the belief that only what is quantifiable can be measured, and only what is measurable in this manner can be scientific, is bound to be passive in its observation of men in their societies, conservative in its reportage, and conformist in its prescriptions. This is a tragedy, for there can be no doubt that our culture has looked, and is still looking to some extent, to the sociological imagination to tell us something that we need to know of ourselves as social beings. The following for sociology at the universities, the popularity of "pop" sociology, the curious effort at a sociological literature in the "new journalism": these are all evidence that there is a profound desire to have ourselves in our societies represented to us with a new imagination. But the imagination that has always been latent in sociology has been stifled.

In all the dottiness of Comte there was an imagination that was trying to get out. "By the aid of Feeling," he said, "an artisan or a woman can without education readily grasp this great encyclopaedic principle" of sociology better than the pure mathematician[24]; and there is a leap implicit in this appeal to "Feeling" that has been arrested from the beginning. Sociology has the wrong ally. Great though the creations and achievements of our science have been, the one thing that is clear is that, in the words of Ortega, "physical science can throw no clear light on the human element. Very well. This means, simply, that we must shake ourselves free from the physical, the natural, approach to the human element. . . . nature is only one dimension of human life."[25] Sociology needs certainly to return to some association with philosophy, but it also needs to be in alliance with the literary, the sociological imagination to be conceived as part of the literary imagination. The influence would be two-way. To put it more sharply, literature and sociology need to inform each other, so that we may again be nourished to reimagine our reality.

THE IMAGINATIVE LIFE OF THE HUMAN REASON

In fact what one is asking for is that the whole breed of priests and acolytes who in our society we call "intellectuals" should determine that they are men of the imagination. By the intellectual, one does not mean any individual who might, with more or less cause, be called an intellectual, but the intellectual as a phenomenon of our age, as a class. Indeed, one may even say that one means that part of us all that is, in our secular age, now the intellectual, as it was once the religious; for all of us now, to some extent, wear the habit of the intellectual, and it is only the intellectual in us that can resist and discipline the artist in us. Nothing is more urgent than that we should be persuaded again that the aesthetic imagination is not the only one, that we can imagine with our minds as well as with our sensibilities, that our thoughts can roam as free as our sensations.

The intellectual was elevated by himself, on a mound of encyclopaedias, to the leadership of the Enlightenment. He would, in the words of one of the *philosophes,* succeed the clergy in its "noblest function . . . of preaching from the rooftops the truths that are too rarely told to sovereigns"; and declare in the boast of another, "Of all the empires, that of the intellectual, though invisible, is the most widespread." This empire was associated with another, as was proclaimed to the French Academy in 1787, ". . . what we have come to call the empire of opinion. Men of letters immediately had the ambition to be its organs, and almost its arbiters. A more serious purpose diffuses itself in intellectual works: the desire to instruct manifested itself." It is worth pointing out in passing that, while the intellectuals in the French Academy were debating the "empire of opinion," the intellectuals in America were engaged in a constitutional convention at Philadelphia.

With the disillusion bred by the course of the French Revolution, the confidence evaporated, but the self-consciousness of the intellectual as a class remained. The intellectual as malcontent was born, not sure of his rank in society, and not certain of the relevance of what he had to say. Whatever else he may understand, he does not today understand his position or his role. He is neither ruler nor subject, he does not lead but he also does not follow. He sees himself as the applier of a method, but the validity of the method and the purposes of its application are not clear. He would be more content if he was still in the service of a church or a sovereign. When instead he serves a politician he finds, not only that the methods of politics are too rough and ready for his own method, but that its purposes are dictated, not by a master with whom he has a relationship that he can comprehend, but by the wishes, real or supposed, of the populace, which he does not know, and which does not seem to know or much care for him. They are "the masses" and they seem to be his master.

Disappointed with the extent of his influence, he still cannot return to the way of truth, to follow where it may, because the truth to him is, by his own definition of his role, something that must be applied: the desire to instruct within the empire of opinion is his mission. So he assists in the subjection of the mind. This is the treason of the clerks. The mind is itself to be despised, the reason to be contemned; and this has, as has been noticed at the beginning, been one of the dominant intellectual themes of the past century and a half. Faith in the human reason is abandoned, and its abandonment is, not only proclaimed, but even boasted. Surrendering his own instrument, the intellectual becomes still more alienated. He begins to envy the artist and to imitate him, bending his ear again to superstition and myth. Existentialism, which is not a philosophy, could not have invaded so many intellectual disciplines if the intellect had not yielded.

What the intellectual—both as a class and as he exists in us all—needs to recover is his sense of the imaginative life of the human reason. It begins in wonder, just as do the "lyrical imaginings" of a Poincaré or an Einstein, and as it has been sung by Ortega:

To be surprised, to wonder, is to begin to understand. This is the sport, the luxury, special to the intellectual man. The gesture characteristic of this tribe consists in looking at the world with eyes wide open in wonder. The faculty of wonder is the delight refused to your football "fan" and, on the other hand, is the one which leads the intellectual man through life in the perpetual ecstasy of the visionary.[26]

Informed by this sense, the intellectual will concede no primacy to religion or art, to superstition or myth. While not denying to other realms their own claims, he will take his stand on the imaginative life of the human reason.

Above all, the intellectual will keep clearly in his mind that the human estate is the centre of his concern, and the arena of his activity; it is there that the empire of opinion is to be found, there that he must influence it, there that he must act, because the intellectual is not in the end an intellectual unless his intention is to act. He is not "pure"; he cannot be innocent. The relationship of the intellectual in America to his society has been a series of infatuations and disillusions. The moments of disillusion are dangerous, to both the intellectual and society. It was against this that Karl Mannheim warned, when he said that intellectuals who "consciously renounce direct participation in the historical process" nevertheless take part in "the great historical process of disillusionment, in which every concrete meaning of things as well as myths and beliefs are slowly cast aside." When thought "turns inwards," he said, "and gives up its conflict with the immediate concrete world, it tends to become innocuous and gentle, or else lose itself in pure self-edification."[27]

We must, it was said earlier, invite the artist back into the estate, for he will not come by himself. But, before that can happen, the intellectual must return to the estate which is his only and his proper arena. He must come back by himself—as did the great spirits of the "golden age" of American philosophy at the beginning of the century—because it is there that he belongs. In other words, he must assist in the restoration of politics as the activity in which the conversation of a society is focussed. Politics is despised by the "intellectual technologist" who believes that society needs only to be managed. But the true intellectual is a political man to the core. It is in politics that he finds, as he must find, the empire of opinion, the public.

The intellectual in America must come out of his closet. It was this that Marías again observed as he gazed on the country:

American intellectual life is not public, but professional in character. I mean to say that the American intellectual is not normally a man in the public eye . . . and if he is it is probably for reasons other than his function as an intellectual. . . .
        . . . the people who know intellectuals are other intellectuals. But even this is saying too much: an intellectual is known only by those who share his special field of interest.[28]

If the intellectual in America is again to become a public man, he must look affectionately at his society, and understand that it was created as a political society, and in that lies its secret.

RESTORING THE CONVERSATION OF POLITICS

One of the clearest signs of the failure in our times to reimagine our estate is the withdrawal from politics. Thirty years ago, the professional middle class of America, as it was described at the beginning of this book, was intensely political; and in its withdrawal from politics both the rebellion of the self and the revolt against their masses are brought to a focus. By the withdrawal from politics, one means the belief that political action is no longer the most effective way, either in which the individual can affect his own society and improve his condition in it, or in which he can assist in the improvement of the condition of others. The meaning of this is perhaps best made plain by saying that the idea of the citizen—which has nourished us since the days of Pericles—is now almost absent from our public discourse.

This situation is passively, as one would expect, described by Dahrendorf: "That there is in fact a withdrawal from politics in modern society, that even among groups which have not changed the direction of their political allegiance, the intensity of political commitment has decreased, is almost a commonplace today."[29] Even as socially committed a sociologist as C. Wright Mills could write that "we need to characterize American society in more psychologic terms"—than the political terms of John Stuart Mill or Karl Marx—"for now the problems that concern us most border on the psychiatric,"[30] which is a way of giving a social licence to the rebellion of the self. Indeed, why not stop trying to amend our societies, and just send everyone instead to a psychiatrist?

All that this political indifference means is political conformism, the abandonment of the effort to change our societies, as J. Valles said in 1882:

> The man who says he has no political opinions confesses to one all the same. He is the collaborator and accomplice of those who hold the whip-hand, who have their hold on the motherland's throat. It is his indifference that supports the slayers of the poor and the butchers of thought.[31]

In fact, the unpolitical man has no right to complain if those in political office do not behave as he would like them to do, whether they bomb Cambodia or pervert the working of the process.

The reduction of politics, which is implied in the retreat from it, is celebrated by an "intellectual technologist" such as Bell, who describes the post-industrial society, as he calls it, as one in which "changes pose management problems for the political system." Politics is diminished to nothing more than management, and the political realm "regulates the distribution of power and adjudicates the conflicting claims and demands of individual groups."[32] This has, indeed, been the teaching of American political science for at least thirty years, of which the emblem has been Harold Lasswell's description of politics as a question of "Who Gets What, When and How."

The allocation of power and resources is, of course, one of the purposes of politics, but it is not the only purpose, not always the primary one, and seldom pursued in isolation from the ideas and aspirations and ideals, which are not merely materialist and often not materialist at all, of those who take part in politics or look to politics for an increase in the satisfaction of their lives. The emphasis on allocation can only reduce the activity of politics either to an amoral pursuit of power—"the distinctive, unifying element of politics," as one American political scientist has put it, "is the struggle for power, elemental, undisguised, and all-pervading"—or to an elitist view of the process—"the authoritative allocation of values," as another American political scientist has called it—or to both.

That politics is a co-operative endeavour of the whole community, the activity in which it most obviously is a community, is not considered.

A situation that is political is complex and subtle, and men act in it from a variety of motives, to a variety of ends, on a variety of levels of apprehension; they are not solely concerned with the allocation of power or resources. This is one of the fascinations of politics. Within its ambiguity there are always more plays than can be seen at once, and one is never quite sure which is the play, and which the play within the play. This ambiguity is its virtue. Politics is the conversation of an entire society at the point at which it is most public, and the value of conversation—what differentiates it from all other discourse—is its tolerance of ambiguity. It is not necessarily meant to have point, or result in a decision. It is the way in which people get used to each other, and without politics there is no other way in which a whole society can do this. Politics is talk; and in democracy it is talk in which all may take part.

Ideas more than interests are at the heart of the talk. The ideas may seem to be only the rationalization of interests or prejudices, or of the situation in which someone finds himself; "ideas in politics," as J. N. Figgis said, "more than anywhere else, are the children of practical needs."[33] But one cannot stop there. The transforming of these interests and prejudices and situations into ideas has the effect of altering them; by generalizing them, a new dimension is added, and the person ceases to act solely from them. The desire for higher wages is transmuted into a conception of human justice which touches much more than the original concern. When the American took the experience of his continent and uttered it as an idea, he altered that experience, and gave it a meaning beyond itself; the local was made universal. The catalogue of parochial grievances in the Declaration of Independence is completely altered by the idea by which they are prefaced.

Politics is the true equalizer, for it is each individual, whatever his quality, who can alone know, as John Strachey said after the Labour government of which he was a prominent member was defeated in 1951, "when the shoe pinches." The settlers in the back-country of Wisconsin were saying much the same when they argued in their petition for statehood that "a fool can sometimes put on his coat better than a wise man can do it for him"; and what must be noticed is that, although they were speaking of their own interests, as they perceived them, these were transformed into an idea, the claim for statehood, round which other ideas were bound to cluster, thus altering the way in which the original grievances were understood.

Politics is the ultimate assertion that things "ain't necessarily so." Disagreement and conflict are at the heart of politics. "In a world of universal agreement, there would be no room for it." The disagreement and conflict occur because there have been changes elsewhere in society, whether in conditions or in attitudes, and the reactions to these changes "never move uniformly towards agreement but, instead, generate new disagreements which communicate themselves to political forces, and sometimes engender new political forces."34 The very activity of politics—its conversation—must necessarily be agitating, because implicit in the conversation is the idea that the human estate can be, perhaps should be, and at times must be, reimagined and remade.

CHAPTER 18

The Pursuit of Happiness in Society

Just as one may say, with some reason, that there are only two "sides" in English history, the Cavaliers and the Roundheads, one may equally say that there are only two "sides" in American history, those who are for the Declaration of Independence and those who are for the Constitution. Of course the two cannot be completely separated; they are twins, but they are not identical ones. Eleven years after the proclamation of the Declaration of Independence that men have a right to the "pursuit of happiness," the Constitution subsituted for that pursuit the right to "property." From that moment, the meaning of the American idea was in dispute; the materialist was set against the idealist.

The pursuit of happiness! It is an impossible idea; at first, it hardly appears to be an idea at all. Voltaire would certainly have turned up his nose at it. Yet it came from the pen of one of the leaders of the American Enlightenment. Jefferson was not a speech writer for himself, throwing out a phrase to capture the audience for a moment. He was addressing a supreme moment in history, and he intended his use of the idea of happiness, and of its pursuits, as a self-evident right of all men. What is more, it was not Jefferson alone who used the idea, and intended it. John Adams in his *Thoughts on Government* reached to a utilitarian formula, that the government which will produce "the greatest quantity of happiness is best"; and he conceived happiness as the dignity of which human nature is capable, it "consists in virtue." Gouverneur Morris wrote to George Washington: "I mean politics in the great Sense, or that sublime

Science which embraces for its Object the Happiness of Mankind." The idea of happiness as a political objective was thus given a universal application.

The happiness whose pursuit was thus guaranteed as a right was a condition to be sought in the public, in society, in the human estate. It was, as Adrienne Koch has put it so well, the "substantial happiness that is achieved by the mature development of man's fullest potentialities"; and that means in his existence as a social being, sustained in that character by his society. The idea can of course be sentimentalized, as when Leila Rogers said before the House Committee on Un-American Activities that *None But the Lonely Heart* was un-American because it was gloomy. But there is something that is unsentimental and penetrating, and in the end irresistible, in the observation of Andrew Burnaby, the Vicar of Greenwich in England, after he had travelled through the "Middle Settlements in North America" in 1759–60, when he said that "America is formed for happiness, but not for empire."

But let us stay with the fundamental assurance of Jefferson that there is a measure of human happiness that is achievable in the human estate, if the estate is so made that this measure may be realized. The simplicity of the idea is something of an enormity to the outsider who is acquainted with "fear and failure at the heart of the world." There is also its concreteness. "Life, liberty, and the pursuit of happiness" is notably less abstract than "Liberté, Egalité, Fraternité." One can go about America and ask, "Are they happy?" in a way in which it is meaningless to go about France and ask, "Are they brotherly?" Even if one's answer is hesitant—as in the observation of Marías: "The smile, for example. Do Americans smile because they are happy? Or in order to be happy?"—the concreteness of the question is still illuminating. One might suggest to Marías, for example, that the smile has something to do with dentistry, with the concern in America that children should have their teeth straightened and whitened, instruments of torture being fastened in their mouths during the years of their growth. Is this a part of the pursuit of happiness? It may well be.

HUMAN HAPPINESS AS A SOCIAL PURSUIT

Unless one concentrates one's attention on the promise of the pursuit of happiness, as a self-evident right to be guaranteed by political arrangements in the society of other men, one will miss forever the exact insight of the founding fathers. They were, after all, alienating themselves from the stays of the Old World, loosing all its bonds, freeing men from all narrow walls; and at that moment they made the tremendous assertion that, although the security of the forms and riches of the Old World was to be snatched from men, human happiness is a social pursuit that can be politically realized. They were meeting the fact of their deliberate alienation from the Old World with a direct response that it demanded the creation of a new kind of social being, one whose claim to pursue happiness must be self-conscious.

This is the answer that the outsider eventually finds to his questions about the solitude of the ordinary American; about the lack of depth in his friendships, and his arresting of a relationship on the level of acquaintance; about the curiosity of his mail, that it is full of communications from strangers, but only rarely brings a long letter from a friend; about the fact that a letter from an American friend, as Howard Higman has put it, is usually only an "itinerary," whereas one from a European friend is usually a "novel"; about the wondering of Marías that "friendship in the United States is usually discontinuous, like a rosary of isolated identical moments, with no progression, no plot, no dramatic route to follow. Friendship for the majority of Americans has no biography: it lacks a biography because no one invents a program for his friendship, a more or less imaginative thread to follow."[2] All of these are common observations, and in the American idea is the answer.

The character of the personal relationships of the European is determined by the fact that he is fixed in his station; even if not literally now, at least still metaphorically, within the "ten minutes' walk." There is assurance and comfort in that; and much can be dared when one is sure of one's place and the places of others. People are accustomed to how to behave. The conventions may make acquaintanceship stiff and difficult, but they also provide the frame within which a friendship, once it is undertaken, may be pursued as an adventure, to any height or depth. But the frame was broken by the Americans in the beginning. They created an artificial society, with no god, no monarch, no rank, no station, and the happiness that men might achieve had to be proclaimed as a social artifact, a creation of the public, its pursuit as a right.

Thus it is, as was said at the beginning, that as an individual the

American is whole only as a citizen, that his private philosophy must be in association with a public philosophy, that the private and the public must in him be joined as they have not been in any society since the ancient world. If these conditions are not fulfilled, the American seems at once to become or to be imagined as Ishmael, as indeed he was given the name of Ishmael as early as 1827 by Fenimore Cooper in *The Prairie*. "I am an Ishmael," Theodore Dreiser once wrote of himself, and Sherwood Anderson said that "sometimes I think that we Americans are the loneliest people in the world." The long tradition in American letters of retreat from society never leads, in spite of the whistling of an Emerson to keep his spirits up, to the personal happiness that is promised, a fact of which at least Hawthorne was aware.

It has always seemed to be more than a coincidence that Jefferson and Adams died on the same day in 1826; "the men of 1776" were passing, with their emphasis on political remedies for what they perceived to be social problems. The new voice that was heard was that of William Ellery Channing, proclaiming the self, as we saw at the beginning; writing in 1828, "It is one mark of the progress of society that it brings down the public man and raises the private man," and in 1842 saying, "The truth is, and we need to feel it most deeply, that our connexion with society, as it is our greatest aid, so it is our greatest peril." For a century and a half this has been one of the most persistent voices in American culture, and its danger is that the pursuit of happiness is thus removed from the society of men to the self in its-self; and the radical failure of so many to achieve even a human measure of happiness in our times ought to warn us of the mistake.

THE ONLY ALIENATION THAT MATTERS

A characteristically American political movement such as the Populists was turned outward to try to reimagine the human estate, the situation of men in their society. An editorial in the *Farmer's Alliance* that was written in 1891 by Jay Burrows in fact approached the question of alienation, but in down-to-earth terms:

The materialism of today does all the time segregate human lives. Take a man for instance who labours hard from fourteen to sixteen hours a day to obtain the bare necessities of life. He eats his bacon and potatoes in a place which might be called a den rather than a home, and then, worn out, lies down and sleeps. He is brutalized both morally and physically. He has no ideas, only propensities. He has no beliefs, only instincts. . . . How can you reach this man? Here is Humanity's problem. It involves all other problems, and all modern life. . . . The tendency of the competitive system is to antagonize and dissociate men.

This was the most profound of the voices of the Populist. Finding men to be "impoverished, voiceless, degraded," he pointed to the society as the place where the causes could be found, and where the evils could be remedied.

There was much at fault in the position of the Populist, but he did not deserve the wholesale disdain of him which became fashionable in the 1950s, and which still influences our attitudes to popular movements. To reimagine the past is, of course, a way of imagining the present, and the intellectual attack on all kinds of popular movements of the past was a part of the propaganda which urged that the country must be governed by "elites" that would hold in check the "authoritarian personality" of "the masses." More recently, a number of historians have worked to rehabilitate the Populist movement, and nothing would be healthier than for their reinterpretations to enter the imagination of the country.

"Woven into the texture of their thought was the insistence," as Norman Pollack has put it, "that men *could* consciously make their future. . . . not the impersonal tendency but men themselves are responsible for contemporary society." From this standpoint, they search for a social order "which not only eliminates poverty but develops and controls technology for the general well-being; one which not only insures widespread suffrage and a fair count but makes participation in the political process meaningful through directly confronting major social problems; and one which not only encourages an ethic of fellowship but goes a good deal further, calling for a transformation of values where the narrow urge of profit gives way to concern for the welfare of all." In short, "they sought to build a society . . . where the individual fulfills himself, not at the expense of others, but as a social being, and in so doing attains a higher individuality."[3]

There were contradictions in their position; especially in office, they revealed a deep suspicion of government, and often acted as fiscal conservatives. But their original inspiration was true; and the United States is in urgent need today of a popular movement that will return men to their social concerns. The elites are interested only in managing the society very much as it now exists, the individuals in it to be distracted by their private concern with their selves.

The alienation of man from god, or man from nature, ought not to be allowed to preoccupy us. The only alienation that matters is that of men from their society, of men from other men; and the primary cause of that alienation today is the character of the work in which most people are engaged. We need to reimagine the nature and purpose of work in our societies, and in doing so we must avoid the mysticism that overtakes too many observers. When we are told by Simone Weil that in what the modern worker does, "only a minute part is played by the miracles of the living body; therefore no gods,"[4] We have to stop and ask how much of a miracle his living body seemed to the industrial labourer in the past, or even to the farm worker. Their bodies were on treadmills.

Calvin Coolidge's vivid memory of the blacksmith who could throw a horse to the ground is an appealing picture of "the miracles of the living body," but one also remembers the village blacksmith from one's own boyhood, and his work was hard, its conditions were filthy and hot, and his life was limited in part by his weariness at the end of the day. It was entertaining to watch him as the sparks flew from his hammer, but one would not have liked to spend a lifetime striking on that anvil, every blow travelling through that living body.

THE UNIVERSAL RIGHT TO SATISFYING WORK

There are few people today who deny that satisfying work is essential to the development of an individual's self-esteem, even to his sense of his-self, of his own identity. Indeed, it is a significant fact that, as the struggle for existence has become less ferocious, and what is generally called the "Protestant work ethic" has consequently become less insistent, the meaning of work has become of central concern to us. We realize that we need work, not in order to exist, but in order to live. Within half a century, the challenge has changed. Unemployment was the deprival of the right to work in order to exist; unsatisfying work is the deprival of the right to work in order to live. The right to work has assumed a meaning that is much richer than it was fifty years ago.

If proof of this were needed, it could be found in the now extensive body of sociological literature about work: this is an example of the exact way in which the sociological imagination at its best can be rewarding; it has helped us to reimagine the nature of work. An even more striking proof is to be found in the report of a Special Task Force on "Work in America" which was made, at his request, to Elliot Richardson when he was Secretary of Health, Education and Welfare. In his own introduction to the report, he said that, after reading it, "one cannot help but feel that, however deeply we have cared in the past, we never really understood the importance, the meaning, the reach of work."

The opening chapter of the report justifies his observation. Starting from a definition of work as "an activity that produces something of value for other people," it reaches far into the manner in which most people are condemned to labour today in activities that do not have the quality of work. "Work plays a crucial and perhaps unparalleled psychological role in the formation of self-esteem, identity, and a sense of order." Work should give a person an awareness of his efficacy and competence in dealing with the objects of work, enable him to acquire a sense of mastery over both himself and his environment, and offer him the assurance from day to day that, by producing something of value to society, he is in turn valued by society.

But the report—to the American government, it must be remembered—goes further. "Basic to all work appears to be the human desire to impose order, or structure, on the world. The opposite of work is not leisure or free time; it is being victimized by some kind of disorder which, at its extreme, is chaos." This is much the same as the observation of Peter L. Berger that "to work means to modify the world as it is found. . . . To work is to mime creation itself." It lends vitality to existence, helps establish the regularity of life, its basic rhythms and cyclical patterns of day and week, month and year. Implicit in this challenging definition of the meaning of work is that the opportunity for such work is the right of all. This is indeed one of the fundamental inspirations of Women's Liberation:

that, deprived of satisfying work in the home, women now need satisfying work in the society at large.

There is no need here to reiterate all the evidence that the great majority of workers, blue-collar and white-collar, are dispirited by their work, instead of being enlivened by it. The persistent malingering and absenteeism are among the commonest signs. "Coffee breaks are costing California about $75,000,000 a year," a state senator said not long ago, and added, "I also understand that male office employees go to the bathroom at least six times a day." An efficiency expert who gave testimony at the same time felt able to confirm that "we've made some preliminary studies which indicate a direct correlation between the two kinds of time-off,"[5] which is the kind of illumination—that the more liquid that is taken in, the more liquid that must come out—that one expects from an efficiency expert. But the coffee break, although it is one of the most prevalent, is also one of the mildest forms of malingering. There is ample evidence that, sullen and resentful at the lack of meaning in their work, a large number of workers have developed many devices of avoiding it.

Neither is it necessary here to examine the ways that have been tried to "redesign the job." There have been many well-documented experiments, in "job enrichment" and "job enlargement," as well as in the kind of "participatory democracy" that has been described earlier, and all of these point to changes of value that can be made, and to imaginative changes that have yet to be made. But this is not the real reimagining that is required. The recognition that work is of central importance in the life of everyone, at a time when the amount of satisfying work that is available seems to diminish year by year, demands from a nation that is committed to the pursuit of happiness a dramatic commitment to solving this problem where it can alone be solved: in the public, in the estate, by a renewed exertion of its political will.

Work is public, it is done in association with others; and when the work is unsatisfying, even demeaning, the individual may be found to retreat more and more into a private sphere that is separated from the public sphere of his work. This private sphere, as Berger says, thus becomes the expression of "who one really is," and the public sphere is where one is "not really oneself": as the son says in *The Glass Menagerie,* when his mother finds that he knows nothing of his workmate: "I only work there." In the disaffection with the public sphere of work is yet another of the causes of the rebellion of the self, and its relation to the revolt against the masses is again clear: the self will rebel in its private sphere, not trying to alter the condition of "the masses" in the public sphere; and that they are both the same person, "the self in its-self" trying to create a tolerable life apart from its-self as "the mass man," has been one of the themes of this argument.

One of the values of work is the enforced social relationships that it demands, different from those of family or friendship. A vivid account of what this can mean has been given by Jack Haas in his description of the relations between ironworkers who work on narrow steel beams high above the ground. A problem that is continually present to them is that of trust; their safety depends on the behaviour of their fellow workers. They use two tests of trustworthiness. The new worker must work alone, high above the ground on a four- to eight-inch beam, with nothing beneath him but it, watched by the more experienced workers who are judging his performance; and he has received no training and no advice to "run the iron." The second test is a continual barrage of verbal harassment often indistinguishable from abuse; under this harassment, the worker must prove his self-control, that he will not break down in a crisis.[6]

In occupations that are less dangerous, the situation may seem to be different, and the tests that are made are certainly less rigorous. Yet this testing is an important part of the social relationships in the sphere of work. "Loyalty?" Harold Macmillan once queried, when the word was used by an interviewer. "Loyalty? There is only one loyalty that matters: that the man next to you on your left, and the man next to you on your right, will not let you down." It was an image drawn from his experience in the trenches in the First World War, but it tells us a lot about the social, as distinct from the personal, relationships on which we rely in our estate. We do not expect to be friends of those with whom we work, but we do expect to be able to rely on them. This is an important lesson to learn: that the milk which our child needs will be delivered by a stranger on time; that on time a stranger will bring us the mail that we hope to receive.

The social has a quality of its own that is significant to us, it keeps us alive in more ways than one; and the social is dependent on the public, and the public is in the end dependent on the political. The importance of work is, among all its other values to us, that it introduces us day by day to the social world, in a way in which no other activity can do. We are forced into daily association with other human beings, whom we have not chosen, as we choose our friends, to whom there is no emotional link, as there is in parenthood or family, but on whom we learn to rely, and they on us. This is associative living, and when deprived of it the human being feels less than he knows that he could be. His friendships and his family are in a way measures of himself; his work is his measure of mankind.

THE DILEMMAS OF LEISURE

It cannot be done in play. Play is something in which one can make up the rules. That is why it is important to the child. He is surrounded by rules that are not of his own making, and he retreats into the world of play, there to make his own rules. "Let's play" is a way of saying, "Let's make up our own rules"; but as he plays, the child discovers that rules are necessary, otherwise there is such discord that even the playing becomes impossible. "You can't do that, it's not how we play the game" is one of the commonest causes of children's squabbles, which the adult is asked to smooth. Adults learn to like rules; they learn that chess or backgammon or bridge are more interesting and more rewarding if the rules are tightly observed. Rules are, not only the recognition of the Other, but the recognition that without the Other there would be no game; and the tantrum of the child, when the game goes against it, is its undisciplined recognition of the Other, in the absence of the rules that could enable it and the Other to continue the game.

The idea that play can satisfy the adult is dangerous because of the increase of leisure that appears to be the promise of our future. It is estimated that in 1937 some 15,000,000 people in Britain took their holidays away from home; by 1962 more than 30,000,000 people were on holiday away from home, and *New Society* mused that, "if all of us in England and Wales exercised our right to go to the coast at the same time, we would each get a strip three-and-a-half inches across." Such a figure could easily be translated into an attack on "the masses," as we noticed earlier. But the situation can occur, of course, only if leisure is assumed to be a time for doing nothing in particular, whereas it ought to be a time for engaging more actively than ever in one's life's pursuit.

Arendt is correct when she says that "the spare time of *animal laborans*"—by which she means much the same as the "mass man" of Ortega—"is never spent on anything but consumption, and the more time left to him, the greedier and more craving his appetites. That these appetites become more sophisticated, so that consumption is no longer restricted to hard necessities but on the contrary mainly concentrated on the superfluities of life, does not change the character of this society."[7] It is all true of the people who surf and lie on beaches, but one has to ask Arendt why it need be. People can be taught to use their leisure in a different way, to imagine their spare time as part of their whole time, so that between their work and their leisure there is a distinction, but no separation.

The celebration of the leisure which we are promised in our futures is usually mischievous. In leisure one can be oneself, so we are told, with the implication that in work one cannot. "To have leisure is to be released for selfhood," says an American writer who is voguish, for "a confrontation with the self in its essential situation."[8] The self is thus placed in its essential situation apart from any social responsibility, for there is no way in which it can be pretended that leisure is an occasion of more social responsibility than work. "What will the rest of humanity do?" asked Ozenfant in 1931, as he confronted the advance of technology. "Have holidays: immense periods of leisure in which to think?"; and he then put the real challenge: "Conceive the frightful emotional and intellectual situation of future humanity, with nothing to do and brains more questioning than before."[9]

It is these brains that are more questioning than before that are at the heart of the problem of work as well as that of leisure. This point is repeatedly emphasized in the report of the Special Task Force on work: "From a workforce with an average educational attainment of less than junior high school, containing a large contingent of immigrants of rural and peasant origin and resigned to cyclical unemployment, the workforce is now largely native-born, with more than a high school education on the average, and affluence-minded." (There is the well-groomed striking mind of our times.) In 1960, 26 per cent of white (and 14 per cent of black) blue-collar workers had completed four years of high school. Only nine years later, 41 per cent of white (and 29 per cent of black) workers in those occupations had completed the full course of a secondary education. "These better-educated workers, quite clearly, are not so easily satisfied as their forebears with the quality of most blue-collar jobs." The quality of education that they have received may not be as high as it should be, but it is difficult to shove anyone's nose into any book for any length of time without his mind asking questions which it did not ask before.

What is more, the increase in the time for leisure means inevitably an increase in the time for education. The celebration of the "under-thirties" during the short career of "The Movement" in the late 1960s was the announcement that a new "age group" had arrived, consisting in those who are today kept in college because the society can find no employment for them. When they eventually go to find employment, they are that much more educated than they would otherwise have been. There is no way in which to turn back this clock. Those who argue the case for a "retreat from education" are avoiding the issue. Since these people are going to be educated any-how, at least in some sense, does one try to educate them well, or merely to half-educate them; does one educate them only to dis-content with their lot and their society, or to the possibility of satisfac-tion with their lot, with their societies, and ultimately with them-selves?

In fact, what we find is that the problem of work and the problem of leisure are connected, and that the link is education. The true purpose of education is to nourish people to a life that is satisfying to themselves and creative of something that is of value to others, whether in their work or in their leisure; and indeed the work and the leisure in this view are one. In the life of the truly educated man, there is no distinction between his work and his leisure; his pursuit is the same at all times, and it is in the most profound of senses the pursuit of happiness. There is no evidence that any but a minute number of the seriously disabled are excluded by their faculties from this pursuit; on the contrary, the evidence from decade to decade is that an unrecognized capacity still lies in most human beings.

RETHINKING THE PURPOSE OF EDUCATION

The reimagining of the nature of work must begin with a reimagin-ing of the purpose of education. Those who would retreat from the American idea are clear in their prescription: "the masses" should be given "vocational education." In 1934, Raymond Postgate identi-fied one of the "spontaneous characteristics" of Fascism: " 'Higher' education is discouraged and technical education ('teaching the working classes to *work*') expected to replace it."[10] But it was John Dewey, as one could easily expect, who gave the most calculated answer to those who would give only vocational education to "the masses." He argued from the premise that education in a democracy is meant to develop the capacity of the individual to choose and make his own career, and he went on:

> This principle is violated when the attempt is made to fit individuals in advance for definite industrial callings, selected not on the basis of trained original capacities, but on that of the wealth or social status of parents. As a matter of fact, industry at the present time undergoes rapid and abrupt changes through the evolution of new methods. New industries spring up, and old ones are revolutionized. Consequently an attempt to train for too specific a mode of efficiency defeats its own purpose. When the occupation changes its methods, such individuals are left behind with even less ability to adjust themselves than if they had had a less definite training. But, most of all, the present industrial constitution of society is, like every society which has ever existed, full of inequities. It is the aim of progressive education to take part in correcting unfair privilege and unfair deprivation, not to perpetuate them.[11]

The only purpose of the present proposals to revive vocational education for "the masses," and preserve a full university education for the few, can be to perpetuate the privilege and deprivation that already exist in the society.

Many elaborate tests have shown that, even in the mundane occupations in which most people are employed, a general education can make a difference in the attitude and the performance of the worker which a technical education does not make. In one study of a manpower training programme in Norfolk, Virginia, it was found that those who had been given a general education as well as technical training were more likely to be employed a year after their training, were more mobile, and were more ready to venture into "different, more profitable, fields." The advantages from which they seemed to have benefited were: the increase in the facility of their language and in their command of number concepts; the sharpening of their insights into the world of work and into the working of the economy; and the improvement in their ability to present themselves and to achieve satisfactory relationships in their work. Accompanying all this, there was the increase in their confidence and self-esteem. "Feel more confident in my work," said one worker of the benefits of his general education. "Reading and math gave new insights," said another. "Communication skills in language arts classes helped a lot," added a third. "Know more about life—want more," concluded a fourth; and with that one is in the realm of expectations, and the need to expand them.[12]

America embarked on its effort to give a general education to everyone at the beginning, in the famous Massachusetts Ordinance, while it was still a colony, compelling every community to provide such an education in order to save the children from "the old seducer," the devil; and the purpose was reaffirmed, although in secular terms, by John Adams in the Massachusetts Constitution more than a century later. At the beginning of our own century, Sara Burstall, the headmistress of the Manchester High School for Girls, travelled from England to America, and concluded: "America believes in education, while England fundamentally does not." The comment of *The Spectator* on her impressions at the time could stand today with little alteration:

> Americans educate the mass, while we have always educated the leaders. . . . It has been the immemorial practice of England to train leaders for the nation. . . . Americans rather concentrate on the ruck. . . . English teachers feel that there is a certain body of knowledge which it is necessary for their pupils definitely to acquire. . . . The American teachers, on the other hand, do not try so much to implant knowledge in their pupils' minds as to produce power and facility of thought.

The alteration that is required—and it is the only alteration that is necessary—is in the last sentence. For "power and facility of thought" one is inclined now to substitute "independence of attitude."

There is a lack of rigour in American education today that is in danger of defeating its purpose. Robert Hutchins once referred to "the great criminal," Charles William Eliot, who, "as President of Harvard, applied his genius, skill and longevity to the task of robbing American youth of their cultural heritage. Since he held that there were no such things as good or bad subjects of study, his laudable effort to open the curriculum to good ones naturally led him to open it to bad ones and finally to destroy it altogether."[13] In the thirty years that have elapsed, the discipline of the curriculum, from grade school to the university, has been further weakened; and much of the justification has been found, mistakenly, in the writings of Dewey.

Few people could have been more emphatic on the point. He argued strenuously that "the notion of a spontaneous normal development" of the innate, instinctive capacities of the child or individual "is pure mythology. . . . There is no learning except from a beginning in unlearned powers, but learning is not a matter of the spontaneous overflow of the unlearned powers. . . . The neglect, suppression, and premature forcing of some instincts at the expense of others are responsible for many avoidable ills, there can be no doubt. But the moral is, not to leave them alone to follow their own 'spontaneous development,' but to provide an environment which shall organize them."[14] There is no "permissiveness" in that.

It is a tragedy at the moment that the great American experiment in universal education should be diverted by its erroneous conviction that the child or the student can himself know what he should learn and how he should learn it. This removes one of the primary social functions of education; it arrests the self in its-self at the very place where it should be brought into strenuous contact with what is Other; it puts the emphasis on the individual as he was born and what he was born with, rather than on what he has learned and can still learn. Not everyone may agree with Auden that "the class distinctions proper to a democratic society" are those of age; that in a democracy it is more important than in other societies that "a distance should be kept between the young and the adult, the adult and the old"; and that "what the United States needs are puberty initiation rites and a council of elders."[15] But there is a danger that, if the I is released in the person of the unformed child in the classroom, even those who enjoy a higher "education" will grow up not to think mechanically, maybe, "but only because [they] cannot think at all," having never learned how.

This in itself, as has already been hinted, can be a form of class distinction, between those who have been taught to think and those who have only been taught to express what they believe to be their own selves, so that they become two classes, of those who are rulers and those who are helots. The more one searches into these questions, the more clear it becomes that, whether one looks at them from the point of view of the individual or the society, the most urgent task that confronts the public mind of America today is to reimagine the meaning of the original promise of education for all, extending that promise into the field of higher education. This most American of all ideas needs to be rethought, with the conviction that America alone has the resources and the political will to make the experiment, with facilities of "amplitude and efficiency." It is here that the reimagining of the estate must begin, because it is here that it is most clear that it is our learned behaviour that matters, and that this can be changed.

THE TRUE AMERICAN CERTAINTY

This book has not been a work of prescriptions; America has enough of prescriptions with too little sense of a common endeavour. If anything, the argument has been the initial response of an outsider to the humanism of the American tradition and experience, even of American society and life today, which is at the moment too much overlooked, and which he has discovered with surprise and reassurance: a response to those uprights that are driven deep through the national consciousness. This humanism has been at the core of that consciousness since Roger Williams set foot on American soil in 1631, often in tension with other ideas, but its expression never for long muted. Whenever it is set aside in favour of religion or superstition or myth, of tradition and hierarchy and custom, America loses its own conviction in itself, and the world its conviction that America is at the prow of civilization.

George Norlin once said that he meant by humanism "an attitude of mind and heart which holds to the preciousness of human life, which has faith in the potential dignity and worth of our human being apart from the trappings of wealth or station, and which strives to create a social soil and climate wherein every human personality may take root and flower and be fruitful, each in accordance with the nature and capacity of each."[16] No statement, with its embedding of the individual in the soil of the social, could be more American. It was, after all, an American philosopher who not long ago, as the French pursued the fatal attractions of the existential gesture, and the English picked at language until they picked all sense out of it, proclaimed that "the job of philosophy is to work out a new kind of materialism, able to do justice to the human scene. Here we have a unique level of existence which has evolved in this planet and is the culmination of biological and cultural developments."[17]

The "social soil and climate," the "human scene": since the "golden age" of American philosophy at the beginning of this century, American thought and literature and art have increasingly disdained these. Although he once made a world, the mind and the imagination of the American have been bent increasingly to consider only the immutable forces that control his life, not to try to negotiate with them in his estate, but only to transcend them. In the early 1950s, Malcolm Cowley said of such writers of fiction as Jean Stafford and Truman Capote:

> The characters in the new fiction are distinguished by their lack of a functional relationship with American life. They don't sow or reap, build, mine, process or sell, repair, heal, plead, administer, or legislate. In a still broader sense they don't join or belong. . . . [They] are exceptional persons who keep away from offices . . . and are generally as unattached as Daniel Boone. As compared with the population at large, the characters include an abnormally large number of persons living on inherited incomes.

His last sentence is to the point, for the preoccupation with personal problems to be personally solved or transcended is for the privileged.

But something is lost even for the privileged, a sense of the day-to-day enduring and, with the enduring, loving of ordinary men and women for it is in this human quality that they in fact find the resource to construct for themselves a happiness and even a peace here that are attainable in spite of the implacability of nature and the cold and the dark of the universe. Americans once had this benign estimate of the individual, placed in his society, and also the faith that he could, in association, use his knowledge to extend the boundaries and the satisfactions of his life. "Knowledge is humanistic in quality not because it is *about* human products in the past, but because of what it *does* in liberating human intelligence and human sympathy."[18] That is the true American creed, which can still teach the world, if it is recovered, and teach once more that the liberation can be, not for some, but for all.

References

PART I: THE SPOILED CHILD OF THE WESTERN WORLD

CHAPTER 1: THE INCITEMENTS TO PERMISSIVENESS

1. Jerry Rubin, *Do It!: Scenarios of the Revolution* (New York: Simon & Schuster, 1970), p. 101.
2. Thomas E. Dewey, speech accepting the presidential nomination at the Republican National Convention, Chicago, June 1944.
3. Lewis Corey, "Problems of Peace. IV: The Middle Class," *Antioch Review*, V, No. 1 (Spring 1945), 87.
4. Robert Nisbet, "Has Futurology a Future?" *Encounter*, XXXVII, No. 5 (November 1971), 20.
5. Calvin Coolidge, *The Autobiography of Calvin Coolidge* (New York: Cosmopolitan Book Corporation, 1929), p. 54
6. Henry Wallace, speech to the Free World Association, New York City, May 8, 1942.
7. Dwight Macdonald, "The Waldorf Conference," *Politics*, VI, No. 1 (Winter 1949), 32–36.
8. Arthur M. Schlesinger, Jr., "The Decline of Greatness," *The Politics of Hope* (Boston: Houghton Mifflin Co., 1962), p. 25.
9. William Graham Sumner, *Folkways* (Boston: Ginn and Co., Atheneum Press, 1907), pp. 50, 205–06.
10. Julián Marías, *America in the Fifties and Sixties* (University Park, Pa.: The Pennsylvania State University Press, 1972), pp. 137–38.
11. George Melly, "Pop World and Words," *New Society*, I, No. 3 (October 18, 1962), 32.
12. Rubin, op. cit., p. 70.
13. Thorstein Veblen, *The Theory of the Leisure Class* (1899) (New York: Modern Library, 1934), p. 188.
14. Patricia Nixon, quoted in *Time*, January 3, 1959.
15. Ronald Atkinson, *Sexual Morality* (New York: Harcourt, Brace & World, 1965), pp. 51–52.
16. Peter Worsley, "The Spread of Jazz," *The Listener*, LXIX, No. 1772 (March 14, 1963), 456–58.

17. Jean Wahl, "Existentialism: A Preface," *New Republic*, CXIII, No. 14 (October 1, 1945), 442.

18. *Times Literary Supplement*, XXII, No. 1123 (July 26, 1923), 493.

19. *Time*, January 10, 1969, p. 68.

20. Iris Murdoch, *The Sovereignty of the Good* (New York: Schocken Books, 1971), p. 27.

21. John Stuart Mill, *A System of Logic, Ratiocinative and Inductive* (8th ed.; New York: Harper & Brothers, 1874), p. 632.

22. Richard Chase, *The Democratic Vista: A Dialogue on Life and Letters in Contemporary America* (Garden City, N.Y.: Doubleday Anchor Books, 1958), pp. 13–14.

23. Alexis de Tocqueville, *Democracy in America* (1835–39), ed. Phillips Bradley (New York: Alfred A. Knopf, 1956), II, 4.

24. Antoine Cournot, *Considérations sur la marche des idées et des événements dans les temps modernes* (Paris, 1872), Bk. I, Ch. 8.

25. Rubin, op. cit., pp. 106–08, 127, 11, 79, 18–19.

26. Irving Louis Horowitz, "Rock, Recordings and Rebellion," *The Anti-American Generation*, ed. Edgar Z. Friedenberg (Chicago: Aldine, 1971), p. 145.

27. André Weiner, "Political Rock," *New Society*, XIX, No. 487 (January 27, 1972), 187–89.

28. Charles Reich, *The Greening of America: How the Youth Revolution Is Trying to Make America Livable* (New York: Random House, 1970), pp. 140–42.

CHAPTER 2: THE GODFATHERS OF THE CHILD

1. George Gaylord Simpson, *The Meaning of Evolution* (New York: Mentor Books, 1951), p. 179.

2. S. E. Luria, *Life: The Unfinished Experiment* (New York: Charles Scribner's Sons, 1973), p. 15.

3. Simpson, op. cit., p. 179.

4. Bruce Mazlish, "Our Heraclitean Period," *The Nation*, CXCII, No. 15 (April 22, 1961), 336–38.

5. Simpson, op. cit., p. 179.

6. Luria, op. cit., p. 15.

7. Karl Popper, *The Open Society and Its Enemies* (1945) (New York: Harper Torchbooks, 1962) II, 201–iii.

8. Rubin, op. cit., p. 130.

9. *Times Literary Supplement*, XXIII, No. 1147 (January 10, 1924), 13.

10. José Ortega y Gasset, *The Revolt of the Masses* (New York: W. W. Norton & Co., 1932), pp. 94, "History as a System," *History as a System and other Essays Toward a Philosophy of History* (1941), (New York· W. W. Norton & Co., 1962) pp. 177–79.

11. Ozenfant, *Foundations of Modern Art* (1931) (New York: Dover Publications, 1952), p. 184.

12. Jacques Maritain, *The Dream of Descartes* (1944), tr. Mabelle L. Andison (Port Washington, N.Y.: Kennikat Press, 1969), pp. 148–49.

13. Coolidge, op. cit.

14. Albert Einstein and Leopold Infeld, *The Evolution of Physics from Early Concepts to Relativity and Quantum* (1938) (New York: Simon & Schuster, 1960), pp. 31, 75.

15. Simone Weil, *First and Last Notebooks*, tr. Richard Rees (London: Oxford University Press, 1970), p. 9.

16. C. Day Lewis, "Robert Frost, 1874–1963," *The Listener*, LXIX, No. 1767 (February 7, 1963), 283.

17. Maurice Merleau-Ponty, *Sense and Nonsense*, tr. Hubert L. Dreyfus and Patricia A. Dreyfus (Evanston, Ill.: Northwestern University Press, 1964), p. 3.

18. Maritain, op. cit., pp. 178–79.

19. José Ortega y Gasset, "Notes on the Novel" (1925), *The Dehumanization of Art and Other Essays on Art, Culture and Literature* (Princeton, N.J.: Princeton University Press, 1968), p. 63.

20. Einstein and Infeld, op cit., pp. 120–21.

21. Frank Lloyd Wright, *Genius and the Mobocracy* (New York: Duell, Sloan & Pearce, 1949), p. 88.

22. Alexandre Koyré, "The Significance of the Newtonian Synthesis," *Newtonian Studies* (Cambridge, Mass.: Harvard University Press, 1965), pp. 20–24.

23. Ortega, *The Revolt of the Masses*, pp. 45–46.

24. Paul Tillich, in an interview, *The Listener*, LXVI, No. 1707 (December 14, 1961), 1026.

25. Eugene Rabinowitz, "Integral Sciences and Atomized Art," *Bulletin of the Atomic Scientists*, XV (February 1959), 64.

26. Susan Sontag, "The Death of Tragedy," *Partisan Review*, XXX, No. 1 (Spring 1963), 122.

27. Merleau-Ponty, "Preface," op. cit., p. 3.

28. Richard M. Weaver, "Individuality and Mortality," *Essays in Individuality, ed. Felix Morley* (Philadelphia: University of Pennsylvania Press, 1958), pp. 76–77.

29. Frank Getlein, "The Ordeal of Mark Rothko," *New Republic*, CXL, No. 6 (February 6, 1961), 29–30.

30. Rubin, op. cit., pp. 98–101.

31. Martin Green, "A Year of Science," *The Listener*, LXVI, No. 1708 (December 21, 1961), 1071.

32. G. W. F. Hegel, *The Phenomenology of the Mind* (1807), tr. J. B. Baillie (New York: Harper Torchbooks, 1969), p. 75.

33. Herbert Read, *High Noon and Darkest Night: Some Observations on Ortega y Gasset's Philosophy of Art* (Middletown, Conn.: Wesleyan Center for Advanced Studies, 1964), p. 12.

34. Nikolaus Pevsner, *The Listener*, LXV, No. 1664 (February 16, 1961), 299–301.

35. Read, op cit., p. 16.

36. Lionel Trilling, "The Modern Element in Modern Literature," *Partisan Review*, XVIII, No. 1 (January–February 1961), 25–26.

PART II: THE PRESENCE OF THE AMERICAN

CHAPTER 3: THE BEGINNING OF AMERICAN TIME

1. Thomas Pownall, *An Memorial Addressed to the Sovereign of America* (London, 1783).

2. Ezra Pound, *Patria Mia* (Chicago: Ralph Fletcher Seymour, 1950), pp. 41–43.

3. Ann Massa, *Vachel Lindsay: Fieldworker for the American Dream* (Bloomington, Ind.: Indiana University Press, 1970), p. 10.

4. Ortega, "The Dehumanization of Art," pp. 50–52.

CHAPTER 4: THE COUNTRY WHICH IS AN IDEA, THE IDEA WHICH IS A COUNTRY

1. W. H. Auden, "Introduction," *Poets of the English Language*. Vol. IV: *Blake to Poe*, eds. W. H. Auden and Norman Holmes Pearson (New York: The Viking Press, 1953), pp. xxii–xxv.

2. Frederick Jackson Turner, "The Significance of the Frontier in American History" (1893), *The Frontier in American History* (New York: Holt, Rinehart & Winston, 1962), p. 4.

3. Jeremy Rifkin, "The Red, White and Blue LEFT," *The Progressive*, XXXV, No. 11 (November 1971), 14–21.

4. Adrienne Koch, *Power, Morals, and the Founding Fathers: Essays in the Interpretation of the American Enlightenment* (Ithaca, N.Y.: Cornell University Press, 1961), pp. 126–28.

CHAPTER 5: THE AMERICANIZATION OF THE WORLD

1. Ortega, *The Revolt of the Masses*, pp. 27–28.

2. Marías, op. cit., pp. 346, 414.

3. John Dewey, *Individualism Old and New* (New York: Minton, Balch & Co., 1930), pp. 21–22.

4. David Riesman, *The Lonely Crowd* (New Haven: Yale University Press, 1950), pp. 20–21.

5. Babette Deutsch, review of Archibald MacLeish's *New Found Land*, in New York *Herald Tribune Books*, VI, No. 43 (July 6, 1930), 4.

6. Karl Jaspers, in *The Future of Mankind*, quoted in the *New Republic*, CXLIV, No. 12 (March 2, 1961), 11.

7. Geoffrey Gorer in a symposium, *The Listener*, LXVII, No. 1725 (March 19, 1962), 669.

8. Daniel J. Boorstin, *The Americans: The Democratic Experience* (New York: Random House, 1973), p. 14.

9. Donald Macrae, "American Sociology: 2½ Cheers," *New Society*, II, No. 47 (August 22, 1963), 6–8.

10. Alvin W. Gouldner, *The Coming Crisis of Western Sociology* (New York: Basic Books, 1970), p. 22.

11. John Russell, "English Education: More Room at the Top," *The Reporter*. XXIV, No. 9 (April 27, 1961), 28.

12. Paul Shrecker, "American Diary, Part I," *Harper's Magazine*, CLXXXIX, No. 1130 (July 1944), 199–200.

13. In Katherine Elliott, ed., *The Family and Its Future* (London: J. & A. Churchill, 1970), p. 38.

14. Peter Hall, "Going American?" *New Society*, XVIII, No. 459 (July 15, 1972), 117.

15. Editorial, *New Society*, III, No. 58 (November 7, 1963), 3–4.

CHAPTER 6: THE QUEST FOR THE PUBLIC IN AMERICA

1. Quoted in F. R. Cowell, *Cicero and the Roman Republic*, (London: Penguin Books, 1948), p. 18.
2. Erich Fromm, *The Sane Society* (New York: Rinehart & Co., 1955), p. 62.
3. Dewey, op. cit., pp. 28–29.
4. George Norlin, *The Quest of American Life* (Boulder: University of Colorado, 1945), p. xiv.
5. William Graham Sumner, *What Social Classes Owe Each Other* (New York: Harper & Brothers, 1888), pp. 113, 120–22.
6. Pound, op. cit., p. 54.
7. Arthur Mizener, "Defining the Good American," *The Listener*, LXVIII, No. 1742, (August 16, 1962), 241.
8. Pound, op. cit., p. 48.

PART III: THE HUMAN ESTATE

CHAPTER 7: IN PRAISE OF SURVIVORS

1. Eric F. Goldman, "This Tree in Bearing," *New Republic*, CXII, No. 24 (June 11, 1945), 819.
2. Lionel Trilling, *Matthew Arnold* (1938), p. 88.
3. Robert Nisbet, "Moral Values and Community" (1960), *Tradition and Revolt* (New York: Random House, 1968), p. 132.
4. Marías, op. cit., p. 444.
5. John Plamenatz, *Ideology* (New York: Praeger Publishers, 1970), p. 23.

PART IV: THE REBELLION OF THE SELF

CHAPTER 8: THE DO-IT-YOURSELF GOD KIT

1. Dag Hammarskjöld, *Markings* (New York: Alfred A. Knopf, 1965), p. 77.
2. Murdoch, op. cit., p. 55.
3. Gilbert Murray was quoting Pliny, *Natural History*, Bk. II: 7, 18.
4. David Thorburn, "The Artist as Performer," *Commentary*, LV, No. 4 (April 1973), 87–93.
5. Ortega, "In Search of Goethe from Within" (1949), *The Dehumanization of Art*, pp. 147–48.
6. Jacques Maritain, "Poetry and Religion," tr. T. S. Eliot, *The Criterion*, January–May 1927.
7. Arthur M. Schlesinger, Jr., "Reinhold Niebuhr's Role in American Political Thought and Life." *The Politics of Hope*, pp. 97–125.
8. Schlesinger, "Liberalism in America: A Note for Europeans," op. cit., p. 63.
9. Judith Shklar, *After Utopia: The Decline of Political Faith* (Princeton, N.J.: Princeton University Press, 1957), pp. 5, 219.
10. Arthur M. Schlesinger, Jr., "The Causes of the Civil War: A Note on Historical Sentimentalism," *Partisan Review*, XVI (1945), 969–81.

11. Editorial, *The Progressive*, XXXV, No. 11 (November 1971), 4.

12. *Time*, January 17, 1969, p. 51.

13. Winthrop S. Hudson, *Religion in America: An Historical Account of the Development of American Religious Life* (2nd ed.; New York: Charles Scribner's Sons, 1973), p. 425.

14. Chase, op cit., pp. 73, 77.

15. W. H. Auden, "Heresies," *Forewords and Afterwords* (New York: Random House, 1973), p. 45.

16. Gilbert Murray, *Five Stages of Greek Religion* (New York: Columbia Unversity Press, 1925), p. 18.

17. Ninian Smart, "Yoga in the Suburbs," *The Listener*, LXV, No. 1659 (January 12, 1961), 73.

18. Salvador de Madariaga, "On the Western God," in New York *Herald Tribune Books*, VI, No. 38 (June 1, 1930), 1.

19. Ozenfant, op. cit., p. x.

20. George Santayana, *The Life of Reason*. Vol. III: *Reason in Religion* (New York: Charles Scribner's Sons, 1905), p. 277.

21. Ozenfant, op. cit., p. xiv.

22. Georg Büchner, *Woyzeck* (1879), *The Modern Theatre*, ed. Eric Bentley (Garden City, N.Y.: Doubleday & Co., 1955), I, 28.

23. Merleau-Ponty, op. cit., p. 5.

24. Robert Birley, Burge Memorial Lecture for 1947, quoted in Nisbet, *Tradition and Revolt*, p. 54.

25. Ralph G. Hendricke in Elliott, ed., op. cit., p. 49.

26. Lionel Abel, "Beyond the Fringe," *Partisan Review*, LXXX, No. 1 (Spring 1963), 111.

27. Weil, op. cit., p. 47.

28. Ortega, "History as a System," *History as a System*, p. 231.

29. Gregory Baum, "Cultural Causes for the Change of the God Question," *Concilium*, VIII, No. 6 (June 1972), 48–57.

30. Jürgen Moltmann, "The 'Crucified God': God and the Trinity Today," *Concilium, loc. cit.*, p. 27.

31. Harvey Cox, *The Seduction of the Spirit: The Use and Misuse of People's Religion* (New York: Simon & Schuster, 1973), p. 167.

32. Ibid., p. 253.

CHAPTER 9: MAKING A FOOL OF NATURE

1. Friedrich Nietzsche, *The Birth of Tragedy* (1872), tr. Walter Kaufmann, *The Basic Writings of Nietzsche* (New York: Modern Library, 1968), p. 43.

2. Ralph Waldo Emerson, "Nature," *Nature: Addresses and Lectures* (Boston: Houghton Mifflin & Co., 1883), pp. 15–16.

3. *Edinburgh Review*, No. 426 (October 1908), p. 355.

4. Stephen Railton, "Thoreau's Resurrection of Virtue," *American Quarterly*, XXIV, No. 2 (May 1972), 210–27.

5. W. H. Auden, *Epistle to a Godson and Other Poems* (New York: Random House, 1972), p. 49.

6. Hannah Arendt, *The Human Condition* (Chicago: University of Chicago Press, 1958), pp. 96–97.

7. Sumner, *Folkways*, pp. 16, 327.

8. Erik Erikson, *Childhood and Society*, Second ed. (New York: W. W. Norton & Co., 1963), pp. 94–95.

9. Judith Hole and Ellen Levine: *Rebirth of Feminism* (New York: Quadrangle Books, 1971), p. 172.

10. Shulamith Firestone, *The Dialectic of Sex: The Case for Feminist Revolution* (New York: William Morrow & Co., 1970), p. 10.

11. John Rees, *Equality,* (New York: Praeger Publishers, 1971), p. 21.

12. *Edinburgh Review,* loc. cit.

CHAPTER 10: THE EXHAUSTION OF THE SELF

1. Philippe Ariès, *Centuries of Childhood*, tr. Robert Baldick (New York: Alfred A. Knopf, 1962), pp. 33–34.

2. Anton C. Zijderveld, *The Abstract Society: A Cultural Analysis of Our Time* (Garden City, NY.: Doubleday & Co., 1970), p. 16.

3. Murdoch, op. cit., p. 67.

4. Lionel Trilling, *Sincerity and Authority* (Cambridge, Mass.: Harvard University Press, 1972), pp. 4–5.

5. Dewey, *Individualism Old and New,* pp. 85–86.

6. Malcolm Cowley, *Exile's Return* (New York: W. W. Norton & Co., 1934), p. 80.

7. O. Fenichel, *The Psychoanalytic Theory of Neurosis* (New York: W. W. Norton & Co., 1945), pp. 110–11.

8. Robert M. Adams, "Fashions in Fiction," *Partisan Review,* XXX, No. 1 (Spring 1963), 130.

9. Mary McCarthy, "Characters in Fiction," *Partisan Review,* XXVIII, No. 2 (March–April 1961), 182.

10. Leslie A. Fiedler, "Up from Adolescence," *Partisan Review,* XXIX, No. 1 (Winter 1962), 127–31.

11. Rubin, op. cit., pp. 12, 86.

12. Thomas B. Morgan, "Brigitte Bardot, Problem Child," *Look,* August 12, 1960, p. 88.

13. Andy Warhol, quoted in *The Progressive,* XXXIV, No. 11 (November 1970), 37.

14. A. Alvarez, "Beyond All This Fiddle," *Times Literary Supplement,* (March 1968).

15. Pamela Smith, "Architectonics: Sylvia Plath's Colossus," *Ariel,* IV, No. 1 (January 1973), 5.

16. Marías, op. cit.

17. Rubin, op. cit.

18. Dewey, *Individualism Old and New,* pp. 143, 32, 53, 61, 70, 81, 82, 167.

CHAPTER 11: "THE MOVEMENT": TRYING TO TURN THE INSIDE OUT

1. Paul Goodman, *The New York Times Magazine,* February 25, 1968, p. 6.

2. David Riesman, "Universities on Collision Course," in Friedenberg, ed., op. cit., pp. 53–60.

3. Fred Davis, "Why All of Us May Be Hippies Someday," in Friedenberg, ed., op. cit., pp. 61–79.

4. Rubin, op. cit., pp. 87–88.

5. Edmund D. Pellegrino, "Of Passions—Hot and Cool," *American Benedictine Review,* Vol. XXIII, No. 3 (September 1972).

6. Rubin, op. cit.

7. C. Vann Woodward, "The Future of the Past," *American Historical Review*, LXXXV, No. 3 (February 1970), 718, 722.

8. Rubin, op. cit., pp. 89, 98, 113.

9. Davis, op. cit.

10. Michael E. Brown, "The Condemnation and Persecution of the Hippies," in Friedenberg, ed., op. cit., p. 110.

11. Rubin, op. cit.

12. Rifkin, op. cit., pp. 17–18.

13. Arthur Lothenstein, "Introduction," *"All We Are Saying . . .": The Philosophy of the New Left* (New York: G. P. Putnam's Sons, 1970), p. 11.

14. Hoffman, op. cit.

15. Rubin, op. cit.

16. Andrew Kopkind, "The Real SDS Stands Up," *Hard Times*, June 30, 1969, reprinted in Harold Jacobs, ed., *Weatherman* (Berkeley, Calif.: Ramparts Press, 1970), p. 15.

17. Rubin, op. cit., p. 84.

18. Mark Rudd, quoted in *National Review*, November 5, 1968.

19. Rubin, op. cit., pp. 37, 82.

20. Kopkind, op. cit., p. 18.

21. Lothenstein, op. cit., p. 16

22. Martin Duberman, "The Agony of the American Left," the New York *Times Book Review*, March 23, 1969.

23. Allen Ginsberg, quoted in Rubin, op. cit., p. 45.

24. Rubin, op. cit., p. 55.

25. Ibid.

26. Hoffman, op. cit.

27. Free, op. cit., p. 10.

28. Rubin, op. cit., p. 122.

29. Kirkpatrick Sale, *SDS* (New York: Random House, 1973), pp. 10–11.

30. Atkinson, op cit., pp. 81–83.

31. Derek Miller, "Marriage and the Family in the Near Future," in Elliot ed., op. cit., p. 63.

32. John Dewey, *Democracy and Education* (1916) (New York: The Free Press, 1966), p. 121.

PART V: THE FICTION OF THE MASSES

CHAPTER 12: THE FICTION OF THE MASSES

1. *Times Literary Supplement*, No. 937 (January 2, 1920), pp. 1–2.

2. Fromm, op. cit., p. 110.

3. Walter Kaufmann, "Introduction" to Richard Schacht, *Alienation* (Garden City, N.Y.: Doubleday & Co., 1971), p. xviii.

4. All quotations from Ortega in this chapter are from *The Revolt of the Masses*, pp. 14, 76, 14, 18, 77, 19, 25, 63–4, 68, 11, 11–12.

5. Louis MacNeice, "American Letter," *Horizon*, I, No. 7 (July 1940), 462.

6. Herbert Read, "Tourism Unlimited," *The Listener*, LXV, No. 1661 (January 26, 1961), pp. 187–88.

7. Marya Mannes, "Penalties of Prosperity," *The Listener*, LXIV, No. 1653 (December 1, 1960), 963–64.

8. Zijderveld, op. cit., p. 88.

9. C. Wright Mills, *The Power Elite* (New York: Oxford University Press, 1959), p. 305.

10. Fromm, op. cit., pp. 133–34.

11. Mahmut Makal, *A Village in Anatolia*, tr. Sir Wyndham Deedes, ed. Paul Stirling (London: Vallentine, Mitchell & Co., 1954), pp. 25, 36, 68, 83, 146.

12. Arendt, op. cit., pp. 59, 45.

13. Nisbet, "Leadership and Social Crisis," *Tradition and Revolt*, p. 55.

14. Marc Bloch, *Feudal Society*, tr. L. A. Manyon (Chicago: University of Chicago Press, 1961), II, 443.

15. Nisbet, various essays in *Tradition and Revolt*, pp. 4, 5–6, 73–74, 137, 41, 106, 75.

16. Kenneth Minogue, *The Liberal Mind* (London, Methuen & Co., 1963), p. 20.

17. Herbert J. Muller, *The Individual in a Revolutionary World* (Toronto: Ryerson Press, 1964), p. 11.

18. Victor Ehrenberg, *The Greek State* (Oxford: Basil Blackwell, 1960), p. 92.

19. Rainer Maria Rilke, *Letters to a Young Poet*, tr. Reginald Snell (London: Sidgwick Jackson, 1945), p. 34.

20. Edgar Z. Friedenberg, *The Vanishing Adolescent* (Boston: Beacon Press, 1959), p. 43.

21. Dewey, *Individualism Old and New*, pp. 28–29.

22. Francis D. Wormuth, *Class Struggle* (Bloomington, Ind.: Indiana University Press, 1946), p. 33.

PART VI: THE REVOLT OF THE PRIVILEGED

CHAPTER 13: THE BOUNDARIES OF AFFLUENCE

1. Sumner, *Folkways*, p. 167.

2. Marías, op. cit., pp. 37–38.

3. J. D. B. Miller, *The Nature of Politics* (London: Gerald Duckworth & Co., 1962), p. 164.

4. John Street, "How to Succeed in Gardening," *New Society*, Vol. II, No. 47 (August 22, 1963).

5. The account of conditions on British and American merchant ships is taken from Stephen A. Richardson, "Organizational Contrasts on British and American Ships," *Administrative Science Quarterly*, I, No. 2 (September 1956), 189–207.

6. Raymond Williams, "Television in Britain," *Journal of Social Issues*, XVIII, No. 2 (1962), 7–8.

7. Ferdinand Lassalle, quoted in W. H. Dawson, *German Socialism and Ferdinand Lassalle* (London: Swan Sonnenheim & Co., 1888), p. 192.

8. John Goldthorpe, David Lockwood, Frank Bechofer, and Jennifer Platt, "The Affluent Worker and the Thesis of *Embourgeoisement:* Some Preliminary Research Findings," *Sociology*, I, No. 1, 11–31.

9. Daniel Bell, *The Coming of Post-Industrial Society: A Venture in Social Forecasting* (New York: Basic Books, 1973), p. 15.

10. Norah Sayre, "Reels of California," *Progressive*, XXXIV, No. 9 (September 1970), 35–37.

11. Wright, op. cit., p. 85.

12. Mark Van Doren, *Liberal Education* (New York: Henry Holt & Co., 1943), p. 30.

CHAPTER 14: CREATED EQUAL BUT EVERYWHERE UNEQUAL

1. Zbigniew Brzezinski, *Between Two Ages America's Role in the Technetronic Era* (1970) (New York: The Viking Press, 1971), p. 111.

2. Isaiah Berlin, "Equality," *Proceedings of the Aristotelian Society*, 1955/1956, p. 326.

3. John Rees, *Equality* (New York: Praeger Publishers, 1971), p. 22.

4. Dewey, *Democracy and Education*, p. 76.

5. Pellegrino, op. cit., p. 276.

6. Dewey, *Democracy and Education*, p. 36.

7. The report on toys was made by Basil Bernstein and Douglas Young in *Sociology*, I, No. 2 (May 1967), 131–40.

8. Dewey, *Democracy and Education*, pp. 20–21.

9. John Rawls, *A Theory of Justice* (Cambridge, Mass.: Belknap Press, Harvard University Press, 1971), p. 100.

10. Robert M. Hutchins, "Introduction" (1963) to *Education for Freedom* (1943) (New York: Grove Press, 1963), p. xvii.

11. Dewey, *Democracy and Education*, pp. 87–88.

12. Peter Viereck, *Conservatism Revisited* (New York: The Free Press, 1962), pp. 34–35.

13. Van Doren, op. cit., p. 31.

14. *General Education in a Free Society, Report of the Harvard Committee* (Cambridge, Mass.: Harvard University Press, 1945), pp. 3–4.

15. Alexander Meiklejohn, *New Republic*, CX, No. 1 (January 3, 1944), 27.

16. Van Doren, op. cit., p. 67.

17. Dewey, *Democracy and Education*, pp. 191–92.

18. Wright, op. cit., p. 7.

19. Eric Ashby, "Investment in Man," Presidential Address to the British Association for the Advancement of Science, August 28, 1963.

20. Daniel Bell, "Meritocracy and Equality," *The Public Interest*, No. 29 (Fall 1972), pp. 66–68.

21. Christopher Jencks *et al., Inequality: A Reassessment of the Effect of Family and Schooling in America* (New York: Basic Books, 1972), p. 102.

CHAPTER 15: FIXING PEOPLE IN THEIR STATION

1. Howard Higman, *Genetic Society* (Boulder, Colo.: Center for Action Research, University of Colorado, Document 36, 1972), pp. 30–32.

2. Leo Kanowitz, *Women and the Law: The Unfinished Revolution* (Albuquerque, N.M.: University of New Mexico Press, 1969), p. 4.

3. Bell, "Meritocracy and Equality," p. 32.

4. Jencks, op. cit., pp. 65–66.

5. Ibid., p. 14.

6. Kathie Sarahchild, "A Program for Feminist 'Consciousness Raising,'" pre-

sented at Women's Liberation National Conference, Chicago, November 28–30, 1968.

7. Marlene Dixon, "On Women's Liberation," *Radical America*, February 1970, p. 26.

8. Robin Fox, "Comparative Family Patterns," in Elliott, ed., op. cit., p. 3.

CHAPTER 16: THE REVOLT AGAINST THE DEMOCRATIC IDEA IN AMERICA

1. Irving Kristol, "American Historians and the Democratic Idea," *On the Democratic Idea in America* (New York: Harper & Row, 1972), p. 51.

2. Kristol, "The Shaking of the Foundation," op. cit., pp. 27–29.

3. Kristol, "Pornography, Obscenity, and the Case for Censorship," op. cit., pp. 41–42.

4. Kristol, "Urban Civilization and Its Discontents," op. cit., pp. 14–16.

5. August Heckscher, "The Fair Deal," *The Reporter*, Vol. I, No. 1 (April 26, 1949).

6. Daniel Patrick Moynihan, *Maximum Feasible Misunderstanding* (New York: The Free Press, 1969), p. 193.

7. R. H. S. Crossman, "The Faith of Arnold Toynbee," *New Republic*, CXVIII, No. 20 (May 17, 1948), 29.

8. Nicola Chiaramonte, "The Will to Question," *Encounter*, I, No. 2 (November 1953), 1–2.

9. The argument of John Stuart Mill is condensed from several passages in his *Representative Government*.

10. George Seferis, *On the Greek Style: Selected Essays in Poetry and Hellenism*, tr. Rex Warner and Th. D. Frangopoulos (Boston: Little, Brown and Co., 1966), p. viii.

PART VII: RETHINKING THE PURPOSE OF AMERICA

CHAPTER 17: THE RESTORATION OF POLITICS

1. Marías, op. cit., pp. 103–4.

2. William Godwin, *Fleetwood* (London, 1805), I, 277.

3. Lewis Mumford, *The Myth of the Machine: Technics and Human Development* (New York: Harcourt, Brace & World, 1967), p. 3.

4. Wright, op. cit., p. xiii.

5. Arendt, op. cit., pp. 4–5.

6. Dewey, *Democracy and Education*, p. 37.

7. Dewey, *Individualism Old and New*, p. 29.

8. Daniel Yankelovich and William Barrett, *Ego and Instinct: The Psychoanalytic View of Human Nature—Revised* (New York: Random House, 1970), p. 84.

9. Brzezinski, op. cit., p. 32.

10. Ibid, p. 102.

11. Bell, *The Coming of Post-Industrial Society*, pp. 29–32.

12. Ibid., p. 13.

13. Arendt, op. cit., pp. 92–93.

14. Brzezinski, op. cit., p. 9.

15. Emmanuel G. Mesthene, *Technological Change: Its Impact on Man and Society* (Cambridge, Mass.: Harvard University Press, 1970), p. 25.

16. Fromm, op. cit., p. 126.

17. Emile Durkheim, *The Elementary Forms of the Religious Life* (New York: The Macmillan Company, 1926), p. 18.

18. Lester F. Ward, "The Place of Sociology among the Sciences," *American Journal of Sociology*, I, No. 1 (1895) 17–25.

19. W. Lloyd Warner and Paul S. Lunt, *The Social Life of a Modern Community* (New Haven: Yale University Press, 1941), p. 15.

20. An American anthropologist quoted without being identified in Muller, op. cit., pp. 4–5.

21. Brand Blanshard, "The Limits of Nationalism," *Contemporary American Philosophy*, ed. John H. Smith (Second Series) (London: George Allen & Unwin, 1970), pp. 24–26.

22. Auden, "Death at Random," *New York Review of Books*, XXI, No. 20 (December 12, 1974), 28.

23. Thorstein Veblen, *The Higher Learning in America: A Memorandum on the Conduct of Universities by Business Men* (The Viking Press, 1918), pp. 186–87.

24. August Comte, *System of Positive Polity* (London, 1875), I, 179.

25. Ortega, "History as a System," pp. 182–83.

26. Ortega, *The Revolt of the Masses*, pp. 12–13.

27. Karl Mannheim, quoted in Loren Beritz, "The Lonely Intellectual," *The Nation* CXCII, No. 3 (January 21, 1961), 50.

28. Marías, op. cit., pp. 73–74.

29. Ralf Dahrendorf, *Conflict after Class* (London: Longmans, Green & Co., for the University of Essex, 1967), pp. 20–21.

30. C. Wright Mills, *White Collar* (New York: Oxford University Press, 1951), p. xx.

31. J. Valles, quoted in Jack Lindsay, *Cézanne: His Life And Art* (New York: Harper & Row, 1972), p. 188.

32. Bell, *The Coming of Post-Industrial Society*, pp. x, 12.

33. J. N. Figgis, *Studies in Political Thought from Gerson to Grotius* (Cambridge, Eng.: Cambridge University Press, 1923), p. 1.

34. Miller, op. cit., pp. 14–22.

CHAPTER 18: THE PURSUIT OF HAPPINESS IN SOCIETY

1. Marías, op. cit., p. 61.

2. *Ibid.*

3. Norman Pollack, "Introduction" to *The Populist Mind*, ed. Norman Pollack (Indianapolis, Ind.: The Bobbs-Merrill Co., 1967), pp. xlii, xix-xx.

4. Weil, op. cit., p. 5.

5. Los Angeles *Times*, quoted in *The Reporter*, XXIV, No. 6 (March 16, 1961), 16.

6. Jack Haas, *American Behavioral Scientist*, XIV, No. 1 (September–October 1972), 27–29.

7. Arendt, op. cit., p. 133.

8. Glenn Tinder, *The Crisis of Political Imagination* (New York: Charles Scribner's Sons, 1964), p. 78.

9. Ozenfant, op. cit., p. 183.

10. Raymond Postgate, *How to Make a Revolution* (New York: Vanguard Press, 1934), pp. 54–57.

11. Dewey, *Democracy and Education,* pp. 119–20.

12. The study in manpower training was reported by William F. Brazziel, "Effect of General Education in Manpower Programs," *Journal of Human Resources,* I, No. 1 (Summer 1966), 39–44.

13. Hutchins, op. cit., p. 25.

14. Dewey, *Democracy and Education,* p. 117.

15. Auden, "Rome v. Monticello," *The Dyer's Hand and Other Essays* (New York: Vintage Books, 1968), p. 326.

16. Norlin, op. cit., p. xv.

17. Roy Wood Sellar, *Reflections on American Philosophy from Within* (Notre Dame, Ind.: University of Notre Dame Press, 1969).

18. Dewey, *Democracy and Education,* p. 230.

INDEX